P9-CJU-909

SPECTACULAR BODIES

While films such as *Rambo, Thelma and Louise* and *Basic Instinct* have operated as major points of cultural reference in recent years, popular action cinema remains largely overlooked within contemporary film criticism.

Spectacular Bodies unravels the complexities and pleasures of a genre often dismissed as 'obvious' in both its pleasure and its politics, arguing that these controversial films should be analysed and understood within a cinematic as well as a political context.

Yvonne Tasker argues that today's action cinema not only responds to the shifts in gendered, sexual and racial identities which took place during the 1980s, but reflects the influences of other media such as the new video culture. Her detailed discussion of the homoeroticism surrounding the muscleman hero, the symbolic centrality of blackness within the crime narrative, and the changing status of women within the genre, addresses the constitution of these identities through the shifting categories of gender, class, race, sex, sexuality and nation. *Spectacular Bodies* examines the ambivalence of supposedly secure categories of popular cinema, questioning the existing terms of film criticism in this area and addressing the multiple pleasures of this neglected form.

Yvonne Tasker is a freelance lecturer and writer in film and cultural studies.

COMEDIA
Series editor:
David Morley

SPECTACULAR BODIES

Gender, genre and the action cinema

Yvonne Tasker

A Comedia book
published by Routledge
London and New York

A Comedia book
First published 1993
by Routledge
11 New Fetter Lane, London EC4P 4EE

Simultaneously published in the USA and Canada
by Routledge
29 West 35th Street, New York, NY 10001

Typeset in 10 on 12 point Baskerville by
Computerset, Harmondsworth, Middlesex
Printed in Great Britain by
TJ Press (Padstow) Ltd, Padstow, Cornwall

British Library Cataloguing in Publication Data
Tasker, Yvonne
Spectacular Bodies: Gender, genre and the action cinema. – (Comedia Series)
I. Title II. Series
791.43

Library of Congress Cataloging in Publication Data
Tasker, Yvonne
Spectacular Bodies: Gender, genre, and the action cinema/Yvonne Tasker.
p. cm. — (Film, media, and cultural studies) (Popular fictions series)
Includes biblographical references and index.
1. Strong men in motion pictures. 2. Sex role in motion pictures. 3. Machismo in motion pictures. 4. Adventure films — United States.
I. Title. II. Series. III. Series: Comedia
PN1995.9.S697T37 1993
791.43'653—dc20 92-44020 CIP

ISBN 0-415-09224-8
0-415-09223-X (hbk)

CONTENTS

List of plates vi
Acknowledgements vii

INTRODUCTION: Gender and the action cinema 1

1 WOMEN WARRIORS: Gender, sexuality and Hollywood's fighting heroines 14

2 BLACK BUDDIES AND WHITE HEROES: Racial discourse in the action cinema 35

3 NEW HOLLYWOOD, GENRE AND THE ACTION CINEMA 54

4 TOUGH GUYS AND WISE-GUYS: Masculinities and star images in the action cinema 73

5 MASCULINITY, POLITICS AND NATIONAL IDENTITY 91

6 THE BODY IN CRISIS OR THE BODY TRIUMPHANT? 109

7 ACTION HEROINES IN THE 1980s: The limits of 'musculinity' 132

8 THE CINEMA AS EXPERIENCE: Kathryn Bigelow and the cinema of spectacle 153

Notes 167
Filmography 178
Bibliography 186
Index 191

PLATES

Between pages 72 and 73.

1 Arnold Schwarzenegger and Grace Jones in *Conan the Destroyer* (1984)
2 Danny Glover in *Predator 2* (1990)
3 Danny Glover's alien adversary in *Predator 2* (1990)
4 Whoopi Goldberg in *Fatal Beauty* (1987)
5 Sylvester Stallone as Rambo in *First Blood Part II* (1985)
6 Bruce Willis in *Die Hard* (1988)
7 Linda Hamilton as Sarah Connor in *Terminator 2* (1991)
8 Sigourney Weaver as Ripley in *Aliens* (1986)
9 Sigourney Weaver with mechanical skin in *Aliens* (1986)
10 Geena Davies and Susan Sarandon in *Thelma and Louise* (1991)
11 Patrick Swayze and Keanu Reeves in *Point Break* (1991)

ACKNOWLEDGEMENTS

The author and publisher would like to thank the following for permission to use stills: the Margaret Herrick Library, Los Angeles for *Conan the Destroyer*; Twentieth Century Fox for *Predator 2*, *Die Hard* and *Aliens*; Metro Goldwyn Mayer for *Fatal Beauty* and *Thelma and Louise*; and Guild Films for *Terminator 2*. Every effort has been made to obtain permission to reproduce the photographs. If any proper acknowledgement has not been made, we invite copyright holders to inform us of the oversight.

I would like to thank Rebecca Barden at Routledge and the Series Editor, David Morley, for their help in producing this book. I would also like to acknowledge the help of those friends who have been involved with the project at different stages, in particular Val Hill, Andy Medhurst and Ken Page. Thanks also to Duncan Webster for his collaboration in the early stages.

This book is dedicated with love to Carolyn Brown.

INTRODUCTION
Gender and the action cinema

The image of Sylvester Stallone as Vietnam veteran John Rambo, brandishing a rocket-launcher whilst parading his musculature, became an icon of American masculinity in the mid-1980s. As the decade went on, though, Stallone was displaced in popularity by the even larger figure of ex-Mr Universe Arnold Schwarzenegger. These two stars provided the most publicised, most visible image of the figure of the muscular male hero who had come to dominate the American action cinema of the 1980s. Many critics saw the success of Stallone and Schwarzenegger as a disturbing sign, signalling the evolution of a previously unseen cinematic articulation of masculinity. At the same time these figures echoed unsettling images from the past, through their implicit invocation of a fascist idealisation of the white male body. Combining an ability to signify both concerns about the future and the horrors of the past, the box-office appeal of the male bodybuilder provided a resonant image for the mid-1980s. Coming at the particular point that it did, the success of these films and stars could be read in terms of a backlash against the feminism of the 1970s, as indicative of a new conservatism in both national and sexual politics. As we'll see, the muscular action hero was, for some, a figure who represented the antithesis of the 'new man', himself a creation of advertising images in the early 1980s, and the feminist gains he supposedly represented. These competing images perhaps indicate the extent to which masculinity itself has been called into question through the 1980s and since. It seems as if, at the same time as the male body on the screen was becoming more and more visible, an excessive parody of an ideal, masculinity was emerging as a visible category within the criticism of the day.[1] Both the films themselves and my analysis of them emerge then from a critical and cultural context in which the multiple meanings of masculine identity, the existence of masculinities, has been made increasingly apparent.

Yet, as much as these films may represent something new, the appearance of what I'll call a 'muscular cinema' during the 1980s calls on a much longer tradition of representation. I refer here not only to the evident appeal which the figure of the male bodybuilder makes to notions of classical culture, but to the existence of cinematic traditions which prefigure the popular action movies of the 1980s. The series of successful films centred on the figure of Indiana Jones, for example, explicitly refer back to the adventure serials of an earlier cinematic moment. What does distinguish the action cinema of the recent past is its transition into big-budget operations. Indeed this is conveyed quite precisely by the difference between the high production values of Spielberg's *Indiana Jones and the Temple of Doom* (1984) and the low-budget adventure serials it takes as a reference point. The low-budget tradition of Italian mythological films, the numerous Tarzan films produced in Hollywood and other action-based pictures had, for many years, provided film roles for star bodybuilders and athletes such as Steve Reeves and Johnny Weissmuller.[2] Though the popularity, in terms of the sheer number of films generated, of a fictional figure such as Tarzan, indicates the centrality of the white male body in these cinematic traditions, black American sports stars such as O. J. Simpson and Fred Williamson have also found film roles within the action-movie tradition.[3] These cinematic traditions produced films that were characteristically low-budget affairs, receiving marginal critical attention and with no advertising budget to speak of. It is by way of contrast to these earlier historical moments that, today, Arnold Schwarzenegger has been vaunted as the highest paid movie star of his day.

It is the sheer *scale* of the budgets, the box-office success, and of the male bodies on display, that seems to have shifted in the Hollywood cinema of the 1980s. In the same period the connotations surrounding bodybuilding as a practice and as a competitive sport have similarly shifted from freakish marginality to the mainstream of western health culture.[4] These shifts form part of a gradual redefinition of images of masculine identity which has evolved partly through the commodification of the male body. Reference to films from earlier periods in Hollywood's history, such as the many versions of the Tarzan narrative, serves to remind us that there are antecedents for the evident commodification of the male body in contemporary culture. Whilst the narratives of these films, as with sub-genres such as the mythological epic, were driven by action, they also offered a set of visual pleasures focused on the display of the male body. Indeed it is the emphasis on *action* in these films which both legitimates, through the affirmation of an active understanding of masculinity, and provides a narrative justification for such physical display.[5] The relationship between action and display, indeed Hollywood's production of action *as* display through the spectacular bodies of its muscular stars, provides a central focus for the discussion of images in the pages that follow.

Initially, whilst researching for *Spectacular Bodies* I became convinced that the figure of 'woman' was in the process of being eclipsed from the

Hollywood cinema altogether. It seemed to me that sets of anxieties to do with gender identity were being inscribed almost exclusively over the tortured figure of the white male body. This conviction was heightened by the rash of fatherhood movies such as *Three Men and A Baby* (1987) and *Parenthood* (1989) which found popular success during the late 1980s. As ever, rather than representing some dramatic final break, such movies can be taken as only part of the seemingly ceaseless process of redefinition and renegotiation operating in relation to images and understandings of gendered identity. Whilst it is possible, to a certain extent, to discern *trends* within the history of American film, we should not attempt to erase the contradictions which movies as well as critics, since both are part of contemporary culture, are having to contend with. As if to prove the point the late 1980s and early 1990s have seen the release of a series of movies featuring aggressive, gun-toting heroines. Films such as *Aliens* (1986), *Thelma and Louise* (1991) and *Terminator 2* (1991) have had highly publicised cinema releases. The success of these films serves to highlight the existence of a cinematic tradition which has placed women at the centre of the action narrative, a tradition that stretches back to the 1970s and beyond. As with the movies featuring male stars that have already been referred to, these new films are distinguished by their accession to big-budget status. Accompanying such hefty production budgets is, amongst other things, a matching advertising budget. Thus images of the action heroine taken from these films have had a very high media profile. While it's true of course that the most reproduced image from *Terminator 2* was that of Schwarzenegger as the cyborg which first brought him cult star status, the image of Linda Hamilton as Sarah Connor has quickly acquired a cult following of her own with, for example, lesbian audiences.[6]

I originally intended to write about gender, masculinity in particular, concentrating almost exclusively on men in the action cinema. The release and success of films such as *Terminator 2* problematise such a schema. These films reinscribe, in different ways, the *female* body in terms of masculinity. It is for this reason that I want to introduce the term 'musculinity'. 'Musculinity' indicates the extent to which a physical definition of masculinity in terms of a developed musculature is not limited to the male body within representation. Along with Jamie Lee Curtis in Kathryn Bigelow's *Blue Steel* (1990), heroines such as Ripley and Sarah Connor are part of an emergent action tradition to which female stars are central, though obviously it is still male stars who command the most money and status within Hollywood. The analyses opened up in Chapter 1 and developed in Chapter 7 deal specifically with the significance of these action heroines. I hope to offer here both a limited account of the recent history of the action heroine, and a specific address to the emergence of a muscular female heroine and the problems that these figures pose for binary conceptions of gendered identity.

Just as a discussion of masculinity and the female action heroine requires something of a different frame of reference than the terms of gender theory can offer, constructions of 'race' are also central to these movies. My analysis of the action heroine in Chapter 1 concludes with a discussion of the role of Whoopi Goldberg as Rita Rizzoli in the cop movie *Fatal Beauty* (1987). This film encounters problems in the positioning of Goldberg as a black performer in the symbolic order of things which operates in the cop movie. The incoherence which results from her casting at the centre of the narrative makes apparent the extent to which the action narrative relies on an equation between blackness and marginality, blackness and criminality. Speaking of the representation of Afro-American women in film James R. Nesteby suggests that the 'most important stereotype of all' may be the 'sheer facelessness', the invisibility, of black women in Hollywood film (Nesteby 1982: 203). Given the symbolic importance of this invisibility, of the black performers who populate the streets and the prisons of action movies, *Fatal Beauty* confronts something of a crisis of representation. Other films, as we will see, attempt to experiment with the codes of representation in order to position either white women or black men at the centre of the narrative, whilst retaining a space of marginality. In *Fatal Beauty* Goldberg is ultimately isolated within the frame to such a degree that she almost seems at times to be in a different film from the rest of the cast.

The centrality of a marginal blackness in American action cinema is picked up in Chapter 2 through an analysis of the role of the black male buddy and the black action hero. Despite the dominance of white stars, it is in forms like the action cinema in which both male and female protagonists are often defined by their *physicality*, that, in fitting with stereotypes, black actors have been given significant, if rarely starring roles. In *Die Hard* (1988), as in other 1980s movies, black characters act as supportive figures for the white hero. The relationship between John McClane (Bruce Willis) and Sergeant Al Powell (Reginald Veljohnson) is central to the development of the narrative, yet Powell is a marginal figure. Similarly by the time of *Rocky III* Carl Weathers's character, Apollo Creed, has shifted from the role of Rocky's opponent, as in the first two films, to that of friend and trainer. Yet at this very point Mr T enters to take up the role of chief villain. It is not until *Rocky IV* that the boxer's climactic battle pits him against a white fighter. Donald Bogle has described the Al Powell figure in *Die Hard* as the 'black-buddy-as-mammy-nurturer', a type he links to a range of representations through the 1980s which paired black and white actors (Bogle 1991: 276). Following on from a discussion of this buddy pairing, Chapter 2 concludes with a discussion of Danny Glover's role alongside Mel Gibson, in the hugely successful *Lethal Weapon* films and, substituting for Schwarzenegger, as Lieutenant Mike Harrigan in *Predator 2* (1990).[7]

Beyond Hollywood it is the Asian stars, both male and female, of the Hong Kong industry who have defined and developed the action genre. Cynthia Rothrock, a western martial-arts star who is discussed in Chapter 1, made her first movies in Hong Kong. Such films are made, by and large, for Asian markets but are also popular in the west where they are generally accessible through video. Whilst the Hong Kong industry is not discussed here in much detail, traces of the innovations for which it has been responsible are evident in the American action cinema.[8] The issues raised through a discussion of race problematise any simple analysis of the working out of gender and sexuality in the action picture. For the black male hero to parade his muscular torso bears vastly different connotations from the display of the white hero. The discussion offered here represents only the beginnings of an inquiry into the complex ways in which the action cinema constitutes 'race', how power is written differently over the black, white and Asian bodies of its heroes and heroines.

My analysis of the contemporary action cinema proceeds from two basic premises. Firstly that the appearance of a muscular cinema, rather than signalling a radical break with the past, inflects and redefines already existing cinematic and cultural discourses of race, class and sexuality. Secondly that it is worth attempting to give an account, rather than an 'explanation', of both the pleasures and the political significance of these popular films. Such an account might allow an attention to the complex ways in which popular cinema affirms gendered identities at the same time as it mobilises identifications and desires which undermine the stability of such categories. These two modes are matched by the operations of much academic film criticism which seeks to politically pin down popular cinema at the same time as celebrating (selected) examples of its ambiguous plurality. Part of the motivation for this book lies in the conviction that the critical colonisation of popular cinema, whose products are judged by the standards of high culture, is intimately bound up with class and with the operation of cultural power more generally. Working within the parameters of feminist criticism, it has often worried me that popular texts and pleasures were somehow subject to analysis only in order to be understood, transcended and moved beyond. Forms like the romance, popular with so many readers, often seemed to be taken to function only as, and I simplify, obstacles on the route to the attainment of high culture, and political consciousness.[9] Part of my concern in this book, then, is to attempt to think about popular form within another framework, one in which these same forms might be taken to have something to say.

Elsewhere, I have characterised the critical construction of muscular cinema as 'Dumb Movies for Dumb People', a phrase which signals some of the issues of cultural power that are at stake in thinking about the status and the operations of action cinema.[10] It raises at an immediate level the significant silence of the heroes, the primacy of the body over the voice in the telling of these stories. More than that, the phrase indicates something of the contempt with which this form of popular culture and its audience has been evaluated. Whilst a desire to think through issues of politics and sexuality in the cinema is familiar, I hope that an exploration of these questions in relation to the action cinema may allow the possibility of a perspective which does not exclusively construct the popular cinema as the object of analysis. As products of particular historical moments, and as formed by and through a variety of political discourses, both popular cinema and academic cultural criticism can be included within a broad definition of 'culture'. The fact that the former tends to address a working-class, dispossessed audience whilst the latter has tended to be the privilege of the middle classes, has sometimes led to the mistaken assumption that one can tell 'us' all 'we' might want to know about the 'other'.

If the phrase 'Dumb Movies for Dumb People' indicates the extent to which the pleasures of the action cinema are primarily those of spectacle rather than dialogue, then this might also help us to understand the contempt with which these films have been critically received. When I speak of the pleasures of spectacle, I do not refer solely to special effects or the staging of spectacular stunts, but to some of the more general visual qualities which define the cinematic experience. By way of contrast, academic film criticism has often placed an inordinate emphasis on the operations of narrative, hence the significance often given to the moment of narrative resolution as a way to decode the politics of a given text.[11] Whilst valuable work has been undertaken on, for example, cinema-going as a social practice, the cinema as sensuous experience is too often neglected. Features such as the breathtaking nature of visual spectacle, or the feelings of exhilaration at the expansive landscapes in which the hero operates, are fundamental to the action cinema. Such features are also, inevitably, rather difficult to render in academic prose. The model I'm working from here is not an opposition between form and content. Certainly within this particular mode, and probably within other modes of popular cinema, the two are bound up together so that the 'action' of action cinema refers to the enactment of spectacle *as* narrative. Instead of an opposition between form and content then, I'm referring here to the contradictory desires to which we are subject as the audience for the performance of a given text. We want to find out, to follow the narrative through to its conclusion and the revelation of knowledge that accompanies this. At the same time we wish to stop and stare, to linger over details. I certainly do not want to argue that spectacle has no content, or that it cannot be commented on in political or ideological terms.[12] Yet popular cinema is as much concerned with visual pleasure as it is with narrative development and in the action cinema visual display is elevated to a defining feature of the genre.

As signalled in its gradual transition to big-budget status, the action cinema has been an immensely successful cinematic venture in the 1980s. Given my desire to eulogise the *cinematic* qualities of the genre in this book, it is perhaps ironic that a key launching pad for this transition has been the success of action pictures on the video market. The multiplicity of films and images circulating on the cinema and video market today provides, however, an important context for thinking about Hollywood in the 1980s and 1990s. The films discussed in this book arise from an internationalised context of media production, distribution and consumption. In Chapter 3 a brief industrial context for talking about recent Hollywood production is sketched out. Features such as generic knowingness, a sense of parody, which are present to varying degrees within action films represent a more widespread aspect of recent Hollywood production. An attention to such formal qualities reveals, in relation to a film like *Die Hard*, the limitations of a content-based form of ideological analysis. I want to signal an understanding of such films as being rather more than a simple enactment of white male supremacism. In Chapter 4 I discuss a range of inflections of the action-hero persona through an examination of different star images and character types. This allows for an understanding of the complex processes of signification at work in the construction of the action hero, through the cinema itself, and through the circulation of star images in other media. Questions of the body, masculinity and power are taken up further in Chapter 6 in an investigation of the significance of the physical display that is emphasised in recent action films.

Rather more than the other films we might refer to, the much publicised release of *Rambo: First Blood Part II* in 1985, signalled a new visibility for the muscular hero of the action cinema. Breaking numerous international box-office records, *Rambo* achieved almost instant notoriety. Reference to 'Rambo' extended well beyond the film's enthusiastic audience, and by 1987 both the British and the American press had begun to speak of the 'age of Rambo'. By the end of the decade 'Rambo' had made it into the updated edition of the Oxford English Dictionary. John Rambo is the hero of three films to date, though the character originally appeared in David Morrell's 1972 novel *First Blood*.[13] An outsider hero, Rambo achieved an immense rhetorical significance in the mid-1980s. When writers, critics, politicians or other spokesmen and women talked of 'Rambo-style films' they were referring to what was perceived to be a disturbing new phenomenon, a type of violent popular cinema to which Rambo could give a name. Cultural and political concerns were intimately bound together by pundits who cast the young male American audience for *Rambo* as the new right-wing voters who had supported Reagan.[14]

With the notable exceptions of the western and the gangster movie, traditions of action cinema have achieved neither aesthetic nor political credibility within film studies. The kinds of critical investigations elaborated around forms such as the western or the gangster movie of the 1930s have been absent in relation to the contemporary action picture, though such studies of popular forms, it is true, have largely been produced retrospectively. And while the success of *Rambo* has generated numerous commentaries, these have largely been framed in terms of an address to the truth, or otherwise, of the cinema's rendition of the saga of American involvement in Vietnam. That is, both the film and the genre of which it is a part have been discussed within a realist paradigm which assesses the narrative in terms of truth. To ask whether a film is 'true' is, fairly obviously, to assume a measure by which to judge. I'd argue though that the realist paradigm, when applied to popular films like *Rambo* as in this instance, presumes an ontology which itself needs to be investigated. The tendency for critics to focus exclusively on the narrative of *Rambo*, judging it against the narrative of the American forces in Vietnam, may well stem from the assumption that the construction and the appeal of the action cinema is *obvious*. Analysis of the films has little significance if one accepts the premise that there is nothing to be said about them, other than to signal the genre's ideological complicity with the operations of patriarchal capitalism; to say, for example, that the film is Reaganite propaganda, or that it is 'lying'. Leslie Fiedler is one of the few critics I have read who attempts to think about the film in terms of the mythical voicing of the unspeakable, in an analysis which opens up questions of whose story is being told, to whom, and why, within the Vietnam narrative.[15] A similar critical operation was often performed in relation to *Thelma and Louise* which was judged, and found wanting, as an account of women's lives. The standards of truth against which popular films have been judged, standards which rarely admit the complexity of terms like fantasy, can also operate to silence the other stories to which they attempt to give a voice.

The action cinema depends on a complex articulation of both belonging and exclusion, an articulation which is bound up in the body of the hero and the masculine identity that it embodies. These dramas of belonging and exclusion mobilise discourses of national, racial and gendered identity through intimate fictional groupings such as the platoon, the police squad or the buddy relationship. Chapter 5 examines the dramatisation of nationhood and masculinity in the American action cinema, specifically in terms of the way in which images of warfare are mobilised. As the chronology might well have appeared to cinema-goers during the 1980s, *Rambo*'s box-office success functioned as a trigger for the release of a 'second wave' of American films concerned with Vietnam. The majority of *muscular* movies, by way of contrast to Vietnam films such as *Platoon*, are not concerned with a specific historical moment or even a specific geographical location. The generalised setting of the action film opens up a discussion of ideas of nationhood in relation to the placelessness which is often a defining feature of the heroic figure.

Various critics have seen the muscular body of the action hero as a triumphant assertion of male power. Others, such as Barbara Creed, have viewed the Schwarzenegger persona in terms of the articulation of a set of anxieties about the very masculine identity that they seem to embody so forcefully.[16] The question of whether these movies and their heroes offer viewers the male body in crisis or the body triumphant, or whether that opposition itself is a useful one, is developed in Chapter 6. It is worth noting, though, that 'physical actors' such as Sylvester Stallone, Arnold Schwarzenegger and Chuck Norris have been represented by some critics as grotesque figures who are potentially out of control, framed by images of the monstrous and the deviant. The critical language with which a popular film such as *Rambo* or its star, Sylvester Stallone, has been discussed has tended to extend that rhetoric of the monstrous, pathologising the film's audience. In this critical process, particular cultural products and forms come to seem dangerous, signifying anarchy or the threat of it. As concerns for the effects of a mass culture on the social body have so frequently testified, such responses are not new.[17] The fear and loathing that muscular movies have inspired in the liberal/cultural elite as well as the popular press in the mid-1980s ('No, No to Rambo' screamed a headline in the *Daily Mirror*) seems to indicate in part a fear of the audience for such films.[18]

In contrast to the images of anarchic violence that have critically accompanied muscular movies, it is, in fact, the values of self-control rather than chaos, and the practices of training and discipline which are extolled as central terms in the definition of bodybuilding and in the image of the muscleman hero of 1980s cinema. The visual spectacle of the male body that is central to muscular movies puts into play the two contradictory terms of *restraint* and *excess*. Whilst the hero and the various villains of the genre tend to share an excessive physical strength, the hero is also defined by his restraint in putting his strength to the test. And it is the *body* of the male hero which provides the space in which a tension between restraint and excess is articulated.[19] As I explore further in Chapter 4 such a tension is mediated through both horror and comedy. It is also important to note though that whilst Stallone, Schwarzenegger, Dolph Lundgren and others are cast as monstrous in one view, they are pin-ups in another, their bodies self-created works of art, constantly worked over and redefined. The active construction of the body invoked within muscular mythology offers the kinds of possibilities for change to which the small ads in men's magazines appeal, the promise that, as reward for time and energy invested, a new image will look back at us from the mirror.

In terms of their relation to issues of gender, these kinds of appeal can usefully be further situated within feminist discourses on women, fashion, and the body beautiful.[20] Feminist writers have analysed the oppressive ideals involved in notions of the body beautiful. Women's magazines, for example, assume 'natural', racially exclusive, standards of beauty, standards which are seemingly made attainable via the cosmetics industry. Bodybuilding and health culture have generated an industry comparable to that of beauty culture, with competing systems and products marketed through different magazines. Whilst bodybuilding was initially directed almost exclusively at men, and certainly the most visible image of the bodybuilder was that of the white male, this image has been modified in recent years. An examination of films such as *Perfect* (1985) and *Pumping Iron II: The Women* (1984) in Chapter 7, serves to show the rather different connotations at work in women's involvement in aerobics and bodybuilding. As many feminist commentators have noted, while the ideal images that are offered in bodybuilding, health culture and beauty culture cannot be replaced with images that simply correspond to the 'truth' of women's experience, these forms offer a range of competing images within which a (limited) physical definition of identity can be negotiated.[21] This is precisely the promise and the desire for change, that is worked on in these images and in the huge industries that they support.

MAKING MR RIGHT

A useful contemporary reference point is provided by Susan Seidelman's film *Making Mr Right* (1988) which operates as a post-feminist reworking of the Frankenstein scenario, situating concerns of creation and control within a new historical context. The film's central character is Frankie Stone, a public relations consultant and image-maker. The plot concerns Frankie's attempts, after ditching the campaign to re-elect South Florida congressman and boyfriend Steve Marcus, to make the socially inept Ulysses android user-friendly enough to pull in much needed congress dollars for parent-company Chemtec. The narrative tension of *Making Mr Right* is structured by two opposing classes or types of creation, as the languages of science and of the world of media and public relations come into conflict. To achieve media saturation for Ulysses, Frankie advises on the need to 'polish up his social graces'. Meanwhile, Ulysses' scientist creator, Dr Jeff Peters (both are played by John Malkovich), rages at the introduction of 'emotional ticks that I have *worked* to get out of my own personality'. Jeff's pet project, his fantasy, is the exploration of deep space, for which Ulysses has been specifically designed in order to cope with the problems of isolation. Yet Ulysses, under Frankie's influence, becomes too humanised. He not only falls in love, but delights in those social occasions and settings in which his creator is so clearly uncomfortable. Ulysses escapes from the laboratory that Jeff escapes *to*. The android wanders around the mall, is wide-eyed at the Miami skyscape, eats real junk food instead of protein paste, does the conga at a wedding and so on.

Ulysses takes to postmodern life with relative ease, learning fast from TV, which is where he picks up Steve Marcus's election slogan – 'It takes a man this sensitive to know your needs' – and quizzing Jeff on the exact relation between sex and love. In the film's final twist Jeff takes the place of Ulysses, fulfilling his own boyhood dream to voyage into space which, for him, is 'truly the most exciting thing in the world'. Jeff's are the final words of the film, heard over images on the TV screen in Frankie's apartment. When asked how he's coping with the isolation he replies, 'I'm not very good with people'. The glib superficiality of the Marcus campaign slogan indicates the film's concern with the territory of identities forged in and through the mass media. Seidelman explores not only different images and versions of masculinity but also the constructedness of these different ways of being a man. The world of PR in which Frankie works relocates the questions raised by the scientific creation of life to a postmodern context in which the activity of *making* rather than meeting the mythical figure of 'Mr Right' is fantasised as a possibility. The construction of the raw material – Ulysses – is only a starting point. The importance of the social skills in which Frankie specialises poses, in basic form, a set of questions about the formulation of identity.

In this context Judith Williamson's comments on Seidelman's film usefully locates it within the 1980s' rubric of the 'new man'. Ulysses, as Williamson notes, is brand new. And, as she goes on to point out, '[t]he key fact about the new man is that he doesn't exist'. As a combination of 'a marketing concept and a projection of modern women's desires, the emotional, sensitive, tender Loving Hunk is no more real than the Living Doll who was, similarly, an amalgam of consumer products and male fantasies' (Williamson 1988: 28). Williamson's analogy between a fantasy of ideal femininity circulating in the mass media of the 1960s and the more recent construction of the 'new man' is pertinent here. Much discussion of the 'new man' has centred on whether or not this figure exists, which is to say whether a figure created within advertising has any correspondence with 'real life'. Yet as feminists discovered in their interrogation of female types like the 'living doll', it is the construction of different definitions of femininity rather than the truth value of particular images that is significant. That is to say, the effects of these types are real enough. Surely that is part of the reason why image-makers, such as Cindy Sherman and Barbara Kruger, have reworked images derived from mass-media sources such as advertising in order to produce a commentary on the formation of identity within and through these same media.[22] While the different images of the 'new man' and the muscular hero may have no, or few, referents, they do have determinants.

Like Seidelman's earlier *Desperately Seeking Susan* (1985), *Making Mr Right* is precisely situated in a world of images, surfaces and lifestyle options. Frankie Stone is the epitome of the post-feminist heroine, successful in business and unlucky in love. We see her as busy, capable and dressed to perfection. The film opens with Frankie waking up to televised images of Marcus clutching a beauty queen. Though she's wearing a T-shirt with the legend 'Marcus is My Man', when the congressman calls round he finds himself locked out. As Marcus drives away, a life-size cardboard cut-out of himself, wearing a smile in the role of sincere politician, sails down from the window to be crushed under the wheels of his car. Here Frankie rejects the first of many versions of masculinity to be offered in the film.

In the credit sequence that follows, Seidelman charts Frankie's transformation from one image to another as she drives to work. Frankie holds up the traffic as she shaves her legs, sprays on her perfume and fixes her face. Striding into a conference room she announces 'I'm always late but I'm worth it' to the waiting representatives from Chemtec. Later, when Ulysses empties out Frankie's bag, he finds a set of accessories familiar to the readers of women's magazines: a copy of *Smart Women, Foolish Choices*, lipstick, cigarettes, hairdryer, diaphragm, tights, snapshots. . . . Meanwhile *Donahue* plays on the TV in the background, with the host quizzing the audience on the search for 'Mr Right'. The bewildering range of objects and images offered to Ulysses, and possibly to us, in this scene echoes Frankie's earlier arrival at work when she reels off an order for 'breakfast as usual' along with '*Cosmopolitan, Glamour, New Woman, Complete Woman, Working Woman* and *Modern Wrestler*'. Frankie consumes mass culture for breakfast. This litany of the modern working woman's reading jokily signals woman as consumer, an important theme for the film. The romance narrative of *Making Mr Right* draws from this context of competing images, a discourse derived in part from women's magazines with the possibilities that they offer of making opportunities, make-up, creation and self-creation. The film thus draws on the kinds of feminist understandings offered through mass-media forms like women's magazines, invoking the kinds of powerful images associated in the 1980s with an aggressively sexual, and image-conscious, figure like Madonna.[23] As Williamson points out, 'the stress is not on women switching images' as in *Desperately Seeking Susan* 'but on women as *consumers* of images – and of men, in relation to whom the film functions like a *Which* guide' (Williamson 1988: 29). There is an accompanying stress on man as image, an attention to the many different definitions of masculinity which are available within contemporary culture. Even Jeff, who prides himself on his isolation from society, reveals that he has *worked* on his personality. We also discover that Jeff knows enough about the signifiers of masculinity to give Ulysses an enormous penis for 'confidence'.

The very texture of *Making Mr Right*, with its bold use of colour and its Florida setting, invokes a sense of the fabrication of social life and of the existence of different, competing identities. Generic awareness and intertextuality are fundamental to these textual qualities though, as we will see, this is far from unique in contemporary cinema. *Making Mr Right* pulls in the romance narrative, screwball comedy, science-fiction and soap opera. The film manages to parody them all, whilst still keeping them in play. A sense of change and transformation is at work here, an awareness of the constant renegotiation of both generic and gendered identities. The postmodern play, with images and identities that characterise both *Making Mr Right* and the figure of the bodybuilder, begins to mobilise metaphors of construction, creation and change.

The intertextuality at work in *Making Mr Right* makes apparent the extent to which gendered identity is formed and transformed through our consumption of images. But the film also draws attention to the operations of form. Picking up on these themes, this book has both a general and a specific project. Specifically, I hope here to deliver an analysis of the action cinema, a genre that is both popular with audiences and critically neglected. Centrally the book is concerned with the *cinematic* qualities of the action cinema, the importance of visual spectacle. Kathryn Bigelow is, in this context, one of the most striking directors working in the action cinema today. Her contemporary rendition of the vampire myth in *Near Dark* (1987) and of the cop movie in *Blue Steel* (1990) involve images of both startling physicality and breathtaking beauty. The book's final chapter centres on an analysis of Bigelow's work, which also provides a way to bring together some of the key themes. Her 1991 film, *Point Break*, represents a fascinating excursion into the territory of male bonding. The sensations evoked in the skydiving and underwater sequences prove as interesting as the obvious play with the intensity of male bonding and homoeroticism. The book ends with a discussion of this film partly because it is so accomplished. The critical reception of *Point Break* though also returns us to the ways in which action-based texts, action stars and the rest of the creative teams associated with them, are so routinely dismissed by the critical establishment.

1

WOMEN WARRIORS

Gender, sexuality and Hollywood's fighting heroines

Pictured alongside Sylvester Stallone, whose box-office success in the roles of Rocky and Rambo represented a particular and very visible inflection of masculine identity in the cinema of the 1980s, was found, for a time, the larger-than-life image of the star's then wife, Brigitte Nielson.[1] Shortly after her arrival in America, Nielson had played the part of a comic-book swordswoman, alongside Arnold Schwarzenegger, in the mythological epic *Red Sonja* (1985). Nielson also played the wife of Rocky's opponent in *Rocky IV* (1985) and had roles in *Cobra* (1986) and *Beverly Hills Cop II* (1987). Though she was associated with the action genre through such roles, it was her marriage to Stallone that gave Nielson extensive media visibility. A six-foot, muscular blonde, Nielson's androgynous image combines 'masculine' characteristics, such as her height, muscular physique and boyish short hair, with an exaggerated female sexuality. Nielson embodies the big-breasted sexualised fantasy woman of comic-book traditions, whilst emphasising the more 'masculine' elements that are an important part of this figure. The stories circulated through magazine gossip and Hollywood hype are indicative of the rather unsettling aspects of this image, in that they often centre on sexuality and on Nielson's location in relation to traditional discourses of womanhood. Along with persistent rumours of both lesbian and heterosexual affairs, questions about her 'fitness' as a mother undermine Nielson's 'femininity', whilst rumours of cosmetic surgery similarly emphasise her constructedness as against some 'natural' notion of womanhood. A regular 'comic' interview question concerns whether men are afraid of her, a formulation which is indicative of the uncertainties generated by her image.

Nielson embodies then a contradictory set of images of female desirability, a sexualised female image which emphasises physical strength and stature. Like the figure of the muscular male hero, Nielson's version of the woman warrior borrows on comic-strip traditions which deal in parodic, exaggerated characterisations of gendered identity. Indeed, the increased visibility of male and female action stars within American movie culture are related phenomena. What then is the significance of the emergence of the action heroine within Hollywood cinema? How has the Hollywood cinema represented the action heroine and how has this changed in relation to the shifting persona of the muscular action hero? At one level the action heroine represents a response of some kind to feminism, emerging from a changing political context in which images of gendered identity have been increasingly called into question through popular cultural forms such as music video. Equally the persona of the action heroine borrows on well-established images such as that of the tomboy, so that the heroine who is cast as the hero's sidekick can be read as a girl who has not accepted the responsibilities of adult womanhood. The heroine of Hollywood action pictures has more commonly been figured as romantic interest for the hero. The female fighter as centre of the action, whilst only emerging relatively recently in American film, has for some time been an important figure in Hong Kong action traditions. It was in Hong Kong that American martial-arts star Cynthia Rothrock, who is considered in more detail below, made her first films.

Ripley, played by Sigourney Weaver in *Alien* (1979) and *Aliens* (1986), represents one of Hollywood's most visible action heroines of recent years.[2] The characterisation of Ripley in Ridley Scott's original film represented a significant development in the portrayal of action heroines, combining icons of the action narrative with borrowings from the horror film. The climactic action sequences of the film, in which Ripley undresses before her final confrontation with the alien, has generated a good deal of debate concerning the limits and possibilities of the cinematic representation of the action heroine.[3] Weaver reputedly dubbed her role in the second film as 'Rambolina', acknowledging the film's rather self-conscious allusions to the Rambo narrative and persona. *Aliens* has Ripley, having been betrayed by the 'company', decked out in weaponry to do battle with the mother alien. Director James Cameron had co-written the screenplay for *Rambo* as well as directing another key muscleman movie of the 1980s, *The Terminator*. The *Alien* sequence of films is discussed further in Chapter 7, alongside the figure of the muscular heroine. The figure of Ripley raises interesting questions of symbolic transgression, of the extent to which the positioning of a woman at the centre of the action narrative generates problems for the genre at the level of connotation. The figure of Ripley also provides an interesting instance of the ways in which image-makers have dealt with the 'problem' of the action heroine, mobilising configurations of motherhood, for example.

By way of contrast to a figure like Ripley, roles such as that played by Patsy Kensit as Rika in *Lethal Weapon 2*, to cite just one example amongst many, provide little for the actress to do but confirm the hero's heterosexuality. If the male body is to be a point of security, the hero a figure who can be relied on, then bodily integrity and heterosexuality in particular, need to be maintained within the action narrative. The figure of the woman as romantic interest performs, in this respect, a key narrative function. She both offers a point of differentiation from the hero and deflects attention from the homoeroticism surrounding male buddy relationships. In these terms the figure of the woman provides a space onto which a variety of desires and anxieties are displaced. In *Death Warrant* (1990) Jean-Claude Van Damme plays Burke, an undercover cop in a maximum security jail. Cynthia Gibb plays Amanda Beckett, a lawyer who, posing as Burke's wife, provides a contact to the outside. The film enacts a complex male psycho-drama in which the prison narrative is framed by Burke's encounter with the ghostly figure of 'The Sandman'. Rape is held up as a threat to Burke, who resists both the sexual violence of his cell-mate and the more seductive temptations of Jersy, a transsexual who lives in the prison's basement. At the same time, the narrative and cinematography insistently sexualises and commodifies the male body. Gay desire is primarily displaced onto a pathologised construction of blackness within the film, but seemingly to further allay the anxieties attendant on the male prison narrative the film includes a scene in which Amanda inexplicably visits Burke in a private trailer for an intimate love scene, which then fades out at the first kiss. This love scene follows an indicative set of sequences in which we cut from Burke being beaten up by the prison guards to a scene in which Amanda arrives at the prison and is sexually harassed by the same guards. In this case the woman functions as a figure where a displaced story of sexual desire – represented in terms of violence – can be voiced. In an earlier visit to the prison, Burke rebukes Amanda for not looking the part, indicating perhaps the extent to which she is out of place in this film.[4]

Whilst the woman in the action narrative may operate as some kind of symbolic guarantee, a place for the fixing of difference and heterosexual desire, she is simultaneously rendered increasingly marginal. Unlike the active/passive division of labour discussed by Laura Mulvey in relation to the classic Hollywood film, in which the male figure advances the narrative whilst 'woman' functions as spectacle, the male figure in the contemporary action picture often functions in both capacities. He controls the action at the same time as he is offered up to the audience as a sexual spectacle.[5] Given the additional importance that images of same-sex friendship have as a source of visual and narrative pleasure within the action narrative, the woman as love interest is in many senses an unwelcome figure. An hysterical figure who needs to be rescued or protected, the heroine is often played for comedy. Sometimes she is simply written out of the more intense action narrative altogether, as in *First Blood*. More often female characters are either raped or killed, or both, in order to provide a motivation for the hero's revenge. It is almost a cliché of the detective narrative that the cop hero has lost his wife or lover either before the film commences, as in *Dirty Harry* or *Lethal Weapon*, or fairly soon after her appearance as love interest, as in *Lethal Weapon 2*.

In films like *Rocky III* (1982) and *Kickboxer* (1989) the figure of the woman mediates the sexual threat that the black or Asian villain represents to the white hero. Mr T plays Clubber Lang, a vicious challenger to Rocky's title in *Rocky III*. Lang challenges Rocky's virility, making sexual suggestions to his wife Adrian and taking his title from him before the film's final confrontation, from which Rocky emerges triumphant once more. In the final fight from *Kickboxer* the Thai kickboxing champion, Tong Po, taunts Jean-Claude Van Damme with both having raped his girl Mylee and holding his paralysed brother Eric captive. Such roles for female characters are very much in line with traditional, even archaic, understandings of women's role within society. The action movie often operates as an almost exclusively male space, in which issues to do with sexuality and gendered identity can be worked out over the male body. It is perhaps no surprise then that the heroines of the Hollywood action cinema have not tended to be action heroines. They tend to be fought over rather than fighting, avenged rather than avenging. In the role of threatened object they are significant, if passive, narrative figures. This role is sometimes also played by a 'weak' male character, a figure who is similarly in need of the hero's protection. This kind of narrative dynamic operates, for example, in *Lock Up*, a film in which the status of threatened object is initially played by the young male convict that Stallone/Leone has befriended in the prison. His nickname, 'First Base', indicates something of the sexualised power relations structuring this friendship, implications not lost on the rest of the inmates at Gateway. Once First Base has been killed, it is Leone's girlfriend on the outside, Melissa, who once more assumes the role of the one who needs to be protected, as the narrative moves to its conclusion.

This much, in terms of the sexual organisation of narrative, is familiar, summarised in the mythological image which Laura Mulvey invokes, of Andromeda tied to a rock awaiting rescue from Perseus.[6] If women are erased from the action, if not the *mise-en-scène*, of the action narrative, where does this leave female performers? I certainly do not want to argue that this results in an unproblematic erasure of female audiences. One of the pleasures of the cinema is precisely that it offers a space in which the ambiguities of identities and desires are played out. This blurring of categories is crucial to understanding the play of femininity and masculinity over the bodies of male and female characters, a process that has been inflected significantly in the action cinema of recent years in which the body is brought so much to the fore. Weakness, vulnerability is expressed through the mobilisation of traits associated with femininity, most particularly a softness or lack of definition which might allow the body to be fatally penetrated. It is in these terms that the scars and wounds which mark the body of the suffering male hero are significant. The muscular male body functions as a sort of armour – it is sculpted and worked on – which is repeatedly breached, an understanding expressed in the image of Achilles' heel, a body with one point of physical vulnerability which betrays the otherwise invincible warrior, and which itself becomes intensely vulnerable.[7] Such images can be interpreted in relation to images of castration within the framework of psychoanalysis, as a dramatising of the pleasures of empowerment and the fear of powerlessness. The narrative dynamic that operates in relationship to the female body in the action cinema is constructed within a similar set of terms. Considered within a psychoanalytic framework women, of course, have less to lose. Whilst there is a symbolic transgression enacted through the feminisation and penetration of the male body, a symbolic transgression enacted over the woman's body emphasises the ways in which her body is rendered impenetrable. It is the play of such qualities in *Alien* that elaborates a distinction between the two female crew members – Ripley, who survives, and Lambert, who does not.

As the construction of the action heroine with reference to images of physical hardness makes clear, the connotations of the term 'heroine' in the Hollywood action cinema have been sharply shifted in recent years. By the beginning of the 1990s a range of images of active heroines had begun to emerge, figures such as Susan Sarandon and Geena Davies in Ridley Scott's *Thelma and Louise*, Linda Hamilton in a muscular reprise of her role as Sarah Connor in *Terminator 2* and Jodie Foster as aspiring FBI agent Clarice Starling in *The Silence of the Lambs*. These roles began to sketch out a different set of roles and new narrative possibilities for women in the Hollywood action cinema so that 'heroine' no longer necessarily signifies passivity. The success of these films, and the sheer visibility of images of their female stars, represents a significant inflection of the action cinema's articulation of gender. Nonetheless these images do emerge from existing traditions of representation, a history that is briefly traced below in an attempt to offer a context for the very public emergence of these action heroines.

THE 'INDEPENDENT HEROINE' AS STEREOTYPE

During the 1970s Hollywood, always eager to cash in on the emergence of new markets, sought to respond to the women's movement in a variety of ways. Films such as *Klute* and *Julia*, which both starred Jane Fonda (an important actress of the period) attempted to redefine existing types and traditions of representation, in order to include the figure of the 'independent heroine'.[8] Such films centred around the stories of women who are independent of men, who are sexually free and who, to an extent, determine their own lives. Forming a recognisable sub-genre these films are also primarily concerned with detailing the problems faced by the independent woman in achieving her independence. Thus the problematic aspects of the 'independent woman's' narrative is repeatedly foregrounded. These fictions can be seen to respond to feminist demands for less stereotypical roles for women, since they offer more developed character parts, even if retrospectively they can be seen to have contributed to a recognisable stereotype. These fictions offer, that is, a new, or at least revised stereotype. During the same period, and forming an allied development in some respects, American television produced such successful series as *Charlie's Angels*, *Policewoman* and *Wonderwoman*. These television series all placed women at the centre of the action narrative, though signalling in a variety of ways uncertainties about such a shift. Thus the three investigators who are 'Charlie's Angels' were oddly positioned as both fashion plates and action heroines, but also as in the service of the central male figure 'Charlie'. Whilst Angie Dickinson, the star of *Policewoman* and a well-established performer, played what was a more sober or 'dramatic' role, these series often emphasised the glamorous sexuality of the heroines, an emphasis which sat uneasily with the need to include action sequences.

What was implicit in a series like *Charlie's Angels*, that these characters were drawn from a stylised cartoon or comic-strip tradition, was made explicit in the televising of *Wonderwoman* with ex-Miss World Lynda Carter in the title role. The cult British television series of the 1960s, *The Avengers*, had mobilised such fantasy traditions, out of pop art, in the leather-clad, tough, fighting heroines played by Honor Blackman and Diana Rigg. In the cinema, films like *Barbarella* (1968) provide antecedents for these 1970s superheroines and for more recent epics such as *Red Sonja* and *Conan the Destroyer*, discussed below, which conjure up a mythological world in which to place the woman warrior, whilst also drawing on camp comedy to undermine the earnest poses of the performers. In crude terms, if images of men have often needed to compensate for the sexual presentation of the hero's body through emphasising his activity, then images of women seem to need to compensate for the figure of the active heroine by emphasising her sexuality, her availability within traditional feminine terms. Hence the rather conventional coding of glamour around characters such as 'Charlie's Angels'. This anxiety also allows us to think about the complex problems of coding posed by the more recent emergence of the muscular action heroine, a figure who is discussed later in the book.

In responding to feminism, image-makers sought to present women as active and as powerful, mobilising already-existing types and conventions, images that were an established part of popular culture, such as the leather-clad dominatrix. That producers reached for such conventions convinced many hostile critics that these representations were exploitative, and were directed at male rather than female audiences. The complex relationship between feminist criticism and images of the action heroine is taken up further in Chapter 7. Here we can note that the combination of supposedly masculine and feminine elements in the gendered images of the 1970s posed all sorts of iconographic problems for television producers and film-makers. Producers often sought to allay, if not resolve, the uncertainties posed by the action heroine through either the sexualisation of her persona or the use of comedy, or both. The production history of a television series like *Cagney and Lacey* is a case in point. Whilst this series became a rallying point of 'quality' television for many feminist critics and audiences of the 1980s, it was initially conceived as something quite different, during the 1970s. Barbara Avedon and Barbara Corday created the characters as a response to the arguments presented in Molly Haskell's book *From Reverence to Rape*, first published in 1974. Haskell had argued that women had been excluded from Hollywood in the 1970s in favour of the 'immature' and unthreatening relationships seen in male buddy movies. The producers got the idea of producing a female buddy movie, with the initial plot functioning as a spoof that had Cagney and Lacey investigating a 'Godmother' figure who runs a joke scam involving male prostitutes and female clients.[9]

The kind of comic role reversal operating here is reminiscent of the polarised 'battle of the sexes' rhetoric through which gender relations were popularly represented during the 1970s. The militancy ascribed to the women's movement can be seen as, in some senses, an extension of such rhetoric. This rhetoric and the images to which it gave rise are part and parcel of an attempt to insist on the retention of a binary understanding of gendered identity – a battle between two sides – which finds its contemporary manifestation in the popular understanding of human nature as made up of feminine and masculine 'sides'. Yet popular representation, indeed the very styling of this particular 'debate' as a 'battle', constantly calls into question such binary constructions. The strategy of role reversal and the stereotype of the independent heroine are very much of the 1970s due to their need to *explain away* the actions of the heroine and to reassert her femininity, at the same time as these actions are offered as pleasurable. This may be achieved through comedy or through narrative justifications which explain the 'accident of fate' by which the heroine occupies her position, if not the rather obvious fact that she is more than able to carry out the role asked of her. A common device has the heroine explicitly taking over her father's role after his untimely death. In terms of the fantastic powers traditionally ascribed to the heroes and heroines of action narratives, such a need to explain can be self-defeating. It is perhaps such factors that have led to the frequent repetition of rape-revenge narratives as a way of producing appropriate motivation for an active heroine in films such as *Sudden Impact, Ms 45/Angel of Vengeance* or *I Spit on Your Grave*.[10] The ideological construction operating in such narratives retains an understanding of the heroine as a vulnerable figure alongside her move into action, into a narrative of revenge. Indeed the two are bound up together.[11]

BLACK ACTION FILMS AND THE 'SUPERWOMAN'

American production companies were equally quick to respond to the success of Hong Kong action pictures with black audiences in the 1970s. *Black Belt Jones* (1973), a Warner Bros/Shaw Brothers co-production, represents a typical response to this phenomenon, casting martial-arts star Jim Kelly, who had just appeared alongside Bruce Lee in *Enter the Dragon*, in the title role. The film also cast Gloria Hendry in the role of Sidney, a character who exemplifies the figure of the black fighting heroine who emerged as a recognisable stereotype in a series of low-budget American action films of the 1970s. Bogle dubs these women 'macho goddesses', arguing that they 'answered a multitude of needs and were a hybrid of stereotypes, part buck/part mammy/part mulatto' (Bogle 1991: 251). Echoing the devices mobilised in television series like *Charlie's Angels*, narratives featuring the black female fighter resort to both the use of comedy and the fetishistic representation of female power. Thus whilst Sidney is revealed to be a fighter skilled in karate, this is at times played for laughs or seen in terms of a certain novelty value. Similarly when she is fighting alongside Jim Kelly in the film's final confrontation with the mob, a semi-comic scene which takes place amongst a deluge of soap suds, Sidney is only half-dressed.

Whilst the phrase 'macho goddesses' acknowledges the complex blend of masculine and feminine elements at work in this stereotype, it is worth exploring this hybridity a little further. It is in part the blackness of these heroines which opens up, through notions of black animality, the production of an aggressive female heroine within existing traditions of representation. Black female stars who have played action roles, such as Tamara Dobson, Pam Grier and Grace Jones, often function as 'exotic' creatures within the narrative. For her role as Zula in *Conan the Destroyer* (1984) Grace Jones is literally given a tail. The *meaning* of the emphasis placed on animality in Grace Jones's film roles is, however, complexly linked to the ways in which her image itself has addressed the stereotypical physicality and sexuality attributed to the black woman. The complex orchestration of signification involved in Jones's performances in film, in music video and as a singer, involves the simultaneous assertion of and challenge to the kinds of racist fantasies posed by Jean-Paul Goude's construction of her as a caged animal. The 'macho' aspects of the black action heroine – her ability to fight, her self-confidence, even arrogance – are bound up in an aggressive assertion of her sexuality. Simultaneously it is this same stereotypical attribution of sexuality to the black woman which generates anxiety around her representation.

Black Belt Jones transfers the martial-arts school-based scenario of many Hong Kong narratives to the States, combining this with a gangster narrative. The film's martial-arts school, with which Kelly's character is involved, is run by Pops, who is wanted by the mob. After Pops has been murdered his daughter Sidney arrives to investigate his death. Both beautiful and self-assured, Sidney causes a stir in her search for information, storming into a mob bar where she takes on and beats all the men there, revealing her own karate skills. The bar-room showdown is a stock scene of the action narrative, featuring a well-established set of codes. These codes can be seen at work in both Hollywood and Italian westerns, science-fiction films and the Hong Kong martial-arts film amongst others. There are bar-room confrontations in action films as diverse as *Star Wars*, *48 Hours*, *Near Dark* and *Terminator 2*. What does this scenario signify, and how has it been coded through gender and race? The bar-room showdown offers a conflict violently staged in a public space. The protagonists self-consciously strike poses, acting out stylised roles, in their desire to either instigate or avoid conflict. In the action cinema, such scenes are showpieces for the ritualised performance of a tough masculinity. Most typically, the hero does not appear to be threatening, whilst his arrogant antagonists clearly believe they have the upper hand. We, on the other hand, know, or at least suspect, the actual strength of the hero. Such generic moments play off conventional expectations, reminding us that appearances can be deceptive. The hero may seem weak, ineffectual or outnumbered, but ultimately he will overcome his opponents.

Given that the bar room has tended to be a male space – in representation certainly – then action films like *Black Belt Jones* can successfully play off the challenge represented by a woman's entry into this space. Such confrontations, developed as a dramatisation of male conflict, are reworked around a female protagonist in the 1970s action film. The antagonists assume the heroine is unable to fight – she is a woman after all – but she is actually able to outclass her male opponents. Variants on such scenes, found in films like *China O'Brien* and *Above the Law*, are played for laughs as well as drawing on established modes for the representation of conflict. In however tangled and awkward a way these narratives do seek, through the inclusion of the female fighter, to acknowledge the shifting ideas bound up in the contemporary black and women's movements. This is largely played for comedy as when, after Black Belt Jones tells Sidney to stay home and do the dishes, she promptly shoots the crockery, pronouncing 'they're done'. Such comically inflected moments represent an explicit, if anxious, address to and acknowledgement of feminist concerns at the same time as they signal the uncertainties, indeed anxieties, generated by the figure of the action heroine.

In a similar vein ex-model Tamara Dobson played Cleopatra Jones, a glamorous government agent cast very much in a Bondian tradition, in two Warner Bros/Shaw Brothers co-productions. The films use a role-reversal device which opposes Jones to a female arch-villain. Stella Stevens plays the villainous Dragon Lady in the sequel *Cleopatra Jones and the Casino of Gold*. Whilst these films form part of a history of action heroines in western cinema, such roles have been limited until relatively recently to either the television series or to low-budget film production. Bogle makes a familiar assessment when judging Pam Grier's movies as 'trash' saved only by her 'grit' (Bogle 1991: 252). Such a judgement expresses both the pleasure and the disappointments to be found in these films. The production teams at work on films such as *Cleopatra Jones* and *Black Belt Jones* rarely demonstrate an ability to work with and productively employ the complex history of conventions which surround the cinematic representation of black women. More often than not, her presence is treated as a joke. These conventions are worked through and played with in a very small way in a more recent film, *Nico/Above the Law* (1988) in which Pam Grier plays Delores Jackson, Steven Seagal's cop partner. We are told that Jackson has only a limited time to serve as she is moving to the District Attorney's department, a clue which classically sets her up in the role of expendable sidekick, a loved character who will die in order to cement the hero's desire for revenge. Imminent retirement or transfer only increases the tension and the danger surrounding sidekick characters in the action movie. Indeed the film plays out this scenario rather self-consciously as Jackson is dramatically gunned down, only to reveal later that she was wearing a bullet-proof vest so that she survives to the end of the film. The survival of Grier's character is set against a long history of narrative sacrifice on the part of both the black female and male sidekicks of Hollywood cinema.

WOMEN IN THE MARTIAL-ARTS FILM

Films such as *Black Belt Jones* and *Cleopatra Jones* in the 1970s, or *Nico* in the 1980s, form part of a martial-arts tradition in American film production either influenced by the work of Hong Kong studios, or actually initiated and co-produced by American and Hong Kong companies working together. During the 1970s Hong Kong films, including those which showcased female fighters, had a massive commercial success in the west. 'Exotic' women gifted in equally 'exotic' forms of the martial arts had featured in such 1960s' and 1970s' products as the James Bond films. In the early 1970s Hong Kong films starring female performers, with Angela Mao Ying the most publicised, began to be distributed in the west.

As Verina Glaessner points out at the time it was assumed that 'her films, *Hap Ki Do* (1970) especially, but also *Lady Whirlwind* (*Deep Thrust*, 1971), were an exotic response to the growing influence of the Women's Liberation Movement' (Glaessner 1974: 74). Instead Glaessner locates these films within longstanding Chinese and Japanese cinematic traditions of swordplay films. In the west, however, where some women had already begun to look to forms like karate for a method of self-defence, it was inevitable that the films would be read in terms of the women's movement.

The differences between the role of the female fighter in American and Hong Kong traditions are made apparent in the role given to Angela Mao Ying in *Enter the Dragon*, the Warner Bros film which sought to package Chinese star Bruce Lee for western audiences as well as existing Asian markets. There is a significant western redefinition of the Bruce Lee persona at work in this film. This involves the construction of Lee as an asexual figure in the service of the British authorities. Jim Kelly, playing a stereotypical black 'stud', bears the burden of the film's discourse about race, dying before the end of the film. The operations performed around the Lee persona in this film draw from a history of western representations of Chinese men as feminised. A comparable set of negotiations operate in a smaller way around the figure of Angela Mao, who appears briefly as Lee's sister in an early flashback sequence. She is pursued by a gang and, finally cornered, kills herself. We see the suicide from her point of view as a shard of glass is brought towards the camera. For Glaessner this is 'a curious scene in which the suicide is at odds with the whole conception of the fight hero or heroine in Chinese films – everyone knows he or she would have gone down fighting' (Glaessner 1974: 80–1). The flashback allows only a contained showcasing of Mao Ying's fighting skill, just as the film as a whole attempts to contain or redefine the figure of Bruce Lee. The mapping of western concerns about the representation of the active heroine onto the fighting fantasies of Chinese cinema are indicative here of the anxieties at work in films of this period. The sequence, in its representation of a lone woman chased by a group of men, invokes sexual violence, a theme which has had a central narrative and ideological significance within the western action cinema. This once again returns us to the centrality of rape within action narratives as a justification for female violence.

Petite and blonde, Cynthia Rothrock, who began her movie career in Hong Kong action pictures, has repeatedly been described as an unlikely action heroine. My discussion centres on three of her films which have been quite widely available in the west through the video market: *Above the Law* and the two American *China O'Brien* films. Rothrock has become an important figure on the video martial-arts scene and has received publicity due to both her talent and the novelty attached to the fact that she is a white woman working in a genre associated with white men in the west and

Chinese performers in Hong Kong. In *Above the Law* Rothrock plays the part of a tough Hong Kong cop. The film follows hero Yuen Biao's decision to turn vigilante, rejecting a career in the law after his mentor has been assassinated and the corruption of the system has become transparent. Rothrock vows to capture him though she ultimately uncovers the corruption of her police chief boss, and helps the hero, fishing him out of the sea after the final spectacular aerial showdown with the villain. Rothrock has some spectacular fights in the film, including a sequence in which she goes into a gaming house and secures three men to a chair with one set of handcuffs. The different conventions and traditions of the Hong Kong cinema allow all sorts of characters, rather than just the major protagonists, to be fighters, a context in which Rothrock's appearance does not seem to require the kinds of narrative explanation so insistently worked through in her American films.

The two *China O'Brien* films cast Rothrock as Lori 'China' O'Brien, a city cop who, when she accidentally kills a child, gives up her badge and gun, taking off in a cross-country drive back to her home town. China finds her sheriff father in the midst of a losing battle with a corrupt judiciary and the town in a state of near anarchy. When both her father and his deputy are killed, China runs for Sheriff, gets elected to office and defeats the bad guys. The film offers set pieces such as a bar-room showdown in which China performs staggering sidekicks whilst wearing stilettoes. In one of the few moments in either film to explicitly draw attention to the potential problems posed by Rothrock's femaleness, she sighs in *China O'Brien 2* that 'It's tough sometimes – being a woman'. Her remark follows from the hysterical insults of an unreliable male character who screams at her 'I bet you enjoy beating up on men'. It is important that China's femaleness be unthreatening to the symbolic world of the film, so that she can come to represent law and order in small-town America. At a town celebration at the beginning of *China O'Brien 2*, she is awarded a plaque for her services to the community and hailed as a great sheriff – 'Not bad looking either' adds a member of the audience. This is typical of the ways in which the film keeps negotiating the role of a female sheriff. Accompanied by her ex-special forces boyfriend and her sidekick Dakota, China's familiarity with the town and the people in it is stressed in both films.

In the language of the trailers, China is 'a sheriff without a gun, a daughter without a father' and 'a woman without fear'. Such images clearly position China as her father's daughter, and her father is constantly invoked as a presence, even after his death. She is a figure who is marked as 'in-between' or 'not-quite'. Her name brings together the imputed exoticism of the martial arts and the East ('China') with her father's name, that of a white, Irish-American family (O'Brien). The figure of the father operates as legitimation for China's transgression in taking on the job of sheriff. Similarly the setting of the action in a small town with figures such as Chester who seem to be taken directly from an old-style Hollywood western, situates China's position of power within a limited space. It is in the big city that she hands over her gun, seemingly resigning from law enforcement. Within Hollywood's symbolic system possession of a gun is a potent symbol of power, partly drawing from an American context in which the freedom to bear arms is constructed as a right of the citizen. The figuring of possession of the gun as a symbol of power for women has been further appropriated and deployed in recent action narratives such as *Thelma and Louise*.

THE HEROINE AS SIDEKICK

The central role played by Julia Nickson in *Rambo* as Co Bao, a Vietnamese agent who is Rambo's contact on his secret return to the country, has not had a corresponding place in many commentaries on the film. Co escorts Rambo to the supposedly deserted prison camp he has been assigned to investigate, explaining that her career as a guerilla has followed from the death of her father. Like China O'Brien then, Co has taken on her father's role, remaining a dutiful daughter at the same time as she represents a powerful female figure who seems to refuse conventional femininity. Shocked to find American POWs in the camp, Co aids Rambo in escaping, taking a prisoner along as evidence. They separate in time for Co to see Rambo abandoned by an American rescue helicopter. Shots of her in close-up are intercut with the shots of Rambo's capture so that she becomes the audience for his suffering within the film. Co proceeds to disguise herself as a village prostitute, a figure we have seen visiting the camp earlier, rescuing Rambo from his captors. In an early conversation about their roles and motives in the conflict Rambo tells Co that he has been sent on this mission since he is expendable. At their first parting she assures him that this is not so and demonstrates this by coming back for him. The film contrasts the hero's betrayal by the American military machine with Co's loyalty.

At this point in the film the relationship between the two characters shifts from that of comrades-in-arms to romance. In a soft focus scene they kiss and talk of going to America together. This, it seems, is a little too much for the film to deal with. Thus, when Co stands up moments later, she is gunned down and Rambo sets out to avenge her death. Through her death Co's active role is transformed into a role that I've already referred to, that of woman as lost object to be avenged. The inflection of this role in performances such as Nickson's is significantly to re-style the woman-as-romantic-interest as an *action* heroine. At the same time it is made clear that the two roles are incompatible, unable to exist simultaneously. Where this does happen, as in *Total Recall*, this is in the context of a narrative which is about the instability of identity and the uncertainty of appearances. Co's death is important for the narrative logic of *Rambo*, which cannot reconcile its outsider–loner rhetoric with the positioning of the hero in terms of heterosexual romance or even within a projected return to America. The film cannot find a place for either the muscular hero, or the kind of woman Co signifies, within its schema of America. The action heroine here is as placeless a figure as the hero, though in a rather different way, since she is often also rendered marginal by the narrative of the film, literally sacrificed. This difficult position is also made evident in *Terminator 2*. After her transformation into an action heroine through the course of the first film Sarah Connor has, in the narrative time that has elapsed, been separated from her son and we find her incarcerated in a lunatic asylum where she works out and plots her escape. Images of the heroine as mother, an image which emphasises her womanhood, come into conflict with images of the fighting action heroine who is defined as insane, without a place in American society.

In understanding this conflict of images we can look to a longer tradition of representation. Distinct from the women who function as the hero's love interest and little else, are the female sidekicks who accompany the hero on his travels. In contrast to Julia Nickson's role in *Rambo*, these women are often comic characters, getting laughs through a reversal of the conventions of femininity. The character played by Karen Allen in *Raiders of the Lost Ark* (1981) is cast in this vein, a woman who can drink men under the table. Grace Jones's role as May Day in the James Bond film, *A View to A Kill* (1985) is indicative of the crudity of this kind of secondary role. As villain Christopher Walken's sidekick, Jones performs a parody of her own sexualised public persona. The film makes jokes about her sexuality with her 'seducing' Roger Moore as James Bond and aggressively climbing on top of him. A more sustained sidekick role is that played by Nancy Allen as Lewis in *RoboCop* and *RoboCop 2*. Allen is introduced through Murphy's eyes in the first few minutes of *RoboCop*, violently slugging a suspect she has brought into the police station. As Murphy's partner, Lewis looks helplessly on, whilst he is blown to bits in graphic detail. As in *Rambo*, the woman provides an audience for the hero's suffering, his powerlessness emphasised by her gaze. Later it is Lewis who recognises the human traits that remain after Murphy's transformation into a cyborg, and it is she who helps him to take his revenge. In the second film Lewis and RoboCop are still partners, with her tough-cop persona played off against his literal metallic toughness. She knows that Murphy has been re-programmed by the company when he compliments her on her appearance and calls her by her first name. For Murphy to acknowledge Lewis's difference signals clearly to her, and to us, that something is wrong.

This kind of joke about the conventions of courtesy may tell us something about the important symbolic role that the female sidekick has within the action cinema. Like the black buddy who is discussed further in Chapter 2, she provides a point of differentiation, emphasising the masculine identity of the male hero. Yet at the same time the female sidekick problematises, to an extent, that same masculine identity which the hero embodies – since she is witness to his failings. The use of comedy and the representation of suffering, as in *Rambo* or *RoboCop*, present two polarised forms for the mediation of anxieties to do with gendered identity. In *Commando* Matrix/Schwarzenegger teams up with Cindy, an air hostess, played by Rae Dawn Chong. He forces her to help him, despite her protests that 'I've got a 7.30 advanced karate class and I can't help you'. After she has rescued him by demolishing a police truck with a rocket-launcher, Matrix asks her 'Where did you learn to do that?'. She provides the punchline: 'I read the instructions'. As with so much of the humour derived from action heroines, this short sequence plays on a joke about how it is possible to *learn* the skills and qualities which go to make up the supposedly natural masculine strength of the hero. This tension is further exemplifed in the Schwarzenegger film *Total Recall* in which we see the hero specify his ideal heroine, represented by Melina. *Total Recall* offers hero Quaid/Schwarzenegger a choice between two women, the wife he is 'placed' with by the 'agency' and Melina, whom he dreams of. In either case these women are, like the hero, very definitely *constructions*, so that at key points in the development of the narrative we are left unsure whether these women, indeed the whole 'world' in which the action takes place, are 'real' or fantasised.

'STRONG WOMEN': COMIC-STRIP HEROINES

The mythological or fantasy narrative situates exaggerated physical types, often derived from comic books, within imaginary locations. Accompanying the boldly drawn physical characteristics of the heroes and heroines are clear judgements between good and evil – there are few moral grey areas. The film of the cartoon series *Masters of the Universe* (1987) represents an extreme version of this stylised battle, pitting Dolph Lundgren as He-Man against arch-villain Skeletor and Meg Foster, who plays his right-hand woman, Evil Lynn. Perhaps inevitably in the transfer of a cartoon to the screen, comic strands are interwoven with the action of these narratives, indeed they are part and parcel of the general muscular excess. Humour is derived from the juxtaposition of the barely clad heroes and heroines (so clearly offered as sexual spectacle) with the intense earnestness of the mock mythologies constructed for these fantasy worlds. Thus, there is a doubleness operating in these films around a tacit acknowledgement of the hilarity with which the narratives, which take themselves seriously, are actually received. Minor characters constantly comment on the action, acting to undercut the overblown figures of the heroes and heroines. In *Conan the Destroyer* Arnold Schwarzenegger's Conan is persuaded to undertake a journey with the young princess Jehnna. She is to fetch a crystal which will unlock a secret mystical power. Her virginity is supposed to give Jehnna a magical power, but at the same time she is clearly constructed in terms of the modern teenager, asking Grace Jones's character for advice on how to get a man. The characters of Jehnna and Jones as Zula are consistently opposed by the film through the sexualised terms of innocence and experience. Whilst Jehnna is blonde, white and clothed, Zula is black and near-naked, so that the mythicised notions of sexual innocence and experience are mapped onto racial constructions of female sexuality, as well as figures of dominance and subservience, through these two figures.

Red Sonja followed on from the Conan films, casting Brigitte Nielson in the title role and Arnold Schwarzenegger as Kalidor. The ideological figures of virginity and magic are once more important to the narrative. At the beginning of the film Sonja wakes from a daze to find a ghostly figure who informs her, and us, of the events that will trigger her narrative search for revenge. We learn that Sonja had rejected the sexual advances of evil queen Gedren, scarring her face, which Gedren covers with a mask for much of the film. Though Gedren orders the slaughter of her family, Sonja survives and is given a magical power which makes her a strong swordswoman. Something of a commercial disaster on release, *Red Sonja* has become a cult curiosity on the video market. It is also one of the few action-based films to explicitly invoke lesbianism.[12] By way of contrast, the homoeroticism surrounding male action stars is a constant presence, acknowledged and played with by films which, as I'll discuss in later chapters, simultaneously deploy an anxious disavowal of gay desire. The prison settings of films such as *Death Warrant*, *Lock Up* and *Tango and Cash* are used as spaces in which to express images of homosexuality in terms of the threat of violent rape. That lesbian desire, personified in the figure of the evil queen, is made explicit in *Red Sonja* represents the voicing of an often unspoken, if central, term in discourses of the action heroine. *China O'Brien 2* also includes glimpses of a recognisable lesbian stereotype in the policewoman, Lucille, who handles the phones at the station. The relationship between the two protagonists of *Thelma and Louise* invokes in more complex ways images of, and associated with, lesbianism – country music, the cowgirl look, the two women's final kiss, the sub-genre of the buddy road movie itself. *Thelma and Louise* was unproblematically billed as a 'lesbian film' when shown at a women's event in London. Which is merely to assert that there is a space for such identifications within action films like this, even if they don't explicitly acknowledge their gay audiences.[13]

The uncertainties which surround the action heroine can be usefully explored in relation to the comic aspects of mythological narratives, such as *Red Sonja*. Recourse to comedy is a more general feature of the action cinema at moments of symbolic tension. The figure of the hero as wise-guy, for example, can be understood in these terms. The wise-guy hero is always ready with a crack, a witticism which may catch his opponents off guard. *Fatal Beauty*, discussed below, casts Whoopi Goldberg as a 'wise-guy', drawing on her talents as a stand-up comedian. An analysis of the ideological terms at work in a film like *Red Sonja* is not difficult – the film follows Sonja's journey to a 'normal' sexual identity, or at the very least the rejection of lesbian desire. After the initial 'threat' of lesbianism, Sonja becomes a masculinised swordswoman who refuses Kalidor/Schwarzenegger until he can beat her in a 'fair fight'. The final image of the film has the camera pulling away from the two who embrace only after they have begun to fight yet again, since he has in turn insisted that Sonja beat him in a sword fight. The comedy and the excess, which permeate the texture of the film, also systematically call into question the very terms deployed – the 'normal' sexual identity to which Sonja is led. The body, and in particular the muscular body, is very much to the fore in these narratives – hence the minimal clothes of the heroes and heroines of these fantasy narratives. The comic/cartoon origins of figures such as He-Man and Conan allow them to exist in close relationship to and, in some senses, to one side of the conventional standards of social behaviour. I'm speaking here of the sense in which exaggeration, which is over-statement, so easily crosses over into parody. Clearly the big-breasted or muscular women found in comic strips are fantasy figures. Yet in companion with their exaggerated sexual characteristics, these heroines have exaggerated physical powers, in swordplay or marksmanship, a strength which marks them as transgressive, as perverse.[14]

As much as anything else, the *tone* of a film like *Red Sonja* is indicative of the play of elements which cannot be understood through an ideological analysis based on narrative structure alone – Sonja's journey to a 'normal' sexuality. The fact that the film visually defines this normalcy through images of Sonja's sword fights with Arnold Schwarzenegger, or that viewers may well be aware of the qualifications posed by both Nielson's star image and the tabloid gossip surrounding her, indicates a possibility of reading the film differently. There are, that is, a variety of elements, both textual and extra-textual, which may operate to undermine the narrative assertion of heterosexuality. These qualifications make the rather basic point that an experience of cinema is not limited to the duration, or content of a particular film, since texts are contextualised in a variety of different ways by the other mass media, and by the more immediate and diverse ways in which different groups appropriate images from those media. Such an understanding has been crucial to a variety of critical discussions of popular pleasure.[15] Instead of seeing the protagonists of action cinema to be emerging as powerful and meaningful figures 'despite' the fictions in which they are mobilised, it is also important to think about what the pleasures of those fictions might be. Such pleasures might explicitly be seen to include the dramatisation of the struggle to become powerful in difficult circumstances.

At a textual level it is also possible to argue that the action film is a form which puts into question the terms of a gendered representation of power. In all sorts of ways action narratives centred on the male hero are to do with a refusal to make the journey to a 'normal' sexuality, a refusal to 'grow up' within an oedipal trajectory in which growing up involves the assumption of authority and the position of the father. The significance of this drama is developed further in later chapters. The transgressive heroine of action narratives is involved in a rather different scenario. In her perversity – her turning away from the father – she is nonetheless thoroughly oedipalised. Heroines like China O'Brien are functioning quite explicitly *for* their fathers. We have seen the emergence of a generation of action heroines who are positioned in a very close relationship to the law. Just as China is a sheriff, we can also think of films like *Blue Steel* in which Jamie Lee Curtis plays a uniform cop, or *Silence of the Lambs* in which Jodie Foster's character is an aspiring FBI agent. These figures may begin to suggest that the heroine's perversity, in assuming the powerful and threatening role of the phallic woman, involves a very different relationship to the law than that which typifies the outsider hero. He is able to both refuse and embody phallic power. These are complex questions, however, in which it is not possible to generalise a schema for the genre as a whole – both *Thelma and Louise* and the *Alien* films, which I have cited together here, propose a different set of terms for understanding the figure of the action heroine. Nonetheless it is possible to signal these themes as defining the terrain on which the genre operates.

WHOOPI GOLDBERG: *FATAL BEAUTY*

The casting of Whoopi Goldberg as the star of an action picture like *Fatal Beauty* provides an indicative example of the contradictory demands of picturing difference within the Hollywood system. Goldberg plays Detective Rita Rizzoli, a narcotics cop with a personal mission against drugs. She is clearly a representative of the law, a casting which in terms of the history of representations of black women in Hollywood cinema, triggers something of a crisis of coding. Goldberg herself has played such roles as that of a bartender in the revived television series *Star Trek*. The mysticism implicit in this role was made explicit in her casting as a medium in the hugely successful romance *Ghost*. Contrasting the success of Oprah Winfrey with Whoopi Goldberg's career, Michèle Wallace points to Hollywood's difficulty in 'coming up with a credible storyline for a black female comedian with dreadlocks, which will commodify racial "marginality" but isn't racist enough to produce a boycott of the theatre'

(Wallace 1990: 219). *Ghost* seems to have performed this operation quite exactly, playing on mythicised notions of racial difference. In thinking about *Fatal Beauty* there is then a general set of issues about the position of black women in Hollywood, as well as the specificity of the action narrative, to consider. If Goldberg is difficult for Hollywood to cast at all, why position her in a genre already anxious in terms of gendered identity? Though racial and gendered discourses are not interchangeable, they are interlocked in their sexualisation of relations of power. The troubling body is fetishised and thus, provisionally, made safe.[16] The figure of the action heroine then, raises a similar set of issues to that of the black hero in the action narrative. How can the over-determined sexual stereotypes, through which both women and blackness have been coded in the cinema, be transformed in order to produce a stable black or female figure around whom the fiction can be centred?

Blackness is understood within Hollywood's symbolic in terms of marginality and criminality. This criminality has been most often expressed in action narratives of recent years not through sexualised images, but through the ideological figure of drugs. Drugs have emerged as a key signifier in a variety of American discourses over the last fifteen years. Representing the 'enemy within', drugs offer a way of speaking about the circulation of capital and relations of dependency and power. Drugs have also represented a key part of American political discourse, with George Bush's declaration of a war on drugs ultimately used to legitimise such acts as the invasion of Panama. For a brief period in the mid-1980s Hollywood produced narratives focusing on wealthy white drug-users, and images of drug use as a signifier of corruption can be found in a film like *RoboCop*. By and large though the association between drugs and blackness, often cast in terms of a 'foreign' element invading the country, has been increasingly invoked in American representations of recent years. In *Fatal Beauty* we learn that Rizzoli was once a drug user and that she bears a burden of guilt since her drug use led to the death of her child. Thus Rizzoli is the bad mother struggling to make up for her transgression. Her construction as a maternal figure allows her to be caring, whilst also legitimating her extreme use of violence. The one moment in which she comes to blows with another woman is when she assaults a rich white woman who is seemingly indifferent to her son's drug use. The lost object that Rizzoli seeks to avenge is her own child, rather than the love interest sacrificed for the male hero's quest. The rape/revenge narrative is triggered by a violation of the woman's body – events which generate a violence directed at the attacker. In *Fatal Beauty* the logic of Rizzoli's revenge must in part be directed against herself. This tortuous logic stems from the difficulty of finding a term against which Rizzoli can be defined. Who, or what, can be constructed as the black woman's Other?[17] This is, of course, precisely where the ideological figure of drugs is introduced.

Fatal Beauty ends up by almost completely isolating Goldberg's character. The few scenes in which Rizzoli and co-star Sam Elliott have a flirtatious relationship come as a relief within a film in which she is so persistently isolated within shot and abused, both physically and verbally, by both crooks and cop colleagues. With the two going through doors together (a key iconic moment of the cop movie) and rescuing each other, there is at least a sense that Goldberg is in the same film as another character. Due to supposed audience hostility a love scene between the two was cut from the film, a rewrite that Donald Bogle takes to indicate the problems surrounding the 'very idea of Whoopi Goldberg as a romantic film personality'. For Bogle, by 'throwing her into male-oriented action films the industry prevented women from being able to identify fully with Goldberg' (Bogle 1991: 298). Whilst *Fatal Beauty* seems uncomfortable with its own project in many ways, the whole notion of the 'male-oriented action picture' invoked by Bogle is deeply problematic, not least because the emergence of action heroines into the mainstream has necessarily redefined the articulation of gendered identity in the action picture. If the film seeks to prevent identification with Goldberg's character, this is not a function of the genre. Bogle also draws attention to the way in which Rizzoli is rigorously defeminised, if not desexed by the film such that her dress 'in oversized clothes or sneakers' suggests a view of her 'as an asexual creature from another universe' (Bogle 1991: 298). Indeed much is made of Rizzoli's clothes in *Fatal Beauty*, in which she oscillates between an outrageous prostitute's outfit and her off-duty leisure clothes. Isn't this reluctance to make Rizzoli a sexual character strange in relation to the over-sexualised image of the black woman produced in Hollywood and elsewhere in western culture? Goldberg's image in the film as both a hyper-sexualised and a de-sexualised cop is of course precisely related to this history of representation in which discourses of sexuality have been mapped onto the black female body.

Karen Alexander, in her discussion of black female stars, cites Goldberg's comment on the cut love scene that if Elliott 'had put some money on the bedside table the next morning, the scene would have been acceptable' (in Gledhill 1991: 53). Goldberg's comment highlights her perception that black women are generally only permitted to be sexual within the Hollywood film when this is framed by a discourse of prostitution. The black woman can seemingly exist only as a commodity on the screen, not as a desiring subject. Yet for Goldberg to actually play a prostitute would position her on the margins of a film in which she provides the narrative centre, a film in which she is the heroine, the star. To return to my original question – why cast Goldberg in an action movie? – perhaps it is precisely in the action cinema, rather than any other

Hollywood genre, that the anxieties attendant on the spectacular sexuality attributed to the black woman can be displaced onto the spectacle of the action which drives the narrative.

2

BLACK BUDDIES AND WHITE HEROES

Racial discourse in the action cinema

Action heroes and heroines are cinematically constructed almost exclusively through their physicality, and the display of the body forms a key part of the visual excess that is offered in the muscular action cinema. Such an emphasis on physicality has, as I've already indicated, opened up a space in the action cinema for black performers who have been almost totally excluded from many other Hollywood genres. Stereotypically defined through the body and through a variety of kinds of performance, blackness is already coded in terms of spectacle. As Kobena Mercer points out in his discussion of Robert Mapplethorpe's *Black Book* though, the display of the black male body has not generally been staged within the high cultural context of the nude in which Mapplethorpe locates it. The black body has instead been figured within popular culture, achieving a visibility primarily through the forums of sports and entertainment.[1] Perhaps it is not surprising then that the black body is a more visible figure in the popular action cinema than in other, perhaps more prestigious forms of Hollywood production. Further, as we've seen in relation to Whoopi Goldberg's role in *Fatal Beauty*, the inclusion of black performers at the *centre* of the action picture poses a range of iconographic problems which are ultimately worked out in terms of sexuality. What emerges clearly from an analysis of such films is the fact that formulations of 'race', constructions of blackness in particular, are central to the American action cinema.[2] Black actors, performers and stars have regularly appeared as both secondary characters and as vital members of the fighting teams that are visualised in the action picture. Only rarely though have they been given the chance to take centre stage, and Danny Glover's performance as Lieutenant Mike Harrigan in *Predator 2* provides one such instance. Discussed in detail in the final part of this chapter, the film exemplifies something of the complexity that has been brought to the action picture by the use of well-established character actors as it has moved into big-budget status, as well as opening up some questions around the negotiations currently in operation around Hollywood's construction of blackness.[3]

Attention has already been drawn to the association between blackness and criminality within Hollywood's symbolic system. Black characters regularly appear in American action pictures as criminal elements, populating the prisons of films like *Lock Up*, *Tango and Cash* and *Death Warrant*. Black characters are also crucial in such narratives as vendors of information to cop and private-eye heroes. A typical example of this role was that played by Antonio Fargas as Huggy Bear in the popular 1970s' television crime series *Starsky and Hutch*. Whilst the show was primarily concerned to offer up Starsky and Hutch as desirable pin-up heroes who occupy themselves with intense male bonding, rather than detecting, Huggy Bear would provide the information needed in order to get the job done.[4] Blackness functions here as a bridge into the corrupt world of crime. The intermediary figure, the snitch or go-between, provides a way for the white heroes of crime narratives to tap into the secret world of black criminality. The relationship between the figure of the hero and the black go-between varies across a range of registers, from friendly banter to seething intolerance, though the pair are rarely seen coming to blows. This narrative device performs a series of functions. Firstly, it enables the business of detection to take place off-screen. Black informants provide white heroes with the information they need, leaving the heroes free to be constructed in terms of a sexualised display. The processes through which evidence and information are acquired are simply effaced. Such tendencies became even more pronounced in *Miami Vice*, the hit television crime show of the 1980s, which devoted much of its screen time to the construction of star Don Johnson as sexual spectacle.[5] Of course the show also commodified the body of co-star Philip Michael Thomas, a move which to an extent redefined the role of the black buddy.

The relationship between hero and informant further elaborates a representational relation of power and subservience. While the relationship between the white hero and his black helper may be initially tense, the black character, already marginal, invariably ends up willingly sacrificing himself. Hence the significance of the simple fact, referred to in Chapter 1, that Pam Grier survives to the end of *Nico*. In *Death Warrant*, Priest, a powerful black figure within the film's prison setting, sacrifices himself for white hero Jean-Claude Van Damme, a sacrifice which negates his earlier hostility and for which the film offers no explanation. The incoherence of this particular film's articulation of racial difference is complexly bound into anxieties about homoeroticism and gay male desire. That is, there are relations of power and desire in operation which the film cannot bring itself to state explicitly, or perhaps cannot find the words to state. The film-makers are able, nonetheless, to fall back on an unproblematic assumption, indeed a cinematic convention, that the black man is willing to sacrifice himself for the white hero. The sexual implications of the relationship between these two figures are taken up further in the discussion below, but this dynamic also has a significant implication for the operation of narrative. Whilst blackness may be constructed as marginal within Hollywood narratives, it has a *symbolic centrality*. This is particularly pronounced in the action cinema, a form that is played out over the terrain of criminality, and one that is often directly concerned with the policing of deviance. Thus, as in the case of *Fatal Beauty*, a black character does not sit easily at the centre of the fiction. The opening sequences of *Fatal Beauty* feature not only Rizzoli, who is introduced to us in her prostitute's guise, but a range of grotesque stereotypical figures against which she can then be defined – an overweight white queen who deals in drugs, a naked and insanely giggling Asian worker in a drugs factory, along with a whole array of vicious white punks. It is partly through such references that the film attempts to construct a new margin against which the centre, Goldberg in the role of a black female cop, can be defined. As we will see in relation to a variety of films, the positioning of black performers at the centre of the action narrative usually involves a re-negotiation, and reaffirmation of the existence of the margins.

THE BLACK ACTION HERO

Before considering more recent black action films, it is worth briefly recalling the blaxsploitation films of the 1970s, which provide a significant point of origin for many contemporary images and narratives. Through a series of commercially successful films produced in the early 1970s, the figure of the black action hero gained a new visibility in American cinema. Performances such as that by Richard Roundtree in *Shaft*, Melvin Van Peebles in *Sweet Sweetback's Baadasssss Song* (both 1971) and Ron O'Neal in *Superfly* (1972) offered an aggressive articulation of black masculinity, forming one part of Hollywood's response to an emergent black audience.[6] Just as Hollywood had sought to produce films which responded to the women's movement, specifically for the female audience it had created, producers saw black film as a good box-office bet, a phenomenon I've already referred to as a significant factor in the development of the black martial-arts film at around the same time.

The muscular movies of the 1980s work with exaggerated images, derived in part from cartoons and comic-strips, of white male identity, images which also provoke a certain anxiety at the level of representation. The characterisation of the black hero in 1970s' film also worked through exaggerating existing stereotypes, constructing the black hero as a powerful figure, but also as hyper-(hetero)sexual and as very much part of an urban culture. The inflation, or parodic exaggeration, of stereotypes proved problematic in this case, due partly to the complex evolution of the very images which these films took up and developed. Such images came from a long visual history through which white western culture has sought to project its fears and desires onto the black body. Complexly inscribed in colonial discourse and written in terms of power as it is, the reclamation and production of images of the black body for a black audience must involve a difficult set of negotiations. For critical commentators at the time of the release of these successful black action pictures, the images provoked just such an uneasy understanding of the politics of representation. Donald Bogle cites a contemporary feature from the magazine *Ebony* which mourned a perceived irony that 'the black marches and demonstrations of the 1960s reached artistic fulfilment in the 1970s with Flip Wilson's Geraldine and Melvin Van Peebles's Sweetback, two provocative and ultimately insidious reincarnations of all the Sapphires and Studs of yesteryear' (Bogle 1991: 236). But as Bogle points out, these films effectively fell into one more stereotypical articulation of black masculinity, the stud, in an attempt to avoid reproducing another, that of the black man as a passive, asexual figure.

The heroes of these black action films are very much located within an urban culture or community, providing a sharp contrast to the often dislocated black heroes and heroines who have featured in Hollywood films of the 1980s. This aspect of the heroes' characterisation can also be contrasted to a tendency in the construction of the white action hero, who is increasingly represented as an alienated figure. Often seeking to distance himself from all representatives of authority or community, the white hero is rarely seen with a family or any other close network of personal ties. *Shaft* seeks to appropriate in some ways the marginal position of the classic private-eye figure. Yet the street is constructed as very much the hero's domain. In earlier fictions centred on white private eyes the street is very much a threatening space that the hero must inhabit, involving a culture from which he is excluded. If thugs don't hide behind every corner in the world of *Shaft*, the film picks up details such as the hero's difficulty in getting a cab. The narrative is framed by Shaft's jokey relationship, if not friendship, with a white detective, Androzzi. His scruffy appearance contrasts with Shaft's impeccable dress. In the film's opening sequences Shaft buys information on some men who are looking for him from a shoeshine man. This exchange is followed by Androzzi's attempt to get information from him, which is also an attempt to position him in the familiar role of go-between. In action narratives, conversations are also verbal battles for dominance. Aware of such conventions the film positions Shaft in the uncooperative, but basically law-abiding, role of the private eye. This role has been established around fictional characters like Marlowe, who were repeatedly arrested but knew and were articulate in voicing their rights. But if Marlowe's name was designed to invoke a chivalric literary heritage, the name Shaft carries aggressively sexual connotations. Indeed the action is framed by images of the sexualised black body as spectacle. John Shaft is a fictional character who is inevitably constructed by and through a history of stereotypes which originate in desiring and fearful white fantasies. As with the production of the action heroine as phallic woman, the construction of the black action hero as a stud both acknowledges, makes visible, and also retains elements of that history of representation.

While films such as *Shaft* worked to produce the black action hero, critics such as Gladstone L. Yearwood, looking back at the films of the 1970s, have called precisely for a demystification of the black hero. Yearwood suspects that whilst films such as *Shaft* and *Superfly* 'attempt to subvert, or at least question, the dominant tradition in the cinema' they are 'effectively harnessed by it in their usage of the Hollywood model as the basis for the development of black heroes' (Yearwood 1982: 48). Yearwood thus recognises that the kind of cinema he is searching for cannot be found in Hollywood traditions, in which the over-determined figure of the hero stands in for a generalised struggle against the powerlessness of his position. His call for a demystification of the black hero echoes the feminist unease which has centred on the figure of the gun-toting action heroine in the recent Hollywood cinema, but fundamentally goes against the archetypes with which the popular cinema works. The films, heroes and heroines of the action cinema mythicise, if not the specificity, then the *fact of struggle* for a popular audience. The black action films may well prove to be so unsettling precisely because they seem to be so acutely aware of the issues of representation that are at stake in their construction of the black hero. That history is a constant presence, informing both the styling of the heroic images and the construction of the narrative.

GENDER AND SEXUALITY: BLACK AND WHITE BODIES IN THE ACTION CINEMA

The construction of the body through racial discourses cuts across and informs the articulation of gender and sexuality in the action picture. The naked display of the black body carries radically different meanings to the display of the white body, which audiences are so frequently offered in big-budget action pictures. In their characterisation of the hero the action films of the 1970s reached for the stereotype of the confident, hyper-sexualised black man. By contrast, the exaggerated physical characteristics of the white hero tend to lead him into narrative situations in which he is subjected to torture and suffering. The boundaries of his body are repeatedly violated, penetrated in a variety of ways, from the scene in which Rocky's eye is cut open in the first film of the series to that in which Rambo sews himself up in *First Blood* or cauterises his wounds in wide-screen close-up in *Rambo III*. Such imagery derives in part from a Christian tradition to which martyrdom and sacrifice are central. In Jean

Claude Van Damme's *Cyborg* (1989) this imagery is carried to an extreme with a scene in which his character is actually crucified. In part these exercises in suffering serve to indicate the self-sufficiency of the hero, the fact that he can survive with little or no help. If *Cyborg* crucifies Van Damme it also gives him enough fantastic strength to kick through the crucifix and thus rescue himself.

As indicated above, the narrative relationship between the white hero and his black informant allows for both the display of the hero's body, largely dispensing with the work of investigation, and the enactment of relations of racially defined dominance and subservience. Indeed the two are intimately bound together, so that the suggestion and demonstration, through the performance of the narrative, of the superiority of the white hero over his black informant functions to allay an anxiety attendant on the sexualised display of the white male body. To follow this point through a little further, we can look at one of the recurrent character types in the recent American action cinema, that of the damaged black man. This figure represents a way of making safe the black man's fantasised hyper-sexuality. It is in relation to these fantasies of phallic sexuality that the frequent appearance of physically damaged black men, cast as key characters in action narratives, can be understood as providing a form of reassurance.[7] In *Death Warrant* Jean-Claude Van Damme's black buddy Hawkins has a dead eye, whilst in *A.W.O.L.* Joshua has a badly damaged leg and a pronounced limp.[8] Alongside Hollywood's construction of the black male as a sexual threat, there exists an established tradition of representation in which the black man is suffused with a passive, Christian imagery. Yearwood points to the coexistence of 'stoic Christian types' with the 'low-comic buffoon', judging it irrelevant whether Hollywood chooses to emphasise 'one castrated image above the other' (Yearwood 1982: 46–7). Here, as we will see in relation to a variety of narratives, suffering and comedy perform similar functions. In action movies, comedy is often used to undermine notions of masculine power, a function which relates to Yearwood's designation of the comic image as 'castrated'. Thinking within the logic of this psychoanalytic framework, we can understand, in a different perspective, the casting of black and Asian women as sidekick to the white hero, women such as Julia Nickson in *Rambo* or Rae Dawn Chong in *Commando*. The woman in this instance is already 'castrated'. Unthreatening to the white hero, she confirms both his difference and his strength.

Within a representational system that constructs black men as either hyper-sexualised or passive castrated figures, the representation of the black action hero is more than a little fraught. A totally passive hero is a contradiction in terms, whilst an aggressively active black hero seems to provoke altogether too much anxiety for Hollywood to deal with. That the representation of the white hero has also provoked a set of anxieties in recent years, though in different ways, represents an important shift. A point in common between the two figures is the use of humour to resolve anxieties generated by the image. The Silver Pictures production of *Action Jackson* (1988), starring Carl Weathers in the title role, represented an attempt to produce a big-budget revival of the 1970s' action formula, a formula which of course means something rather different in the late 1980s. The credit sequence offers a sort of montage-homage to Detroit, introducing in the process a young, black and rather ineffectual petty criminal, Albert Smith. The two arresting officers talk of handing him over to 'Action Jackson', giving the hero an incredible build-up and terrifying the kid. This produces a running gag through the film, with Smith fainting or running away every time he sees Jackson. This is a joke about Jackson as an embodiment of masculine power, in which even a glance can induce panic in young Smith. Jackson is a tough cop, but he also has a law degree from Harvard. We learn that Jackson has been demoted, a fact which indicates the insubordination characteristic of the action hero. He has also lost both his wife and the right to carry a gun, a couplet which links the loss of two kinds of symbolic, and actual, power for the male protagonist. This weight of loss was due to the intervention of influential (white) businessman and criminal Peter Dellaplane, against whom Jackson bears a not inconsiderable grudge. This Bondian arch-villain provides a clue to the film's strategy which is to play the fast-paced action drama for laughs.

In the best action tradition the plot of *Action Jackson* is almost impossible to follow, the film being centred around its humour and the staging of spectacular stunts. Jackson gets information from a diverse range of sources including, amongst others, Robert Davi as a nervous union man who is soon after assassinated, Sharon Stone as Patrice Dellaplane, the villain's wife whom he murders when she begins to suspect his schemes, Vanity as Sydney Ash, the villain's drug-addicted mistress who teams up with Jackson, and a poetic female hairdresser. Even though Jackson is a rogue cop he is set up in the film as an embodiment of authority, of the law. This is significant when set against the extent to which action heroes of recent years have been constructed as very much outside such institutions. At the time of the original black action pictures, in the early 1970s, the most famous and controversial policeman hero was the embittered rogue cop Dirty Harry. The police, FBI and other institutions of law enforcement have been constructed since this point, in a variety of films, as at best incompetent, and more usually corrupt. Indeed this tendency is already there in *Dirty Harry*, with the hero throwing away his badge at the end of the movie. Jackson's demotion and his antagonistic relationship with Captain Armbruster (Bill Duke) refers to this tradition of representation, in which the hero is problematically situated within the hierarchy of the law.

Whilst contemporary white action heroes are pumped-up figures, their ability to embody masculine power is repeatedly qualified through the narratives in which they appear. Most particularly it is increasingly rare for the hero to represent state power. The over-statement of masculine identity operating in *Action Jackson*, in which, in the final moments of the film, Armbruster reinstates Jackson to the rank of lieutenant, is locked into the over-determined representation of the black action hero. Jackson is explicitly threatened with castration at one point in the film, a danger from which he escapes by pretending to be an hysterical religious fanatic. Again this is played for laughs, with Weathers's hamming up a recognisable black stereotype. The film offers a magical resolution to the problems it has constructed, but one in which the terms are indicative. Not only is Jackson restored to his former rank, but his glamorous sidekick Sydney informs him that she is now off drugs. Throughout the film Sydney's drug-use signals her degradation, but also, complexly, her sexuality. Her addiction is revealed in a bedroom scene with Dellaplane, in which the exchange between the two, which begins as a sex scene, is that of drugs. Drugs provide a symbolisation of Dellaplane's power over Sydney. We see him inject her with a needle in an image of bodily violation. Recalling the symbolic link between drugs and blackness established within Hollywood, these scenes and characterisations are significant. Drawing on this set of connotations, the film also locates the white villain/businessman as a central, threatening, figure within this symbolic circuit. Dependence (on drugs) is explicitly linked to the operations of power. By the end of the film, with Sydney's refusal of drugs and the place to which they assign her in the film's world, the stereotype of the sexually available black woman has been in a sense 'cleaned up'. Yet this transformation is only possible in terms of her relationship to Jackson. With the final confrontation taking place in Dellaplane's bedroom, where Sydney is a prisoner, the battle between hero and villain is enacted in terms of a competition for the possession of the woman's body.

I've already discussed how a film like *Death Warrant* uses the figure of the woman as a space through which to locate a displaced homoerotic desire. The film also invokes the stereotypical damaged black man, figuring blackness as a pathologised space of deviant desire. Old-timer Hawkins is represented as damaged through his 'dead' eye, a flaw which perhaps makes him unthreatening enough to be able to live to the end of the film. The second key black figure in the film, Priest, is, by the way of contrast, figured in terms of an ambiguous sexuality. Priest inhabits the lower floors of the prison, a space that is restricted. The hero, Burke (Van Damme), is told that the guards will not visit this part of the prison and his cell-mate's warning that he should 'cover his ass', 'literally', is a moment that more explicitly voices the fact that the threat faced by Burke in this film is rape, gay desire re-presented as a threatened violence to the body.

Priest offers Burke one of his 'ladies', sexually ambiguous men/women, more as a challenge than a sign of friendship. Burke tells Jersy he'll 'take a raincheck', though s/he is later killed for warning him of his danger, and the promise is never fulfilled. If Hawkins survives, Priest, who has decided inexplicably to help Burke and thus sacrifice himself, is violently killed. 'The Sandman', a frightful, ghostly figure who functions as the hero's super-ego, dispenses with Priest as he is helping Burke to escape, planting an axe in his stomach. The centrality of black buddies to the symbolic schema of *Death Warrant*'s prison drama stems partly from the need to inscribe difference within an all-male setting. This leads us to the centrality of the inter-racial buddy relationship in recent action cinema more specifically.

'RACE', DIFFERENCE AND THE BUDDY MOVIE

In contrast to the construction of the hero as a lone figure, one of the key devices in the action narrative of recent years has been to call on the conventions of the buddy movie. The male pairing allows for comedy to develop through verbal repartee. This kind of interplay is central to films like *Tango and Cash* in which Sylvester Stallone and Kurt Russell move from hostility to friendship. *Thelma and Louise* picks up on this tradition for women, with one-liners and gags, as when a panicked Louise shoots out a car radio, instead of the police radio as Thelma instructs her. Through the 1980s the male buddy pairing has frequently been that between the white hero and his black partner, with the black figure occupying either a secondary or largely supportive role. This pairing has clear antecedents in the American cinema. Whilst it is not strictly a buddy movie, such images of bonding form an important part of the relationship between Gunnery Sergeant Highway (Clint Eastwood) and Stitch Jones (Mario Van Peebles) in *Heartbreak Ridge*. The two meet early on in the film, though they are unaware of each other's identity (since neither is in uniform). Their initially antagonistic relationship ultimately becomes one of respect, as they fight together in Grenada. This film reverses the relationship between Lou Gossett, Jr and Richard Gere in *An Officer and a Gentleman* (1982), a movie similarly concerned with military rites of passage. Beyond the male camaraderie of the military, Mel Gibson and Danny Glover were successfully paired in the *Lethal Weapon* cop films. Don Johnson and Philip Michael Thomas fought crime together in the hit 1980s' television series *Miami Vice*. In the *Rocky* films Stallone and Carl Weathers as Apollo Creed move from enmity in the first and second films to buddies in the third and fourth. In *Rocky IV* Apollo dies in the ring and Rocky takes it on himself to avenge his friend's death, challenging the huge Russian champion who killed him.

When Joe Hallenbeck's daughter in *The Last Boy Scout* asks if she can show off her dad's famous footballing friend Jimmy Dix (Damon Wayans), Hallenbeck (Bruce Willis) points out that he isn't a puppy. But what is the role of the black sidekick in the buddy action movie? On one level he is there to marvel at the hero's achievements and to support him through difficult situations. He operates as a supportive, sometimes almost fatherly, figure. Donald Bogle suggests that a kind of servicing role is being performed by these black buddies, so that in scenarios of 'interracial male bonding, black men are a cross between toms and mammies: all-giving, all-knowing, all-sacrificing nurturers' (Bogle 1991: 276). For Bogle the relationship between Al Powell (Reginald Veljohnson) and John McClane (Bruce Willis) in *Die Hard* represents an extreme enactment of this scenario. Certainly the relationship between the two is central to the film. Not only that, the relationship develops through an articulation of gendered identity which draws on the stereotypical history to which Bogle refers. Powell is the personification of the good-natured, chubby cop. Plump and friendly, he senses that McClane is also a good cop and defends him against his idiotic and ineffectual boss, Dwayne T. Robinson. Powell is first to arrive on the scene, sent to investigate McClane's report of a terrorist takeover of which the police are suspicious. Everything seems calm at the Nakatomi skyscraper, until McClane throws the dead body of a terrorist down onto Powell's car, in a desperate bid to alert him. We see the body descend in slow motion from Powell's point of view as the music reaches a crescendo. Willis exclaims through the broken window, 'Welcome to the party, Pal', as Powell's car is riddled with bullets from the terrorists in the building above. Powell soon establishes radio contact with McClane and, though they do not meet until the final scene, they speak to each other throughout the film, becoming closer as they swap family and police stories. During their conversations Powell reveals that he is a 'desk-jockey', a policeman who only does paperwork, explaining that he had once accidentally shot a kid and that he can no longer bring himself to fire a gun.

In terms both of established traditions of representation of black masculinity, and the iconography of the action cinema, Powell's refusal to fire a gun signals his emasculated status. The refusal to carry a gun is also a refusal of the policeman's role on the streets – Powell has become a figure in an office rather than a figure in a landscape. He is thus also rendered the object of humour. We first see him, singing to himself, buying twinkies in a convenience store. When the guy at the counter jokingly asks why he isn't buying donuts – which are after all real policeman's fare – Powell tries to explain that the twinkies are for his pregnant wife. The checkout man looks disbelieving, and though Powell is good-humoured, laughing the comment off, he is also the butt of the joke. All of this works to establish Powell as a friendly, reliable but essentially unthreatening figure. Yet he is the only one outside the besieged building to appreciate the threat posed by the 'terrorists' within, with the police and the FBI acting in an arrogant, bureaucratic manner. Powell keeps up an ironic commentary on their actions, complementing Willis/McClane's wisecracking. *Die Hard* seeks to tie up all the loose ends, and when McClane has rescued his wife and battled his way out of the building, he and Powell finally meet. Their eyes meet in the crowd and they embrace in what is an emotional moment, with soft music on the soundtrack. After the introductions one of the villains, Karl, emerges half-dead from the building. He is screaming and brandishing a rifle. Karl is shot repeatedly and the camera pulls back from a close-up of the barrel of a gun to reveal that Powell has fired the fatal shots. Operating as part of the film's restoration of narrative order, Powell is significantly re-masculinised in this moment, made iconographically a cop, and a man, once more.

A gendered dynamic operates in *Die Hard*'s buddy relationship, a dynamic through which Powell is constructed as an initially passive figure who is, through his relationship with McClane, masculinised. This echoes Bogle's characterisation of the relationship between the two figures in terms of active and passive gender stereotypes. But the relationship is also indicative of the ways in which concerns of sexuality are mapped through Hollywood's buddy friendships. The buddy movie, particularly as it developed in the 1970s, with films such as *Butch Cassidy and the Sundance Kid*, offered, amongst other things, a space for the covert exploration of the homoerotic possibilities of male bonding. The use of female sidekicks like Sydney in *Action Jackson*, allows for a more explicit play of (hetero)sexuality. As an example of male bonding we can consider the *Lethal Weapon* films. The inter-racial pairing of Mel Gibson as Martin Riggs and Danny Glover as Roger Murtaugh operates without any explicit reference to racial difference. And as Bogle points out, Murtaugh functions in the film as 'the good black man' who 'brings to his white loner friend an element of calm control and a budding maturity' (Bogle 1991: 276). The film operates to both negate and assert difference between the two men. In *Lethal Weapon 2* issues of racism and racial difference are raised in a displaced form, through the figure of unqualified evil that is represented by the film's South African villains. The repeated reference to apartheid, situated in another place, helps to ease over some of the difficulties of the inter-racial pairing. It is a liberal America, contrasted throughout to South Africa, that is the stage for the buddies' drama.

The *Lethal Weapon* films manage to avoid any homoerotic inflections of the buddy pairing by reinscribing difference within the terms of 'race'. In fact, a range of differences are established between the two – the unlikely combination which works out is a convention of both the buddy movie and the romance. Riggs and Murtaugh are paired in the first film very much against Murtaugh's wishes. He is older than Riggs (Glover is given greying hair for the part), repeatedly muttering 'I'm too old for this shit' through the course of the film. Riggs has a bad reputation, as a cop who either has a death wish or is faking insanity in order to claim a 'psych pension'. Either way Murtaugh is not happy with his new partner, but as the film progresses the two become friends. Both films work through a series of verbal reassurances that the relationship is definitely not gay. When a nearby building explodes, Murtaugh jumps on Riggs in order to extinguish the flames on his jacket. Even such an 'explicable' moment of physical contact is framed by Riggs's protests about 'fags'. As the first film progresses, Murtaugh's family comes under threat and he and Riggs join together to defeat the bad guys. The end of the film is an action movie showpiece. As is the case with so many fights in this genre, the participants are soaking wet – a device which either reveals half-naked bodies or allows for clinging costumes. Here Riggs takes on the villainous Mr Joshua, fighting him half-naked on Murtaugh's front lawn. The scene offers an image of the sexual–power relations of the inter-racial buddie pairing in microcosm. Whilst the white hero shows off his body, his black buddie stands back, a protective figure who watches from the sidelines. The fight, of course, also functions as a key moment of spectacle, emphasising the hero's strength. The setpiece fight channels the concerns of the narrative into a physical conflict. The epilogue features Riggs's inclusion within the Murtaugh family, as he is invited in for a Christmas meal, so that by the second film he is clearly one of the family.

The opening sequence of *Lethal Weapon 2* picks up where the first film left off, emphasising the centrality of the buddy relationship between Riggs and Murtaugh. The film opens on a car chase with a close-up of a gleeful Riggs, who thumps the roof of the car and screams 'I love this job'. Riggs's enthusiasm is juxtaposed with Murtaugh's long-suffering look of disbelief and his refusal to drive any faster. Back in the police station, the other cops are taking bets on who will apprehend their quarry first – all the odds laid on Riggs are reversed when they find out that Murtaugh is driving his wife's station wagon. The jokey contrast between Murtaugh as a cautious family man, worried about home and car, and Riggs as a reckless, rootless figure, is pursued at some length through the film. The station wagon is demolished bit by bit as the film unfolds. Reprimanding the team at the station house, Murtaugh plays the grown-up to Riggs's adolescent stunts – escaping from a strait-jacket by dislocating his own arm for a bet. Affectionately harassed at home, Murtaugh is thinking about easing himself into retirement. He is old-fashioned, embarrassed at his daughter's debut appearance in a television commercial for condoms. Attempting to assert himself he orders her boyfriend, George, out of the house, telling him that he has a gun. In turn Riggs reassures George, telling him that 'it's an old gun and he's not a very good shot'. This sequence comically reprises a set of associations, between potency, masculinity and weaponry, which are common in both the action picture specifically, and American cinema culture more generally. The film's audience will probably be aware that Murtaugh is, in fact, an excellent shot. Both men are further defined in the film against Leo Geetz (Joe Pesci), a witness they are assigned to protect. Leo's comic role functions to produce a figure who is both feminised and trivialised by his hysterical speech. Anxieties about masculinity, sexuality and the buddy movie are played out in the final scene of *Lethal Weapon 2*, in which Riggs pretends to be dying in Murtaugh's arms. The parodic enactment of a war movie death scene makes the conventions of that genre comically explicit. Picking up on the cinematic convention which only allows men to embrace if one of them is dying, the film both plays with and averts the possibility of desire between the two men. Playing to and subverting an audience's generic expectations has often provided a source of comedy in Hollywood films. If anything, this strategy has become more exaggerated in recent films, a tendency that is taken up in more detail in the next chapter. It is not despite, but *through* comic moments that the device of inter-racial male bonding functions in the *Lethal Weapon* series, comedy which plays off generic expectations as well as a range of stereotypes. Yet if these devices reinscribe the difference between men, at the same time a political history of racial difference within America is negated. The discussion below of Danny Glover's role in *Predator 2* takes up questions surrounding the inscription of 'race' within the American action cinema.

'WELCOME TO THE WAR': DANNY GLOVER AND *PREDATOR 2*

Predator 2, the sequel to John McTiernan's 1987 science-fiction/jungle patrol movie starring Arnold Schwarzenegger, is one of a very few big-budget action pictures to centre on a black hero. Actually, there is a small team at the centre of the film's action. Danny Glover as Lieutenant Mike Harrigan, heads up a team made up of Danny (Ruben Blades), Leona (Maria Conchita Alonso) and Jerry (Bill Paxton). Jerry is the last to arrive, and we listen with him to Harrigan's lecture on teamwork. The emphasis on teamwork in Harrigan's policing philosophy stems from the warzone conditions in which law enforcement is conducted in the film's world, that of Los Angeles in 1997. Harrigan's team is picked off one by one – though Leona does not die – with the hero left to battle the Predator alone in the final part of the film. In terms of the film's articulation of racial discourses, there are two striking features. Firstly, the jungle metaphor, which operates through the film's construction of Los Angeles, but which also relates to a construction of blackness through stereotypical images of the primitive. Secondly, the ideological figure of drugs, which, as we've seen in relation to *Fatal Beauty*, forms an important feature of many contemporary action and crime narratives. In *Predator 2* drugs are part of the scenery, not used as part of some personalised moral crusade as they are in *Fatal Beauty*. Nonetheless they are significant within the film's articulation of blackness and criminality.

The opening sequence of *Predator 2* sets up the LA-as-jungle image that is pursued throughout the film. Over a black screen we hear a variety of bird and animal noises and gradually percussion-based music fades up. This is archetypal Hollywood 'jungle music' and since the original *Predator* was set in the jungles of Central America this comes as no surprise. We cut into green images – the camera rapidly moving in an aerial shot looking down on the tree tops. Suddenly the city skyline is revealed behind the trees with the locating text, 'Los Angeles, 1997'. The image cuts abruptly into the Predator's point of view. The creature detects movement by heat, represented on screen by shifting patches of red and yellow on a blue background. The Predator seems to be tracking the city streets with speed – the animal noises with which the soundtrack began merging into the noises of the city; cars, screams, voices, music, radio and television. Finally we pick out the sound and heat images of gunfire and cut into 'real' (film) images of an explosion, finding ourselves in the middle of a chaotic street battle between the police and the city's drug gangs.

These opening sequences set the tone for the hectic pace at which the film moves. Multiple textures of sound and image are juxtaposed. In this first gun battle, 'real' film images are intercut with the Predator's point of view and with television coverage. We repeatedly shift from seeing flickering video images of news reports to their 'originals' on which the rest of the action intrudes. Elsewhere in the film we see and hear computer screens and computer-generated voices. More insistently, conventional two-shots of conversation between Harrigan and his team, between gang members and so on, are disrupted by the intercutting of the Predator's point of view. We still hear the characters' voices over these computer-generated screen images, but they are distorted, rendered sinister. It is with a variety of fast-paced techniques, such as rapid camera movements, quickfire editing and jump cuts that we are steered through an 'alien' and dangerous future landscape. The city is both recognisable and at the same time rendered strange as it is seen from a variety of perspectives.

The plot of *Predator 2* incorporates many of the ideological figures that we've seen to be standard elements of the action picture. Lieutenant Harrigan is a tough cop but also a team man. His team is loyal to him, and the members are all united in opposition to the constricting hierarchy of the police department. Harrigan ends his initial pep talk to new team member Jerry with an ironic congratulation, saying 'Welcome to the War'. As in *RoboCop*, where Murphy is deliberately assigned to a deadly part of Detroit so that he will be killed and recycled as cyborg material, the precinct that Harrigan polices represents the warzone of Los Angeles. It's pretty clear to the audience from the opening sequences, that Harrigan's characterisation of the streets as a warzone is accurate. Our knowledge thus positions us with the police team, against the authorities. The police department bureaucrats of *Predator 2* are, in classic action movie tradition, defined by their inability to see that they are involved in a war, and a consequent reluctance to give their officers the support that they need. The film casts Robert Davi as the officious police chief Heinemann, an actor who played one of the FBI 'by the book' men in *Die Hard*. The theme of institutional blindness is doubled within the narrative of *Predator 2*. Not only do Harrigan and his team have to deal with the Predator *and* the police department, but they are also caught up with a federal team headed up by Peter Keyes (Gary Busey) who wants to capture the creature alive.

It is no surprise that amidst all these confusing elements the characters, if not the audience, are unsure as to what it is that they are fighting. As a sequel the film must deal, as *Aliens* had to, with the fact that an audience probably knows already what the narrative's monstrous element is. The problem is one of sustaining tension until the characters find out what the audience already knows. A tense narrative of knowledge and appearance was played out in the first *Predator* in which Arnold Schwarzenegger's crack unit think they're up against a human enemy. Many of their mistakes come from this initial misrecognition. Again reminiscent of *Aliens*, much of the original film *is* coded through the conventions of the American Vietnam movie. The barbarous way in which the members of the patrol are picked off and murdered – the Predator *skins* its victims and leaves them hanging upside down – is attributed to the viciousness of the enemy. Accusations of brutality form a central part of wartime propaganda, drawing like the horror film on the figure of a monstrous other. *Predator* conflates these two discourses whilst at the same time demonstrating the danger of being taken in by them. The explanation of the killings in *Predator* in terms of enemy action will not wash for long. Billy, the Indian member of the patrol, turns to a spiritual explanation in an unsuccessful attempt to ward off the alien – a strategy that we see repeated in the second film – whilst others panic and run to their deaths. The threat in this film is constructed, through the codes and conventions of the Vietnam/jungle/patrol movie, in terms of a specifically racial otherness, before 'he' is revealed to be an actual alien – an 'Other World Life Form'. Thus elements like the invisibility of a barbarous enemy, the uselessness of high-tech equipment within a guerilla war, as well as the treachery of the military leaders who have set up the mission, are all found in *Predator*. These Orientalist fictions, through which the narrative of America in Vietnam has been repeatedly rendered in the cinema, become intimately associated with the mysterious and monstrous figure of the Predator.

In *Predator 2* this construction of the alien is mobilised once again through the use of a sustained jungle metaphor, but also through cinematic codes associated with blackness, rather than the imagined East invoked in the first film. A set of associative links already exists within Hollywood culture between blackness, Africa and images of the jungle, with Tarzan movies a key point of mediation in cinematic terms.[9] The Los Angeles of *Predator 2* is constructed, within familiar terms, as an urban jungle. It is also made explicit that the Predator is 'on safari'. He is hunting for trophies which we ultimately see assembled in a trophy room on board the alien ship. We have got the point well before Keyes, who is infuriated at Harrigan's repeated interference, finally spits out an explanation at him. An indicative moment comes when Harrigan, after making a phone call (from a call box, rather than from his office, visually positioning him outside the institution) stands outside the window of a taxidermist's shop. His head is framed as a reflection in amongst the stuffed animals that we see there. The image is held (a rare moment of stillness in this hectic film) before Harrigan looks uncomfortable at the thought and moves away. This narrative device reprises a common science-fiction theme in which the most sophisticated sites of human culture – science, weaponry, the city – stand as nothing but a primitive hunting ground for a superior alien threat. This transformation is emphasised through the very selection of Harrigan as the Predator's opponent, a selection that draws on symbolic associations between 'blackness' and the 'primitive'. Harrigan is both singled out as special – he is the hero – but is also associated with images of the primitive, situated within the 'jungle' of LA.

Initially the Predator's killings are mistaken, as in the first film, for the activities of a human agency. The film's action, sited in the midst of urban warfare, opposes two drug gangs: the Colombians and, the force on the ascendant, the Jamaican voodoo posse. The Jamaicans, led by King Willie (Calvin Lockhart), are located within a specific black cultural identity. It's made explicit – Leona explains this to the newcomer Jerry – that the gang use voodoo partly to scare the opposition, appropriating a history of fearful stereotyping as a weapon. In a gruesome scene the Jamaicans stage an attack on a Colombian gang-leader's penthouse apartment. The Colombian is strung up from the ceiling, just as the Predator's victims are, as the Jamaican gang members proceed to act out a ritual which involves daubing him with blood and cutting his heart out. The savagery is intended to frighten. When the Colombian offers two million dollars for his life, the Jamaican points out that the killing is not 'about money – it's about power'. But immediately after this 'ritual' slaying, the Predator attacks. When Harrigan's team arrives on the scene, all are strung up from the ceiling, though only the Jamaicans have been skinned. The film then draws on images of a fantasised black barbarity, whilst at the same time acknowledging that these images function as myth. Though the references to voodoo rituals are clearly marked as masquerade, they also form part of a rhetoric of 'race' in which Harrigan's heroic blackness is played off against images of a quite different, a 'primitive', black culture.

One of the Predator's most recognisable physical features is his 'hair'. Perhaps it is unsurprising, given the repeated links established between the monstrous and blackness within Hollywood's symbolic, that the Predator is given dreadlocks. This is but one of a series of associative links drawn between the Predator and the Jamaican gang, links that are established through appearance, actions and editing. Further, whilst the Predator is clearly a creature from a high-tech culture his weapons, like Rambo's nuclear bow and arrow, are iconographically primitive. Though he has a nuclear auto-destruct capacity, the Predator wields knives and spears, weapons which recall an imagery of the primitive, particularly when articulated through the film's jungle/safari metaphor. The Predator then is partly constructed as threatening through codes of blackness-as-primitive-as-other. A crucial set of sequences in this respect is the meeting between Harrigan and the Jamaican drug gang's leader, King Willie, a scene that is immediately followed by the appearance of the Predator, who takes King Willie's head as a trophy. Harrigan is leaving the police station with Jerry when a car, its top designed in a zebra pattern, pulls up in front of them to take Harrigan to King Willie. A joke is made out of the different images of blackness played out through the figures of policeman Harrigan and the Jamaican drug gang – figures already opposed as representatives of the law and of criminality. The car that transports Harrigan to his meeting is literally oozing marijuana smoke. 'Want some ganga?' they ask Harrigan, laughing. When Harrigan gets out of the car in a dark alley he coughs, telling them 'Y'know, you guys really ought to cut down'.

In the meeting that follows between Harrigan and King Willie, the gang leader is closely identified with voodoo, through his costume and his talk of spirits. He tells Harrigan that the thing doing the killing is 'from the other side'. In this, Willie comes closer to understanding the plot than Harrigan has at that point – acknowledging the other-world qualities, the power of the Predator – though this does not help him any. The meeting between the two men, followed by the Predator's attack, brings together the film's radically opposed constructions of blackness. King Willie addresses Harrigan as 'Babylon, Mr Policeman', whilst Harrigan says of the Predator 'He killed *your* people, now mine'. In appealing to a conventional crime or mob movie distinction, that between cops and robber, Harrigan also invokes here the cultural gulf separating the two. Whilst the voodoo posse is constructed within the film as overwhelmingly deviant, it is characterised by a kind of cultural rootedness, an identity, however perverse. By contrast, Harrigan is not located within any community in particular, even that of the police, and he is certainly not seen at home or with friends.

King Willie's death screams bleed over on the soundtrack into a close-up of his severed head, mouth and eyes wide open, swinging by his dreadlocks at the Predator's side. The skull is cleaned and placed in the Predator's gruesome trophy room. These scenes, with the primitive look of the spaceship and the collection of skulls, reinforce the iconographic links between the Predator and the Jamaicans. It is the projection of the monstrous onto the savage figure of the Predator and the Jamaican drug gang, which allows Harrigan to enact an heroic blackness. A key moment in this respect comes when Harrigan is inspecting the seemingly dead Predator. As Harrigan murmurs to himself that the Predator 'sure is an ugly mother . . .' the creature comes to life, grabbing Harrigan by the neck and spitting out in its distorted speech the expected word – 'motherfucker'. The creature is a monstrous double, able to mimic even colloquial human speech. Perhaps because it remains recognisable, the distortion of the Predator's speech, vision and appearance, works to produce it as radically other. In addition to the work of these discourses, however, the film is also structured through Harrigan's opposition to an FBI which is characterised as all-white. The identity of both the Predator and Peter Keyes present themselves as problems for Harrigan, problems that he mulls over out loud and sets his team to help him solve. While King Willie offers the spirit world as some explanation for the Predator, Keyes's federal team offers a fetishised commitment to science and technology, inviting Harrigan to simply sit back and 'enjoy the show'. The team members have set up an elaborate, and completely ineffectual, trap for the Predator. If blackness signifies, and is signified through, marginality and deviance in *Predator 2*, then whiteness signifies, and is signified through, an authority that is not to be trusted. The federal team is positioned firmly within government bureaucracy. Early in the film we see the team arrive at the scene of the Predator's crime, excluding Harrigan and his men. They are all white and all dressed in the same pale trousers, dark flying jacket and shades: offering a façade of a uniformity that is instantly suspicious. Stereotypical FBI men, they represent a faceless authority. Keyes seems to enjoy sneering at Harrigan, telling him that the 'concept of what you're dealing with is way over your head'. He also has the power to erase his existence – Harrigan is warned that he could easily 'turn up missing'.

Harrigan and Keyes repeatedly come into conflict, battling, in a conventional way, over 'territory' and 'jurisdiction'. One of the ways in which the action hero is defined as heroic is precisely through his refusal to accept official boundaries, ignoring the 'Keep Out' signs posted by those in power who seek to hide their own corruption. The contest between Harrigan and Keyes is filtered in *Predator 2* through codes of both gender and race. That the action picture's familiar contest over territory is concerned with masculine identity, is summed up rather succinctly by Harrigan, who tells his captain that his insistence on federal control of the case 'means you're cutting off my dick and sticking it up my ass'. Though a team man, Harrigan is ironically reprimanded by his superiors for his 'John Wayne attitude', an archetypal image of white masculine identity. The designation is fitting in terms of the strength of Harrigan's character. The Predator picks only well-armed people for its opponents, relishing the additional challenge in the hunt for trophies. That, from the very beginning of the film, it is Harrigan who is singled out marks him as a correspondingly powerful figure. By contrast Leona, the female member of Harrigan's police team, is spared when the Predator's scan of her body reveals her to be pregnant. The only survivor of the massacre in the Colombian drug leader's apartment was a woman – presumably too weak to be of interest. When Harrigan has killed the Predator, he finds himself surrounded by aliens who do not attack him but simply carry off the body of their comrade. One Predator remains behind and gives Harrigan a gift – an antique gun inscribed with the date 1715. Whilst this allows for the film's punchline – a sort of 'I'll be back' motif – it is also, within the system of associations between guns and masculine power, a moment of recognition for Harrigan's heroics. This recognition is followed, after a mega-explosion, by one more brief confrontation with the surviving leader of the disgruntled FBI team which has been denied its prize. In the complex permutations of hunter and hunted offered in this film, Harrigan and the Predator are allowed a brief point of contact, whilst the film's representatives of authority vacate the scene in their helicopter.

Predator 2 produces in Harrigan a masculinised black hero who refuses the stereotypes of hyper-(hetero)sexuality. At the same time, however, blackness is repositioned in terms of the monstrous within the film's symbolic hierarchy. These two elements actually work together, with the latter in some senses making space for the former. It is in relation to such complex, and contradictory, articulations that both the political reading, and the pleasures, of popular texts need to be understood.

3

NEW HOLLYWOOD, GENRE AND THE ACTION CINEMA

The aesthetic and industrial development of Hollywood cinema in recent years provides an important context for thinking about the action cinema. An examination of contemporary American film production reveals both changes and continuities with the 'Classic Hollywood' of the past. New Hollywood films work to stitch together sometimes seemingly contradictory genres, styles and star images from past and present in a variety of complex ways. In more academic parlance, we might term this a process of *bricolage*. Such a term, with its sense of the creative play of postmodernism, captures something of the infinite, and often far from playful, recycling of which the mass media is capable, indeed on which it thrives. Yet *bricolage* is a term more often invoked as a characterisation of tendencies in postmodern art, rather than popular practice, or with reference to the consumption of the popular as a form of production in itself. Involving the collection and transformation of disparate elements, *bricolage* signals the ways in which audiences can appropriate, and in the process redefine, aspects of popular culture. Thus, whilst the language of postmodernism has often been used to address the world of high-art practice, or the audiences-as-producers of popular culture, only selective examples of popular cinema have been associated with the term.[1] Notions of postmodern culture have been used to analyse specific cinematic developments, for example the reprise of *film noir* represented by films such as *Body Heat* in the early 1980s, rather than allowing the formulation of a more general theory of the popular cinema within a postmodern context.[2] How then, might the language and debates associated with postmodernism prove useful in an analysis of the contemporary American cinema as a mass media?

The fragmentation of aesthetic boundaries has been central to the postulation of a postmodern culture. Such fragmentation has been analysed in terms of intertextuality, in an attention to the complex relations between media and texts, as well as with reference to the chaotic visual devices at work in forms such as music video. Aesthetic fragmentation has, in turn, a central significance for thinking about the functioning of contemporary popular genres. Generic production and criticism, after all, depends on the construction of boundaries between forms. Conceptualising the popular, which is to say generic or formulaic, cinema has always presented problems of definition for critics, not least because critical methods and evaluative criteria have been evolved and employed primarily in relation to high art. The images and texts of high art are often valued precisely for their unique qualities, rather than their relationship to a generic category. Writing on detective fiction in 1966, Tzvetan Todorov sketches the dichotomy between high and popular art quite precisely, observing that

> As a rule, the literary masterpiece does not enter any genre save its own; but the masterpiece of popular fiction is precisely the book which best fits its genre. Detective fiction has its norms; to 'develop' them is also to disappoint them; to 'improve upon' detective fiction is to write 'literature', not detective fiction.
>
> (Todorov 1977: 43).

What then is the relationship between repetition and generic production? Genre is in fact a mobile category, and the bounds of generic purity cannot be clearly drawn within an industrial context which is constantly developing, shifting the terms of popular narrative. Generic production functions through the play of familiarity and difference, rather than the repeated enactment of any static criteria.[3] The development of generic hybrids, along with other forms of intertextuality, adds a further complexity to our understanding of genre in the contemporary Hollywood cinema.

The term 'Hollywood' now seems something of a misnomer, no longer a site of production but an imaginary space which is itself relentlessly referred to within American and other films. The 'collapse' of the studio system, which made way for a myriad of independent production companies, forms only one aspect of the development of a New Hollywood cinema over the last thirty years. 'Independent' production, a term which once carried connotations of an oppositional cinema, encompasses a range which spans the Australian production of *Mad Max* (1979), a film which successfully cut into American markets, to *The Evil Dead* (1982), a cult success put together on a shoestring, and *Rambo III* (1988) with its rumoured $60 million budget and massive promotional backing. The development of companies set up to oversee the production of a single film project represents one vital economic aspect of the contemporary industry.[4] This has been accompanied by the fine-tuning of the sequel into a distinct form, with films made back to back or featuring endings which beg for the characters' return to the screen. The 1970s, and more spectacularly the 1980s, have seen some memorable sequel cycles ranging from the *Star Wars* trilogy and five *Rocky* movies, to the horror cycles, such as *A Nightmare On Elm Street* and its sequels, and the comic *Police Academy* series. The *Nightmare On Elm Street* films have in addition generated a television show, *Freddy's Nightmares*, as well as an incredible range of associated merchandising.[5]

Such industrial and formal developments have been understood in a variety of ways. Two of the factors we might most usefully point to, in thinking about the development of the action cinema, are the advent of a television-literate viewer, and the vitality of the video market. Indeed the video market has been crucial to the action cinema, which existed for so long within the low- to medium-budget end of feature-film production. A different kind of success is possible for both films and stars within the video market. Here movies get a second chance to make money and reach a different audience to those which they might address in the cinema.[6] Similarly, new action stars of the 1980s and 1990s like Jean-Claude Van Damme or Dolph Lundgren, have gradually acquired a reputation and a following through video. Thus the video market offers a range of low- to medium-budget films which showcase new performers. Such productions sit alongside the mega-budget cinematic events represented by films such as *Terminator 2*, films with an extremely high visibility on the mainstream market. The availability of video technology represents a distinctive shift in the distribution and production of images. The possibilities offered by video as a form, with its domestic context, and fast forward and replay facilities, also operates as an eloquent image for cultural critics concerned to champion the audiences' potential appropriation of popular culture.[7]

The cultural criticism of recent years, which has highlighted the diverse uses that audiences make of popular forms, provides a valuable qualification to a political understanding of popular texts as an uncontested space for the play of dominant ideology. Further, this work allows an address to the complex ways in which marginalised audiences have always sought to position themselves within a visual mainstream that denies their existence. Nonetheless, the language of postmodernism has been seen to evade those crucial questions as to the political status of popular images within a context in which access to the media remains limited. Critics and audiences may delight in the self-referential play of popular texts, the surreal qualities of prime-time television or, as a more specific example, Ridley Scott's construction of stylised, imaginary future worlds in films like *Alien* and *Blade Runner*. Indeed, the recognition of aesthetic changes across the American cinema in the age of television and video technologies, represents an important critical step. But it is equally important to remember that specific formal devices do not carry an innate or essential meaning. It seems that an equation between aesthetic strategies and political worth, associated in film studies with various theorisations of the classic realist text, is also involved in a critical enthusiasm for the textual rupture and chaos so typical of much contemporary (big-budget) cinema. In drawing attention to this issue, I want to emphasise that the practices and formal features associated with *bricolage* cannot, any more than modernist framing devices, provide an aesthetic guarantee of the 'progressive'.[8]

This is to say that, whilst recognising change, we should also recognise continuity. Indeed, none of the above should be taken to imply that 'Old Hollywood' didn't wheel, deal and steal quite shamelessly. Star publicity and genre cycles, as well as a variety of tie-ins, cashed in on previous successes and heightened public interest around particular cinematic releases. Indeed a central issue for contemporary film study is precisely how to distinguish the raiding, reference and allusion taken by some critics to typify the contemporary American cinema, from the recycling of images in which popular cinema has been engaged throughout its history. Whilst the popular generic cinema tells formulaic stories, genre is nonetheless a complex signifying system. It would certainly be a mistake to hark back to the mythicised simplicity of a cinematic past from the supposed sophistication of a contemporary vantage point. I do, however, wish to acknowledge formal and industrial changes, to point to the ways in which New Hollywood operates within a changed context of production, distribution and consumption, and to open up some of the implications of this for the analysis of contemporary American cinema culture. In this sense, developments in film production and changes in the economic and institutional organisation of Hollywood, seem at times to have outstripped developments in film studies. The classic Hollywood that has for so long been the object of study has gradually disappeared from view, turning up only as a set of flickering images on the television sets which repeatedly feature in the productions of those cine-literate New Hollywood directors. Yet sub-genres, such as the recent group of movies centred on serial killers, or rape revenge movies, appear out of the larger generic histories of 'horror' or 'thriller' movies.

The bratpack western *Young Guns*, discussed later in this chapter, reveals a tendency in recent Hollywood production towards the development of hybrid genres. The film constructs its narrative with reference to the western, but combines this tradition with reference to a range of other iconographic and narrative traditions. The terms employed by film reviewers and movie magazines in describing contemporary action pictures indicate the diversity of the cinematic field within which they have to locate specific films for their readers. Thus descriptive phrases such as 'feminist road movie', 'post-apocalyptic thriller' or 'boys-behind-bars action' may refer to genre, but often in a qualified way, in order to function more effectively as a guide to the viewer. Generic hybridity can involve the combination of potentially contradictory modes and genres, as in the production of comic horror films, such as *Reanimator* or *Return of the Living*

Dead during the 1980s. Such a combination also involves a transformation, as the terms of a genre shift, taking on new connotations. Many recent action movies also seek to integrate comic routines and one-liners, such that comedy operates as an explicit part of the entertainment. In the Indiana Jones films this is quite clearly part of an attempt to appeal to both children and adult audiences. Yet comedy is also used in action films with more restrictive certificates, such as the *Lethal Weapon* films, a strategy to which I return at various points in this book.

Genre criticism, in the initial moment of its development in film studies at least, came in part from a populist impulse. This populism is implicit in the desire to study the whole of popular cinema, rather than selected examples which can then be constituted as exceptional. Such a study did not necessarily mean producing surveys or taxonomies, but meant trying to think about popular forms in terms other than those produced by the inappropriate analytical frameworks of high art.[9] In a similar vein, writing in the mid-1970s, Steve Neale argued for the need to develop an understanding of the New Hollywood text equivalent to the vast amount of work undertaken on the classic cinema, so that its 'rules and meanings, and hence its gaps and spaces' might be understood (Neale 1976: 122). Such an analysis is only gradually emerging. Some critics, such as Robin Wood and Andrew Britton, have attempted to generalise about the period though, commenting on the political characteristics of popular American cinema in the 1980s. These writings, in particular the accusation of new right conservatism levelled by Britton against popular films of the period, provide an interesting way into the more general critical field in which the action picture has been situated. In fact, the action picture has been debated during the 1980s almost exclusively in terms of an imputed ideological conservatism.

For Andrew Britton, there is no difference between the majority of film texts that he considers, and dismisses, in his elaboration of a notion of 'Reaganite Entertainment'. He asserts, for example, that the 'structure, narrative movement, pattern of character relationships and ideological tendency of *Star Wars*, *Tron* and *Krull* are identical in every particular: the variations, if that is the word, are mechanical and external' (Britton 1986: 2). These remarks are situated within Britton's understanding of the changed production context of Hollywood, a context which, he argues, no longer allows for 'the complex reflection of standardised generic motifs' typical of classic Hollywood. For Britton 'genre', with all the productivity it implies, is no longer an appropriate term with which to discuss the American cinema, a cinema which he sees as essentially based on repetition. The charge of repetition has often been levelled at the action cinema. Films such as *Rambo* and *Missing in Action* are criticised for their 'predictability', as well as for an ideological and political complacency. Both Wood and Britton share the view that the 1980s has been, by and large, a period of utter cinematic banality. For Wood 'reassurance is the keynote' and, he comments, 'one immediately reflects that this is the era of sequels and repetition' (Wood 1986: 162). Again repetition appears as a key term in the analysis. Britton contrasts such repetition to the productive elaboration of conventions that he locates in the classic cinema, with the contemporary cinema representing only a stultifying sameness. Here the formulaic present is played off against the more 'creative' past.

For both Britton and Wood a suspicion of repetition and sameness is tied into the popularity of the big-budget cinema of spectacle that developed in the late 1970s and through the 1980s. In particular, they single out those films associated with Steven Spielberg and George Lucas, as well as the cheaper imitations that followed them. Such films include *Star Wars*, the Indiana Jones films, *ET* and, in addition, the disaster movie, since Britton locates the release of *The Towering Inferno* (1974) as a symptom of decline. The distinction, between the cinemas of the past and present, has repeatedly been drawn in terms of a certain 'knowing' quality, a knowledge of cinema and popular culture which is shared between texts and the audiences which they address. Both Wood and Britton, in surveying the scope of the cinema of the 1980s, see the development of self-referential forms of entertainment as ultimately in the service of a right-wing ideological project of hegemonic self-effacement. Wood indicates how 'peculiarly difficult' it is to discuss such films 'seriously', since they 'set up a deliberate resistance' to analysis. Indeed 'they are so insistently not serious, so knowing about their own escapist fantasy/pure entertainment nature' that they 'consistently invite the audience's complicity in this' (Wood 1986: 164). Films such as *Star Wars* are seen to infantilise their audience, an effect that is achieved in part through their very self-referentiality, their awareness of themselves as fiction and as spectacle.

The question of the audience's position in relation to the text, raised again here, has been a crucial one for cultural criticism in recent years, as we have seen. If Britton is concerned to stress the changed context of production within which Hollywood now operates (indeed he attributes much of the 'decline' to such factors) a changed context for *consumption* should also be assigned a significance. Aside from some desultory remarks on the audience for stalk'n'slash horror, the analysis of 1980s cinema that Britton offers (including the ways in which the audience is constructed by that cinema) seems instead to negate issues of consumption, assuming the audience to be both unified and passively positioned by the text. This is precisely the critical paradigm through which the action cinema has been most often addressed. Though their political suspicions of the self-aware cinema of spectacle, which they both discuss, ultimately lead Wood and Britton to dismiss the films, both critics nonetheless attempt to develop an analysis that is not grounded exclusively in narrative content or structure. Rather, the analyses offered seek to draw attention to the elusive qualities of *atmosphere* and *tone* which are crucial for an analysis of a spectacle-based cinema. I am not seeking to suggest that an attention to narrative content is critically invalid, but that other elements of the films are equally important, particularly in the context of an analysis of the popular, entertainment cinema. Such an analysis necessarily involves an attention to the experience of cinema.

The structural analysis of narrative reveals how the vast number of stories which are told in myth and popular culture can ultimately be reduced to a small number of narrative elements, which are combined and articulated in a variety of combinations. Repetition is at the heart of both the significance and the pleasures of narrative. Yet the repetition that is involved in genre is also bound up in difference, and if all popular movies appear to look the same, then film criticism may well be viewing them through an inappropriate framework. Whilst the location of the action cinema within the broad sweep of generic analysis is important, a detailed attention to the texts of popular culture is also fundamental to the understanding of any form. As the hero and villain of *Die Hard* come face to face for their final confrontation, the villain taunts hero John McClane, sneering that 'this time John Wayne does not walk off into the sunset with Grace Kelly'. Sure enough, McClane is able to correct his textual ignorance, saying 'Gary Cooper asshole' before dispatching him out of the window. Within the film, Gruber's ignorance gives us further evidence of his *foreignness*, his un-American frame of reference in both moral and popular cultural terms. This moment also comically reprises our awareness of the populist hero's attention to the details of American popular culture.

Of course it is easy to get details wrong, but does this matter? Perhaps it can indicate an attitude, a framework of understanding. One instance can be found in Rowena Chapman's analysis of the television series *Moonlighting* which refers to Cybill Shepherd's character as 'Abby', rather than as 'Maddy'. Small details such as this do not have any especial significance. More telling, however, is Chapman's suggestion that 'a glance at a clutch of recent films and soaps' will illustrate the points about gender relations in the 1980s that she wishes to make (Chapman and Rutherford 1988: 243–7). For Chapman it seems the programme's ideological project is so *obvious*, so easily diagnosed, that there's really no need to look that closely: a 'glance' will do. Such textual contempt is noticeable in a great deal of journalistic and academic commentaries on popular cinema and television. This is related in part to the need to give overviews, to summarise ideas within a few paragraphs, yet it also indicates the assumption that critics can unproblematically read off an understanding of something as complex as, for example, the articulation of gender in a given moment in history, from a glance at a few images. My point is not to single out Chapman in particular, but to think about the implications of such a common practice for the study of popular culture. To suggest that meanings are *obvious*, necessarily excludes something of the complexity of popular films. As good products, *efficient commodities*, films are polysemic, speaking or not speaking to different audiences in different ways.

DIE HARD: 'SUSPENSE, EXCITEMENT, ADVENTURE ON EVERY LEVEL!'

Thus ran the slogan for *Die Hard*, the 1988 skyscraper, office party nightmare extravaganza directed by John McTiernan and starring Bruce Willis. The knowing pun invoked here on the many levels of both the skyscraper's and the text's construction is apt. The movie's producers specifically acknowledge their debt to the 1970s disaster movie. Michael Levey, president of Silver Pictures, comparing *Die Hard* and *Die Harder* to *The Towering Inferno* and *Airport*, joked that the third film 'has to be the *Poseidon Adventure*' (*Premiere*, September 1990: 27). It is precisely this sort of smug jocularity that Andrew Britton finds most detestable about New Hollywood products. To add insult to injury it is *The Towering Inferno* from which *Die Hard* borrows, a film that Britton locates as signalling the beginning of the Hollywood cinema's decline into mindless spectacle.

Die Hard centres on the Nakatomi Corporation's building in Los Angeles, which is taken over by group of assorted European 'terrorists' who end up having to take on New York cop John McClane. The film exemplifies both classic and post-Hollywood techniques. In its narrative and stylistic construction the film is astonishingly tight. There's not an inch of flab in its construction or a loose end in sight: a genuinely muscular movie. In this sense *Die Hard* functions as a *classical* narrative with all the elements introduced in its initial scenes, such as Holly's Rolex, having a significance that is ultimately revealed by the end of the movie. This watch, a reward for and symbol of Holly's achievements within the Nakatomi Corporation, is finally unclasped by McClane so that the villainous Gruber (Alan Rickman), who is holding onto Holly, falls to his death. *Die Hard* is also held together by a range of generic and other references, both visual and verbal. Like classic Hollywood productions, the film depends for its intelligibility on genre. Yet at the same time the film, as other generic hybrids, operates in a sense beyond the categories to which genre refers. Hybridity, that is, allows films to both draw on and redefine a range of genres, through the forging of new associations between them.

Like *Predator*, McTiernan's 1987 feature, starring Arnold Schwarzenegger, which combined the patrol movie with science-fiction/horror, *Die Hard* looks both backwards and forwards generically speaking. Through its visual and verbal references and raidings, the movie invokes the urban thriller, the Vietnam war movie, the disaster movie, the police thriller and the western. As the Nakatomi building becomes a warzone, the central foyer's showpiece fountain and pool become the river/jungle setting from which Willis emerges with machine gun in hand, in a parody of a classic action movie image. Hans Gruber, *Die Hard*'s chief villain, taunts McClane over the radio in an attempt to discover his identity – 'Just another American who saw too many movies as a child? An orphan of a bankrupt culture who thinks he's John Wayne, Rambo, Marshal Dillon?'. Gruber finally settles on a contemptuous 'Mr Cowboy'. McClane responds by characterising himself as Roy Rogers, a significantly dandified version of the cowboy. Such an identification already connotes the male body as spectacle, offering up an image of the hero as performing a pre-existing image of masculinity. This kind of self-aware performance fits nicely with Willis's own star image. Characterised by a self-mocking bravado and verbal wit, Willis's image is writ large in his performances in recent action films such as *Hudson Hawk* and *The Last Boy Scout*, though the latter is much bleaker in tone than the former. This kind of performance also echoes the self-aware aspects of the text's construction, the ways in which *Die Hard* seeks to position itself within popular culture.

The 1980s action cinema has retained and embellished the figure of the hero-as-outsider which has for long been a key feature within the various traditions of 'heroic' narratives, traditions such as the Western and the Epic. The populist heroes of the 1970s and 1980s are only very rarely associated with the established forces of state or government. In movies such as *Die Hard*, where the hero is a cop, they have, at best, a strained relationship with the police authorities. The hero stands out from and to one side of, the establishment of which he is a part. Thus Sylvester Stallone in *Cobra* (1986) though a cop, can't be seen to wear a uniform. The image of the uniformed cop is both invoked and undermined in *Thelma and Louise*, when the two are stopped by a state trooper who is decked out in macho regalia of sunglasses and emotionless expression – 'Oh my God, he's a Nazi' moans Louise. In a comic scene the two apologetically lock him in the trunk of his car. The cop's initial appearance of cool self-assurance collapses as he begins to cry, a joke constructed, as at other points in the film, through reference to recognisable caricatures of masculine identity.

In the films of the 1980s and early 1990s we see little or no evidence of the redemptive community which backed up the hero against the state in earlier tales of American populism. Thus the hero's only ally in the three *Rambo* films is the lone, and rather ineffectual, figure of Colonel Trautman. The military does not provide a supportive community for the hero, but betrays him[10]. Chuck Norris's three *Missing in Action* films, which the star is reported to have described as 'less anti-government' than Stallone's version of the American prisoner-of-war narrative, have to negotiate a similar set of problems. These are primarily to do with the construction of any kind of motivation for a hero who has been betrayed by his country.[11] In *Die Hard* McClane's interventions are unwelcome not only to the 'terrorists' but to both the Los Angeles police and the FBI. The terrorists' entire plan, of course, revolves around the FBI men (Johnson and Johnson) sticking to a well-worn operational routine for dealing with a hostage situation ('sounds like an A7 scenario', they remark sagely). This leads them to cut off all power to the building, in the process breaking the final time-lock on the company's safe, a lock which can't be cut from within the building: 'You asked for a miracle. I give you the F-B-I' gloats Gruber.

The central plot device of *Die Hard* is based on a mis-recognition. The FBI, thinking the gang are terrorists, act according to the book. In the process, the authorities provide the missing link in the smooth running of the heist. Both the gang and the FBI try to play a double-cross and the lone cop hero is stranded, caught in the crossfire. This mis-recognition mirrors the problems faced by a traditional political criticism, when applied to New Hollywood products – the difficulty that Robin Wood finds in taking seriously films which employ a humour that pre-empts analysis. Maurice Yacowar's 1989 *Jump Cut* critique of *Die Hard* functions as a useful example in this respect. Entitled 'The White Man's Mythic Invincibility', Yacowar reads the film in terms of sexism, racism and xenophobia. The film's narrative is seen as a dramatisation of a certain macho self-indulgence which depicts the triumph of the white male hero over female and black characters, as a re-run of Vietnam in which America wins, as a re-run of various other contemporary films (including *First Blood, Rambo* and unspecified Chuck Norris movies), *and* as a dramatisation of the destruction of corporate Japan/Europe by American individualism through the figure of Willis as hero. All of these questions pose important areas for analysis, and they certainly relate to more general trends in popular American fictions – such as fears around a notion of 'Japanisation'. Yet the articulation of power relations offered in a film like *Die Hard* is not unproblematically available for the critic to simply read off. Yacowar lays on a template, producing a text-book analysis (which might be dubbed a 'Category A' scenario) which attempts to sketch the operation of oppressive discourses within the film. In the process such an analysis runs the risk of missing the point, just as the authorities in *Die Hard* are revealed as incompetent organisation men because they fail to see through the masquerade, fail to grasp that the 'terrorists' are really burglars. One might argue, of course, that either way Gruber and his men are villains, though this misses the nuances of a play on male identity as different types of performance in the film.

Die Hard's box-office success, suggests Yacowar, is 'primarily due to its breakneck action' but, he adds, 'it may also be striking a popular nerve in its reactionary politics', for when 'the ruggedly individualist hero thwarts a terrorist take-over of an LA office tower, he lives out a macho pipedream on two political fronts – the international and the sexual' (Yacowar 1989: 2). Whilst such an analysis is able to speak about *levels* of meaning, and therefore suggests some complexity, it can fundamentally only admit the existence of two levels – the *overt* pleasures of the text and the *covert* ideological project. Thus, for Yacowar, whilst the 'open appeal of *Die Hard* lies in its snappy wit and crisp action' the film 'has a deeper appeal in its political assumptions which speak to the sexist who craves to have his obsolete delusions reaffirmed' (Yacowar 1989: 4). This shift in critical register, from an acknowledgement of the open appeal of the film to a laying bare of its underlying (reactionary) assumptions is by now a familiar strategy of the ideological analysis. I don't want to suggest that there is nothing to be said about the contemporary cinema at the level of a political analysis. Yet, if Yacowar's reading of *Die Hard* is akin to the FBI's reading within the film, it is worth considering what happens to the FBI. What we might call Johnson and Johnson's 'obsolete delusions' come from what McClane's police buddy Powell calls the 'terrorist playbook'. The gang play up to expectations so well, with Gruber's apposite use of terrorist rhetoric, that the FBI fail to realise they're using the wrong framework. This is made explicit as they chopper in to take out the 'terrorists' in a doublecross. The white Johnson whoops with elation 'Just like fucking Saigon' to which the black Johnson replies 'I was in Junior High, dick-head'. That is to say, this isn't Saigon, this isn't the 1960s and there's no point behaving as if it were – a moment that provides a jokey commentary on the character's militaristic fantasies.

Yacowar maintains a particular idea of what is going on in the film and what its audience might take from it, partly through the exclusion, the writing out, of the film's black, female and other audiences, and the complexities of the responses that different audiences might have to the film. *Die Hard* can thus be read as a fantasy of white male dominance rather than one of, say, empowerment. Elements that do not fit can be conveniently ignored. The film itself, as with other contemporary productions, attempts to pre-empt such criticisms, partly through a certain playfulness. For example, in the film's opening sequences McClane is angry that his wife has chosen to use her own name since moving to LA. By the end of the film he is reconciled to this and introduces her as 'Holly Gennaro'. Yet this is precisely the point at which she accepts his name, correcting him, 'Holly McClane'. The end credits, however, stand on the fence, listing Bonnie Bedelia's character as 'Holly Gennaro McClane' indicating an awareness of the tangled nature of this final compromise. Such a compromise takes off from Bruce Willis's wise-cracking star image, derived from his role in the hit TV series *Moonlighting*, which centred around a series of verbal confrontations that mediated the sexual tension between Willis and Cybill Shepherd. Whilst Yacowar sees Willis as playing 'roughly the same character' in *Die Hard*, he suggests that 'in the TV series the light characterisation and self-reflexivity undermine his macho pretensions and authority' whereas 'the larger-screen epic allows them unquestioned sprawl' (Yacowar 1989: 4). Just as *Predator* turns Schwarzenegger's image around by pitching him against the kind of robotic alien that he played to such effect in *The Terminator*, *Die Hard* has to negotiate with and, if possible, *capitalise on* Willis's image. An analysis of such strategies needs to take into account the fact that audiences are in possession of a whole series of extra-textual and intertextual knowledge. That is, criticism should recognise that a certain textual self-reflexivity is in operation, though it may not be as overt, which is to say coded in highly particular ways, as in a television series like *Moonlighting*.

The critical view that self-reflexivity functions within popular culture only when it is unmistakable is a familiar one, complementing the more general unease expressed by liberal and left-wing critics when dealing with the action, indeed the popular cinema. To take an example, Derek Malcolm's review of *RoboCop* (1987) distinguishes between his own ability to discern the subtleties of director Verhoeven's grim vision, from that of an audience of young people who disturbingly 'delighted in every bit of violence' at the screening he attended (*Guardian*, 4 February 1988). What is significant about this comment, and about more general critical attitudes to the action cinema, is the reworking of an old notion, that narrative content is somehow simply separable from form. *RoboCop* is often picked up as an 'interesting' film precisely for those moments which overtly seek to ironise the dystopic future that the film imagines. Yet the knowing bleakness of *RoboCop*, its incisive cynicism, is manifest precisely in its hero's use of violence. The violence, and particularly the visceral qualities of the destruction of the hero, form an important part of the film and are not just thrown in as a crowd pleaser. As a populist hero of the 1980s Murphy/RoboCop doesn't (and can't) go to Washington to argue his case before the government. When all else fails, then, it is the body of the hero and not his voice, his capacity to make rational argument, that is the place of last resort. That the body of the hero is the sole space that is safe, and that even this space is constantly under attack is a theme repeatedly returned to in the action cinema of the period.

Muscular action movies have been seen to represent the emergence of something new, to be specifically a product of the 1980s in their articulation of national and sexual politics. It is important to recognise, within any analysis of the films, the historical context in which figures such as Stallone and Schwarzenegger have been so successful. While muscular movies may be something new, they are new within a changed context of both production and consumption, one within which critical models formulated in relation to classic Hollywood are not appropriate. However, such powerful images do not spring from nowhere. The display of the male body and the articulation of versions of masculinity associated with this display in the cinema of the 1980s does have a clear set of generic roots.

'SIX REASONS WHY THE WEST WAS WILD': GENERIC TRANSFORMATION AND *YOUNG GUNS*

Christopher Cain's *Young Guns* (1988) reworks the well-worn Western fable of Billy the Kid. Though ostensibly a western, *Young Guns* announces itself through its credit sequence as a film that is much more concerned with its bratpack stars than with rehearsing an exercise in generic nostalgia. The stars situate the film rather oddly in relation to the western, drawing on the connotations of their appearance in other films, particularly the teen movie (Emilio Estevez in *The Breakfast Club* (1984), Kiefer Sutherland in *The Lost Boys* (1987)), but also the Vietnam movie (Charlie Sheen in *Platoon* (1986)). Combining aspects of the 'realist' western, with its 'authentic' period detail, with techniques developed in music video, *Young Guns* delights in striking visual images, stylish setpieces which foreground the stars over the genre in which they appear.

A symptomatic moment is the sequence in which, following the murder of their 'protector' John Tunstall (Terence Stamp), the six 'Regulators' are deputised in order to hunt down and arrest those responsible. The Justice initially refuses Lawyer McSween's suggestion that they be taken on as deputies, but is forced to look over at the boys who are framed by the camera, posed beautifully with McSween's wife at some distance. Presumably this melts the Justice's heart as, without any voiceover, we see in quick succession a series of images which confirm the boys' deputisation: a close-up of the Justice, his face pale against the darkness of an interior; an extended bible bathed in light over which the boys lay their hands; the camera pulling back as the boys form into a line looking out at us with rifles raised in an echo of the film's opening sequence; the Justice's face once more, and finally a shot of the barn doors as they burst open for the boys to ride out. The modern, electronic, music used over this sequence emphasises the borrowing of techniques from music video. A sequence such as this foregrounds the young stars who seem to be acting out the western here.

Young Guns is concerned not only with youth but also, quite unmistakably, with the figure of the teenager. The youth of the film's six heroes is most obviously stressed by the title and the choice of stars, but is relentlessly insisted on throughout the film. The six 'regulators' are shot to look small beside 'adult' figures like Tunstall, McSween and Pat Garrett. Tunstall acts as a father figure, providing for the boys and tutoring them in reading. He rebukes and then pats Billy (Estevez) on the head, promises a soda to Doc (Sutherland) who wants whiskey instead. Billy expresses his anger at the actions of the big landowners (a familiar inflection of Billy's story, through which he is cast as the people's champion) by saying that he wants 'to get some attention'. His career is expressed in terms of the star system, success measured by the achievement of a media reputation. Billy envies Pat Garrett this reputation, saying 'I bet I get to be as big as him –

nah, bigger'. Against this Doc plays the part of the angst-ridden poet, the sensitive youth caught up in circumstances beyond his control, a type who is very familiar from the teen movie. At moments his commentary is excruciatingly laboured, as when he notes 'God, this country needs a hero' on reading the exaggerated newspaper accounts of Billy's exploits, or the conversations on the importance of being 'pals' that run throughout the film. In all this, the film draws on the figure of the teenager as rebel, as a misunderstood and angst-ridden individual. The figure of the teenager was constituted during the 1950s, a time when Hollywood was undergoing radical change. Stars and films aimed at a new, younger audience – James Dean, Elvis Presley and Marlon Brando – became icons of popular culture. These three figures are also bound up with complex articulations of masculinity and sexuality. In *Young Guns* the teenage rebel is recast as a literal outlaw. Rock music provides a point of mediation between the figures of the outlaw and the teenage rebel. This has been brought very much to the fore in *Young Guns 2* with the brief appearance and soundtrack music contributed by rock singer Jon Bon Jovi.

Despite its plot and setting, *Young Guns* does not seem to be a western at all. Such a judgement is made not from the standpoint of an insistence on generic purity, which maintains that the western cannot change or evolve. Rather it is in terms of the ambiguous questions of tone already referred to. What position does *Young Guns* occupy in relation to the western as a genre? To classify such movies we can begin to introduce sub-genres. Here we could talk of the movie as a teen-western, coming out of a tradition which includes films such as *Flaming Star* (1960) which starred Elvis Presley. In that film the difficult position of the young man, as a rebellious teenager, within the world of the western is expressed through racial discourses of difference and conflict. *Young Guns* employs the grey-tinted landscapes and muted colours of the realist western. Iconographically it is also close to the 'spaghetti' western with the long coats worn by the heroes. However, a key element of the spaghetti films was the music, and this film looks to a different source for its soundtrack. In addition the grubby long coats serve in part to emphasise the diminished stature of the young cast.

Young Guns offers a different level of performance to the parody of the western found in *Back to the Future 3*, which literally takes the teenage hero back to the 'old west', getting laughs from the juxtaposition of his movie-derived expectations and twentieth-century knowledge with the 'reality' of that time and place. By way of contrast, *Young Guns* offers a self-conscious *performance* of the western, a performance made more evident by the seemingly out-of-place heroes who look so small against the expansive setting in which they find themselves. The film has a strange quality which stems from its combination of the 'historically authenticated' western narrative with the teenage rites-of-passage movie. *Young*

Guns can be seen as a teen movie that performs the western in a similar way, though without the same ironic quality, to John McClane's performance of the role of the hero in *Die Hard*, a performance which self-consciously chooses its popular cultural reference points. Perhaps this indicates something of how we, as film audiences, understand genres. Our recognition takes place not in relation to individual films, but to a total field which includes a range of contemporary forms, including MTV. It is not so much that *Young Guns* points to the effective disappearance of the western from the cinema of the 1980s, but that its aesthetic strategies indicate how the kind of generic classification implied within film criticism by 'the western' have become increasingly problematic.

CLINT EASTWOOD AND THE 'END OF THE WESTERN'

The decline of a form such as the western has an importance, partly due to the very significance that this genre has had within the history of film theory and criticism. Pointing to the significance of historical events, Jeanine Basinger locates the downfall of the genre in relation to 1960s' cynicism and the conflict in Vietnam, essaying that 'this may be why Westerns are temporarily dead. Vietnam killed them' (Basinger 1986: 213). Such an acknowledgement of cultural shifts, whilst offering an interesting perspective on the relationship between cinema and the social, runs the risk of constructing an over-simplistic rendition of cinema history, something that Basinger indicates by placing her proposition in parentheses. The western series which had dominated the television schedules of the 1950s had been replaced by the 1970s largely with the crime series and, in America, the ongoing televisual saga of the Vietnam war.[12] The associations of the western lay with an older, parent culture which was to be debunked along with everything else. The old western stars were also fading, to be replaced by the nihilism of the Eastwood persona or the lighthearted jocularity of male stars like James Garner and Burt Reynolds. The western hero comes increasingly to seem anachronistic, as in John Wayne's appearance in *The Shootist*.

Clint Eastwood's movie career provides a bridge from the 1950s to the present. Eastwood's association with action genres stretches from his early, freshfaced appearance in the television western *Rawhide*, through his persona as 'The Man with No Name' in Leone's westerns of the 1960s and as 'Dirty Harry' in a series of films through the 1970s and 1980s. More recent films such as *Tightrope* (1984) or *Heartbreak Ridge* (1986) attempt to address and, to a certain extent, undermine, Eastwood's tough-guy image. A more conventional use of parodic humour is found in *City Heat* (1984), with Burt Reynolds, and the 'Any Which Way' series in which Eastwood stars with an orang-utan. Looking back though, it is apparent that there is more than a little irony in Eastwood's persona, as the Man with

No Name, in the three 'Dollar' films which made him a star during the 1960s. In these films the western hero is prevented from seeming anachronistic through being recast as an anti-hero, a bounty hunter and amoral killer. There are only remnants of the morally superior western hero of earlier Hollywood films.

The spaghetti western, in common with most contemporaneous American westerns, told a different kind of story to earlier examples of the genre. The stories typically told in these films employ both parody and irony, and a commitment to a certain authenticity in period detail. It is, in part, from such a visual tradition that *Young Guns* emerges. Leone's epic *Once Upon A Time in the West* (1969) shares with other Italian westerns an excess in visual terms which is both celebratory and parodic. This is combined with a meticulous acknowledgement of the varied ethnic groups present in the western landscape. The Chinese, Mexicans, Irish and other historical protagonists of the west come to feature, alongside the reconstruction, in other Hollywood fictions, of the history of the American Indian, as guarantees of the historical authenticity of the western. It is in this context that the success of the eastern/western television series *Kung Fu*, in the early 1970s, can be located. This featured David Carradine as Kwai Chang Caine, a Chinese-American Shaolin priest who wanders about the old west. The idea for this series was partially triggered by the success of Hong Kong martial-arts films in the west at that time. Images of an imagined Oriental culture and religion are fetishised in the show, the producers of which, as I have discussed elsewhere, refused to cast a Chinese actor in the lead role, famously turning down Bruce Lee for the part.[13] It is precisely Orientalist stereotypes, through which Chinese culture is constructed in the west, that are invoked in *Kung Fu*. In relation to Chinese men these function in terms of what Richard Fung has called a 'desexualised zen asceticism' (in Bad Object Choices 1991: 148). In *Kung Fu* these images function to *partially feminise* the western hero, who becomes a gentle, pacifist figure who is able, at the same time, to take on anyone who challenges him. In the same period, a favourite Hollywood theme was that of a white child or adolescent, taken in by an Indian tribe, who is ultimately able to speak on their behalf.[14] These strategies keep white men at the centre of the old west, whilst attempting to acknowledge a landscape of racial difference.

The themes enshrined within the western have been preserved in a range of settings, from the Australian outback to the urban landscape. In this context, it is common to find reviewers and critics who remark of a given film that it is 'really a western', only one that is presented to us 'in disguise'. The comparison can, it seems, be pursued to some lengths. A reviewer of Michael Winner's *Death Wish* (1974) described the film as 'really no more than an updated Western, a revamping of the one about the upright citizen, liberal and peaceloving . . . who takes the law into his own hands to avenge the butchery of a loved one' (*Monthly Film Bulletin* 492, January 1975: 7). If this provides one, potentially useful, view of the film, it is just as important to note the centrality of a contemporary urban iconography in the look of the text and the evolution of the narrative, particularly in terms of the shifts in racial discourse that marked the westerns of the period. A similar evaluation was made of *Rambo*, a decade later. One review interestingly reassures us about the film, thus:

> After all the hysteria, the banner *Sun* headlines, the hype and calls for it to be banned, 'Rambo' turns out to be a Western set in the East, where the goodie beats the corrupt Sheriff and the Indians and rescues the trapped Pioneers.
>
> (*Video*, January 1986: 28)

Here the film is made safe by reference to the security of the western as a genre, located in the comfortable past, an interesting strategy given the 'hysterical' responses to the film in Britain. Of course, such assessments are not necessarily intended to be accurate, functioning as they do as a form of cultural shorthand. As Jeanine Basinger points out, a statement such as '*Star Wars* is a Western' forms a way of observing that it is 'a story from one genre moved to another'. We can, that is, find the traces of an earlier, and recognisable form, within its narrative pattern, images and characterisation. Nonetheless, for a criticism which seeks to see the social or cultural significance of the development, success and decline of particular genres, it is important to look to contemporary shifts as well as to the traces of the past. As Basinger notes, *Star Wars* takes the form of 'a science fiction fantasy, because people don't want to see it as a Western' (Basinger 1986: 276–7). When critics note that a film 'really' belongs to another genre than at first appears, a cultural shorthand is invoked which highlights the importance of intertextuality in the way we read movies. A science-fiction romance like *Star Wars*, that is, might well be read in relation to the western. Like *Young Guns*, however, it can also be read within the context of a teenage rites-of-passage tradition. Such perceptions allow us to recognise that whilst the roots of, say, the urban action film of the 1970s may lie in the western, its changed location also significantly alters that tradition.

Clint Eastwood's career spans not only the decades since the demise of Hollywood, but the development of film studies as an institutionalised discipline. Eastwood's films have often been criticised from the viewpoint of cultural conservatives on the one hand, who object to a violent nihilism apparent in many of the films, and from left/liberal critics on the other. The 'Dirty Harry' films in particular were seen by many commentators to function as fascistic, implicitly endorsing police violence.[15] Writing at the time of *Dirty Harry*'s release, Anthony Chase termed the film an 'elegiac, necrophiliac, fascist love poem'. The film is defined as 'worrying' due to its popularity, with Chase mourning the fact that a knowledge of director Don Siegal is 'no longer the sole possession of a handful of action movie fanatics and auteur film critics' (Chase 1977: 18). As the 1980s progressed, Eastwood's persona was critically situated within those feminist-derived perspectives which drew attention to masculinity, its effects and representations as a topic of study. Eastwood's *Tightrope* recognises this positioning to a certain extent, and the film has been the subject of much comment within film studies. Eastwood's character, Wes Block, is a detective and single father of two girls who becomes more and more intimately dragged into the sexual violence of the film's criminal force. Using a traditional *doppelgänger* device *Tightrope* attempts to problematise, and possibly purify, the Eastwood persona.[16]

The paternalistic critical tone evident in Chase, the concern for the tastes of others which are also the problems of popularity, remains a key ingredient of much contemporary cultural commentary. The twin critical trajectories which mobilise an ideological analysis in the consideration of cinema, taking 'law and order' and 'masculinity' as their object, continues into the 1980s in relation to *Rambo*, a film that is held up as symptomatic of Reaganite values, of hawkishness and of a Neanderthal masculinity. The fear and distaste which surrounds the popular cinema is indicative of a complex set of issues bound up with class, taste and judgement. Equally, a political cultural criticism should not necessarily reverse these judgements, valorising popular forms simply because they have been so despised. Yet, as I hope to demonstrate in the following two chapters, the political meaning of a contemporary popular figure like the muscular male hero, is far from stable or unambiguous. Similarly, my comments on the popular film *Die Hard*, both here and in Chapter 2, are by no means intended to suggest that the popular cinema is beyond ideology or the political analysis of meaning. Rather, I want to suggest that such films cannot be taken to simply equate with any simple political position. Critical approaches which recognise textual ambiguity and the complexity of possible and actual audience response do exist, with Valerie Walkerdine's comments, on the figure of the boxer hero Rocky, often referred to in this context. Walkerdine observes of *Rocky IV* and *Rambo*, for example, that while 'it is easy to dismiss such films as macho, stupid and fascist, it is more revealing to see them as fantasies of omnipotence, heroism and salvation'. Instead she offers an understanding of the popular entertainment action-based cinema as 'a counterpoint to the experience of oppression and powerlessness' (Burgin *et al.* 1986: 172). Here she precisely picks up on what the experience of watching these fictions from a particular culturally located position *feels like*. The triumph that these action heroes experience at the end of the narratives offers a particular exhilaration to audiences, an exhilaration which Walkerdine reads through the dynamics of class. Our involvement with the characters and situations that are portrayed is exaggerated, intensified as are the fictional scenarios and the characters themselves. In the highlighting of emotional responses to fiction, though Walkerdine also locates this within a notion of fantasy, this analysis is reminiscent of Richard Dyer's discussion of the musical film as entertainment.[17] In particular Dyer's analysis of the utopian sensibility offered in the Hollywood musical, whilst outlining the limits of the form, acknowledges the values and the pleasures of these fictions. Thus, at the level of narrative, we can see how many action narratives carefully orchestrate social problems, representing inequalities that will be overcome in fantasy form. However, a recognition of these processes does not necessarily exhaust the experience, nor the popularity, of the films.

PLATES

1 Arnold Schwarzenegger and Grace Jones in *Conan the Destroyer* (1984, Margaret Herrick Library, Los Angeles)

2 Danny Glover in *Predator 2*

3 Danny Glover's alien adversary in *Predator 2*
(© 1990, Twentieth Century Fox Film Corporation. All rights reserved.)

4 Whoopi Goldberg in *Fatal Beauty*

5 Sylvester Stallone as Rambo in *First Blood Part II* (1985)

6 Bruce Willis in *Die Hard*

7 Linda Hamilton as Sarah Connor in *Terminator 2* (1991, Guild Films)

8 Sigourney Weaver as Ripley in *Aliens*

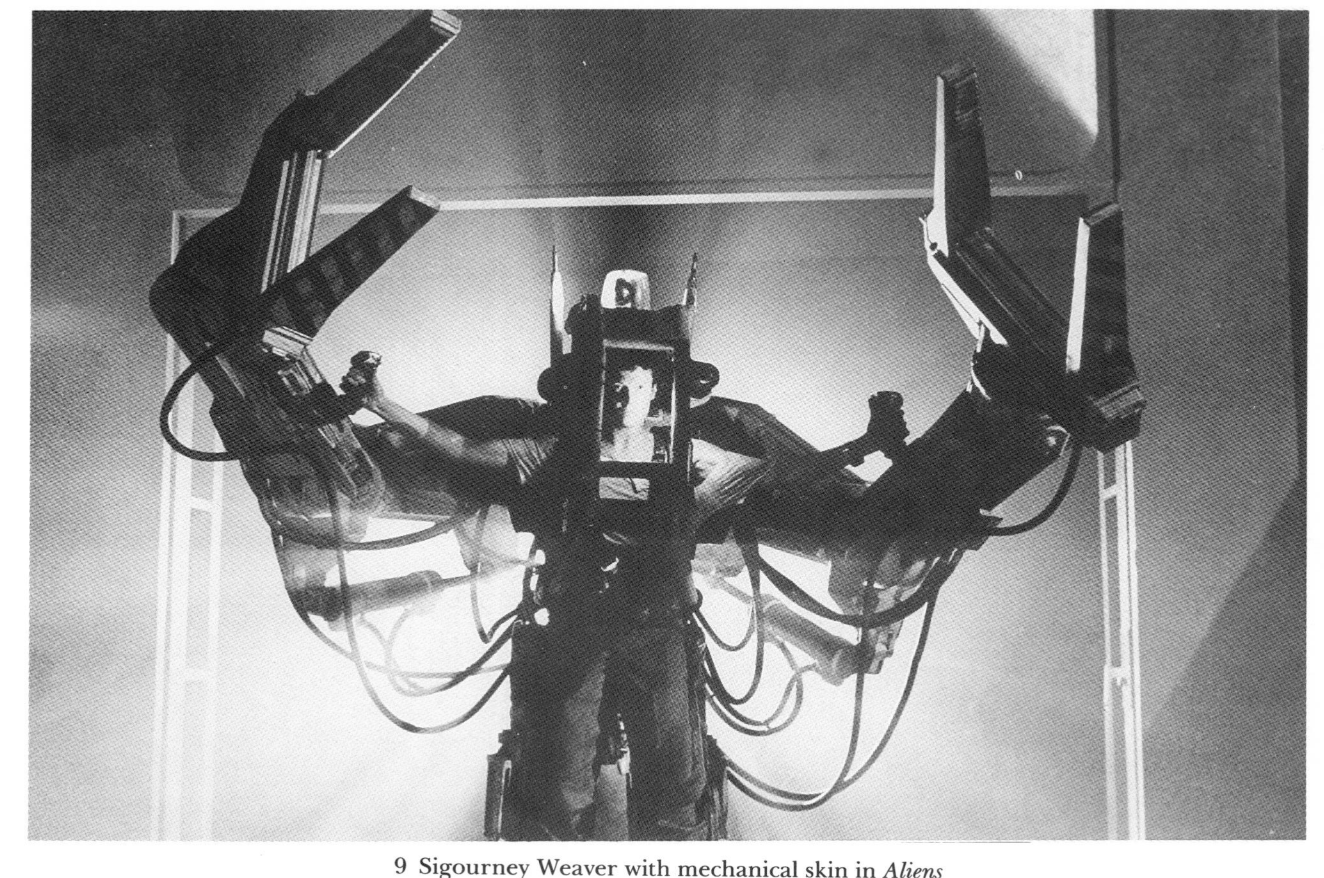

9 Sigourney Weaver with mechanical skin in *Aliens*

10 Geena Davies and Susan Sarandon in *Thelma and Louise*

11 Patrick Swayze and Keanu Reeves in *Point Break*
(© 1991, Twentieth Century Fox Film Corporation. All rights reserved.)

4

TOUGH GUYS AND WISE-GUYS

Masculinities and star images in the action cinema

The box-office success of the white male bodybuilder as star has been one of the most visible aspects of recent American action cinema. The visibility of the built male body, in both film and advertising images, represents part of a wider shift in the male image, and in the range of masculine identities, that are on offer in western popular culture. In terms of the action cinema more specifically, the figure of the bodybuilder as star can be contrasted to the male stars of the Hong Kong action tradition, in which an elaborate, quick-fire, physical performance has come to form a central part of the visual pleasure that is on offer. The distinction is that between images of the body in action, so central to fight-films, and images of the top-heavy, almost statuesque, figure of the bodybuilder who essentially strikes poses within an action narrative. This distinction clearly has implications for the kinds of action, and the sorts of display, that action films offer. American films showcasing the western kickboxing star Jean-Claude Van Damme, for example, are increasingly moving away from the emphasis on contact fighting found in his Hong Kong films, replacing this with an emphasis on the built muscular body. As is perhaps already apparent, the moves through which bodybuilders became movie stars through the 1980s, whilst other male stars began to build their bodies, offers a site through which to explore the changing articulation of masculinities in the contemporary action cinema. This needs to be set against a cinematic context in which narratives of fatherhood and family life, in films as diverse as *Parenthood*, *The Good Father*, *Parents* and *The Stepfather*, have proved extremely popular. Images of the built male body, that is, form only a part of the new visibility that surrounds male bodies and masculine identities within both popular culture and academic inquiry.

The political meaning of these images has, in turn, been fiercely contended. The proliferation of images of the built male body represents for critics like Barbara Creed the kind of deconstructive performativity associated with postmodernism, whilst for others they articulate, in their 'promotion of power and the fear of weakness', traditional images which are also 'deeply reactionary' (Foster 1988: 61). The relationship between star image, genre and masculinity is considered in this chapter through an examination of specific star images. Within the action cinema, the advent of the bodybuilder as star poses quite complex questions for the development of narrative, largely to do with the need to incorporate moments of physical display. The bodybuilder also offers specific formulations of an heroic male identity in the cinema, formulations which are explored below with reference to two key muscular stars of recent years, Schwarzenegger and Stallone. The films in which these stars appear draw on comedy, and, in stark contrast, on those Christian traditions of representation which offer up the suffering white male body as spectacle. These modes have been continued and developed in the films of more recent action stars, such as Dolph Lundgren and Jean-Claude Van Damme. As the title of this chapter indicates though, the action cinema is populated by wise guys as well as tough guys. The strong silent type finds his complement in the kind of wise-cracking action hero played by Bruce Willis in films like *Die Hard*, *Hudson Hawk* (1991) and *The Last Boy Scout* (1991). Whilst these are still big-budget spectacular films, Willis is known for his voice as much as his body, and his role in these films as a wise guy enacts a different kind of masculine performance to that associated with the bodybuilder. The relationship between the body and the voice is central to the action cinema's articulation of male identity. Involving questions surrounding the ability to speak and act, which are also inevitably questions of power, an attention to the relationship between the body and the voice brings to the fore questions of race and class, as well as the more apparent issues of gendered identity through which the muscular action stars have been discussed.

The figures referred to thus far in this book are differently positioned as stars, actors and performers, with these three terms bearing very different connotations of both masculine and artistic identity. Schwarzenegger and Stallone, for example, are very much movie stars, complex personas made up of far more than the texts in which they appear. The star image exceeds the films and other media that showcase it, is cut loose for an unofficial existence within complex circuits of signification. Chuck Norris and Jean-Claude Van Damme are perceived much more as performers, their talents in the cinema deriving from a showcasing of martial-arts skill. The possibilities of shifting from one category to another, or existing across them, is indicated by Schwarzenegger, who initially became famous within the world of bodybuilding, though he is now known primarily as a movie star. Harrison Ford, whilst a star who has appeared in a variety of action roles has, as his career has progressed, increasingly been seen as an *actor*. The different cultural capital associated with stars, performers and actors is a factor which recurs throughout cultural criticism, as well as forming a key part of the American cinema's discourse about itself. Action stars, for example, often express a desire to be 'taken seriously' as actors and/or as film-makers. In part these protestations relate to the impossibility of carrying on physically-based performances indefinitely. As the musclemen stars of the 1980s begin to creep into middle age, they can be seen to be seeking a new niche for themselves, just as female stars have, for so long, needed to redefine themselves as they age. Thus Rocky finally retires, after a fashion, in *Rocky V* (1990). Whilst an ageing Clint Eastwood built up his body for *Heartbreak Ridge*, he has also moved into directing films and has taken on more 'dramatic' roles. More strikingly, action star Mel Gibson took on the key classical actor's role of Hamlet in Zeffirelli's film version, before returning to the part of Martin Riggs for *Lethal Weapon 3* (1992).

Within western traditions the definition of a 'good' cinematic actor centres largely on the ability to develop the sustained portrayal of a complex character. Set against such a standard, neither the action cinema, nor the performers who feature in it, have fared very well in critical terms. The enactment of the role of the action hero requires a different set of qualities and, despite critical disdain, remains hugely successful at the box-office. As a male star who made the transition to being 'taken seriously' during the mid-1980s much more successfully than most, Harrison Ford is an interesting figure. Though he had already appeared in several films, the role which made Ford a major star was that of Han Solo in *Star Wars* (1977) and its two sequels. Here he plays the classic action hero, a persona he took on once more as adventurer and archaeologist Indiana Jones in *Raiders of the Lost Ark* (1981) and its sequels. Jones is an action hero who is successful with women, knowledgeable, quick-witted and physically strong. He is also very clearly positioned in the past, constructed with nostalgic reference to past cinematic fictions and, possibly, past masculine ideals. As an action hero who wears glasses (though only sometimes) Jones displays, like the character of Solo, both a physical and a verbal agility. This wisecracking image made it easier for Ford to make 'serious' movies like *Witness* (1985) and *Mosquito Coast* (1986) with director Peter Weir. In addition, of course, Ford starred in one of the few action movies of the period to score a critical hit, Ridley Scott's *Blade Runner* (1982). This film, with its implicit social criticism, carefully orchestrated visual style and references to valorised moments of cinema history such as *film noir*, takes its place within that part of the popular cinema that is able to pass as high culture.[1]

The phenomenon of stardom provides a useful starting point for thinking about the performative aspects of masculinity in the cinema, perhaps because spectacle, performance and acting all function as both constitutive components of stardom and significant terms in those writings concerned with the sexual politics of representation. Within the action cinema the figure of the star as hero, larger than life in his physical abilities and pin-up good looks, operates as a key aspect of the more general visual excess that this particular form of Hollywood production offers to its audience. Along with the visual pyrotechnics, the military array of weaponry and hardware, the arch-villains and the staggering obstacles the hero must overcome, the overblown budgets, the expansive landscapes against which the drama is acted out and the equally expansive soundtracks, is the body of the star as hero, characteristically functioning as spectacle. Indeed it is this explosive and excessive cinematic context that provides a setting for, even *allows*, the display of the white male body. Such display generates a range of uncertainties, as traditional signifiers of a masculine, colonial power are constituted as sexual spectacle. Sexuality, so often displaced within western images onto a 'savage' landscape which awaits colonisation and civilisation by the white hero, is more explicitly invested in the muscular body of the white male star.[2]

Richard Dyer locates the 'central paradox' of stardom as the instability of 'the whole phenomenon' which is 'never at a point of rest or equilibrium, constantly lurching from one formulation of what being human is to another' (Dyer 1987: 18). Particular star images are no more stable than the phenomenon as a whole. Embracing contradictory elements and constantly shifting the ground, star images present themselves as composed of so many layers, as so many slippages between fantasised, fictional identities and the supposed guarantee provided by the star's 'actual' embodiment of those identities. Performances in films, gossip in newspapers and magazines, publicity that is both sought and unlooked for: all these elements work to constantly displace and reconfirm our understanding in an endlessly played out revelation of 'the truth behind the image'. In this sense the territory of the star image is also the territory of identity, the process of the forging and reforging of ways of 'being human', or of 'being a man', in which a point of certainty is never ultimately arrived at. In this shifting landscape of identity, stars nonetheless perform, or more properly constitute through performance, particular types. Thus 'John Wayne' signifies not only this particular star's image, but a type of masculine and political identity. Thus in *Predator 2*, Danny Glover's character is accused of having a 'John Wayne attitude' to law enforcement, a phrase which immediately means something definite to its audience, however complex Wayne's image may be.[3] Invoking Wayne, who is often taken as an embodiment of a hawkish, white masculinity, to describe Glover's character adds a complex racial dimension to this particular version of a cop in conflict with police bureaucracy.

MUSCLE CULTURE: THE BODYBUILDER AS HERO AND STAR

The hero of the action narrative is often cast as a figure who lacks a place within the community for which he fights, a paradox familiar from the Western genre.[4] In the recent action cinema, problems of location and position are increasingly articulated through the body of the male hero. In this sense, the figure of the bodybuilder as star has a special significance, raising here a more general set of issues to do with activity and passivity and their relation to masculinity and femininity in film. These issues centre on the problematic aspects of the construction of the male body as spectacle, an issue that has generated much commentary and criticism. The male pin-up is certainly of a different order to the female pin-up, shot through with a different set of anxieties, difficulties and pleasures. Richard Dyer links these uncertainties to the problematic processes through which male power is maintained in western culture, processes that involve the disavowal of the very fact that the man is being looked at, and the use of an insistent imagery which stresses hardness, partly through muscularity, a quality traditionally associated with masculinity. Dyer's analysis draws attention to the way in which any display of the male body needs to be compensated for by the suggestion of action. Thus sports pin-ups and the portrayal of the feats of near-naked action heroes both offer the body as to-be-looked-at whilst refusing the 'femininity' implied by that quite passive position (Dyer 1982). This work provides a useful framework for analysis, and may tell us something about the choice of the *action* movie as one of the privileged spaces for the display of the male body.

An analysis of the figure of the male bodybuilder as a movie star, needs also to acknowledge that as the muscular hero is caught by the camera, he is both posed and in motion at the same time. The medium serves to emphasise the contradictions that Dyer finds in the male pin-up. The combination of passivity and activity in the figure of the bodybuilder as action star, is central to the articulation of gendered identity in the films in which they appear. It also represents one of the distinctive qualities of these films. This combination allows us to problematise any clear set of critical distinctions between passivity, femininity and women on the one hand and activity, masculinity and men on the other. The figure of the muscleman hero dramatises the instability of these categories and equations, combining qualities associated with masculinity and femininity, qualities which gender theory maintains in a polarised binary. Bodybuilding as a sport is defined by pleasurable display, but is also criticised as clumsy or ugly, as precisely lacking in the classical grace to which it aspires. It is sometimes seen as positively pathological. An article in the *Sunday Times* in 1988, speculating on a link between the 'Rambo cult and sex crimes', points to the cases of various murderers and rapists, seen by the writer as 'social misfits who spent hours in front of a mirror, flexing muscles or posing in combat gear'. Bodybuilding is here taken to signal a disturbing narcissism, a narcissism which is inappropriate to familiar definitions of manhood. In other words the bodybuilder, obsessed with his appearance as he is, is not a real man. This pathologising discourse is quite familiar, and in part sets the context for the uncertain tone of George Butler's film *Pumping Iron* (1977) in which the heterosexuality of the bodybuilders interviewed and portrayed is repeatedly reaffirmed. Heterosexuality here operates as a more general sign of 'normality', denying the supposed perversity of a man's interest in male flesh.

In some senses the bodybuilder is precisely unnatural, being as he is so clearly marked as *manufactured*. Bodybuilding offers the possibility of self-creation, in which the intimate space of the body is produced as a raw material to be worked on and worked over, ultimately for display on a public stage. Thus critics have seen stars like Stallone and Schwarzenegger as 'performing the masculine', drawing attention to masculinity and the male body by acting out an excessive caricature of cultural expectations. Barbara Creed, for example, speculates on these figures as 'simulacra of an exaggerated masculinity, the original completely lost to sight, a casualty of the failure of the paternal signifier and the current crisis in master narratives' (Creed 1987: 65). The 'current crisis in master narratives' is not seen by Creed as the inability to tell a good story, but in terms of the failing of the key terms around which stories are constructed, terms which include a coherent white male heterosexuality, along with the rationality and binary structures it is often taken to propose. For Creed it is the sheer physical excess of the muscular stars that indicates the performative status of the masculinity they enact. If bodybuilding draws attention to different ways of being a man, to definitions of manhood, it has also been characterised, along with any male concern with the body and appearance, as feminised and rather ridiculous. As I discuss in Chapter 7, women's involvement in the sport is conversely seen to *masculinise* them. For both men and women, the activity has been characterised as perverse in that bodybuilding, as a practice and in its results, transgresses supposedly 'normal' gendered behaviour.

The ridicule directed at bodybuilding stems in part from the ambiguous status of the musculature in question – what is it all for? As one critic commented, these 'baroque muscles' are, after all, 'largely, non-functional decoration' (Louvre and Walsh 1988: 96). They do not relate to the active function that the hero is called on to perform, indeed can be seen as positively disabling. Rather muscles serve as just one component of the excessive visual display that characterises the action cinema. Producer Mario Kassar is reported to have jokingly said of the search for a location for *Rambo III* (a search which eventually led to 'Afghanistan') that 'It's got to be hot so Stallone can show off his body'. If this comment functions partly at the level of a joke, it is also telling in other ways. Stallone has been insistently framed and marketed in terms of the body. One of the publicity images for *Rambo III* self-consciously punned on the phrase 'Stallone's Back' heralding both his return as Rambo and the stylised visual image of his body. It is this emphasis on the body which distinguishes a muscular cinema from other action films, though other features may be held in common. Stallone functions quite clearly as an object of spectacle both as a movie star and within muscle culture. *Muscle and Fitness* magazine lovingly describes his workout with a feature in which he is set up as an example of the 'Great Body', getting the cover story and a pin-up centrefold. The text on the cover invites, or challenges, the reader to consider 'How Masculine Are You?', promising also to reveal the star's secrets – 'Stallone: How He Gets Muscular' (June 1989). Body culture, as manifest in magazines like this, represents a vast, and expanding, industry selling a variety of products to aspirant bodybuilders.

The industry surrounding bodybuilding plays on male insecurities in a form that could be seen as analogous to the ways in which women are addressed by beauty culture. Male readers are asked to judge themselves against the bodies portrayed in the pages of muscle magazines. The presentation of the male body as commodity represents, then, the creation of new markets for a consumer culture. The commodification of the male body that is involved in this process, could be read as 'contained' within the framing narrative images of male activity, the activity of 'working out'. Alternatively, the two, contradictory, processes can be seen as working together in the images generated by body culture. This kind of commodification also intersects with, and draws upon, a long history of representation in which the terms of class and race are mapped over the male body, with sports, for example, traditionally providing an arena for working-class men and for black men to succeed when other routes are denied them. Within these terms, we might note that the kinds of male body – black and white working class – that have traditionally been displayed within western culture are those that are *already sexualised*, perceived through an accumulated history of sexual myths and stereotypes. The body is constituted through such myths, written through the terms of sex, class and race. Within the action cinema, these male bodies also tell powerful stories of subjection and resistance, so that muscles function both to give the action hero the power to resist, at the same time as they confirm him in a position that defines him almost exclusively through the body. As with the figure of the showgirl that Laura Mulvey refers to in classic Hollywood films, contemporary American action movies work hard, and often at the expense of narrative development, to contrive situations for the display of the hero's body. If the performance of a show functioned to produce the showgirl as spectacle, then the equivalent sites of the action movie are the gym, a space for rehearsal, and the arena for a fight, whether that be the boxing ring or a more expansive 'natural' setting. The other key site which has repeatedly been used to provide a narrative excuse for the hero's nakedness is not the bedroom but the prison. The prison is also, crucially, a site of punishment, a place designed to separate off those elements perceived as socially undesirable or dangerous. All these sites involve a mapping of themes of punishment and triumphant resistance onto the male body.

In both academic and journalistic commentaries, the built body, both male and female, has often been the object of disgust and humour rather than admiration. There is, for example, a marked hostility towards the physical display involved in the films of muscular stars. A feature in the *Guardian* on *Rambo* suggests that 'Stallone's only preoccupation in the film is exposing his preposterous body', while his 'enormous breasts loom over the screen like Jane Russell in *The Outlaw*' and the 'acting is performed mostly by his biceps'. Here both the body, and the desire to display it, are seen as comical. This critic's reference to Stallone's 'enormous breasts' operates to define his masculinity as ridiculous, questioning the status of his maleness through the suggestion that when the male body is displayed it is revealed as womanly. Taking this further, Jeffrey Walsh cites a *Times* review which playfully describes the camera lingering over Stallone's muscles 'with an abandon not seen on the screen since Joseph von Sternberg made movies with Marlene Dietrich' (Louvre and Walsh 1988: 56). The Sternberg/Dietrich partnership, referred to here, has formed a central point of reference for a feminist film criticism concerned to explore the work of voyeurism and the sexualised performance constructed around the female star within Hollywood film.[5] If, for some, the figure of the bodybuilder signals an assertion of male dominance, an eroticising of the powerful male body, for other critics it seems to signal an hysterical and unstable image of manhood. The muscular body of the action star seems to provide a powerful symbol of both desire and lack. The body is offered for display as both a static object of contemplation and, in the acting out of the hero's achievements, as both subjected and triumphant. In this sense there are no easy links to be made between the action hero, the muscleman and some unproblematic endorsement of a nationalistic macho. With critics caught between breasts and biceps, it is clear that both active and passive, both feminine and masculine terms, inform the imagery of the male body in the action cinema.

ARNOLD SCHWARZENEGGER: 'HEROISM AND HEALTH'

With the headline 'Arnold: Fit for Fatherhood' an image of Arnold Schwarzenegger, posed casually and not as a bodybuilder, adorns the cover of the American man's style magazine *GQ* for May 1990. Having just been appointed head of the President's Council on Fitness by George

Bush, Schwarzenegger is cast here as living out the American dream: he is rich, relaxed and a father. In this profile Alan Richman describes Schwarzenegger as the man who 'transformed the image of body-building from one of excessiveness and narcissism into one of heroism and health' (*GQ*, May 1990: 204). These two poles, of excess and narcissism on the one hand, 'heroic health' on the other, can be seen to provide the limits for the meaning of the muscular male body, both within the cinema and as an image circulated within popular culture more generally. It is on this fragile tightrope that the action hero is poised. Thus the different components which go to make up Arnold Schwarzenegger's star image have been given both conventionally positive and negative inflections. In one view, he is the good immigrant, a newcomer to America who amassed a fortune in real estate before going into the movies. Within the terms of American mythology his wealth signals his positive qualities, his status as an astute businessman. Schwarzenegger's marriage, to a Kennedy, is also a key aspect of his persona here, signifying a certain hyper-normality. That is, not only is he seen to enact the 'normality' of marriage and fatherhood, his marriage to an American celebrity, like the rest of his image, is larger than life. On top of this is the star's evident physical health, which remains a signifier of *moral* health in western culture.[6] *Commando* (1985) goes to great lengths to present Schwarzenegger/Matrix as 'well adjusted'. Matrix is, in the credit sequence which pictures him with his daughter, seen to be a good father, indulgent if old-fashioned in his foolish comments on Boy George ('Why don't they just call him Girl George?').

Against such 'positive' factors stand the low cultural status of the violent movies in which Schwarzenegger has starred, and, in particular, an unease about the political implications of his persona. Indeed the very value that is often attributed to the way in which Arnold Schwarzenegger constructed himself is sometimes reversed, seen as an overly mechanical enactment of the formula for success. The tone of Ian Penman's profile, in the *Sunday Correspondent*, is very much within this mould. Penman sees Schwarzenegger as 'American Fascist Art exemplified, embodied', speaking of the way in which the star 'epitomises the American dream':

> an Austrian immigrant with an unwieldy name, he literally built himself up, bit by bit: economics degree, acting lessons, bodybuilding. Now he has mega millions from acting *and* from real estate, and is big buddies with Milton Friedman. And now there is talk of politics. . . . This will be a case of 'power or nothing'. . . . Things are that simple in his movies and perhaps that is the reason why he is so popular in an America that is military hardware-worshipping, illiterate and demoralised.
>
> (Penman *Sunday Correspondent*, 1 July 1990)

Admiration quickly shifts into unease, which shifts into speculations on the appeal of Schwarzenegger to the masses of America. In particular Schwarzenegger's foreignness, his immigrant status, carries for Penman disturbing associations of a Nazi past, a Europe from which so many fled, escaping to America. In an associated fashion Schwarzenegger's very look reminds us of the appeal that Nazi art made to an idealised classical culture. Even in the case of these briefly sketched instances, we can see that the same elements can be inflected in very different ways, so that the meaning of elements like bodybuilding or 'foreignness', as they operate within Schwarzenegger's image, cannot ultimately be secured. The double advertising images used to promote *Kindergarten Cop* (1990) successfully exploited the good/healthy versus bad/dangerous aspects of Schwarzenegger's star image. In the first he is cast as the tough cop, wearing shades, stubble and brandishing a shotgun, with a tagline that tells us he's 'the toughest undercover cop in LA'. In the second, Schwarzenegger, dressed in casual clothes, is mobbed by small children with the accompanying slogan 'Go ahead – *you* try telling him you didn't do your homework'. The comedy of the film comes from the very redundancy of Schwarzenegger's muscles when dealing with a class of small children. Violence figures in the film as a way of dealing with child-abusing fathers. For organising the children, Schwarzenegger must find the next best thing and teaches the kids some marching, physical discipline.

Arnold Schwarzenegger moved to cinema stardom when he was already a famous figure in the world of body-building. Not surprisingly, therefore, his star image has almost exclusively been defined through the body. In the mythological *Conan* films Schwarzenegger brought to life a comic-book version of muscular male heroism. He also appeared as a bodybuilder in Bob Rafelson's *Stay Hungry* (1976). Schwarzenegger's character, Joe Santo, is a contender for Mr Universe, a contest being staged in the American south in which the film is set. The 'simplicity' and 'gentleness' of his European immigrant persona, combined with his huge frame, are played off against the corruption of wealthy southern society. Thus he is seen playing the violin with his friends in a folksy scene in the woods. Later, when commissioned to play for a society party, he is patronised by the wealthy. Such movies used the fact of Schwarzenegger's body in a variety of ways, a body which had made him famous before his entry into movies. As seen with the advertising images for *Kindergarten Cop*, the fact of his size, and the toughness this is taken to imply, remains a fundamental aspect of Schwarzenegger's image.

Towards the end of the 1980s Schwarzenegger attempted to re-define and extend his image, largely through the use of humour. *The Terminator* (1984) had already featured a certain black humour, derived in part from the relentlessness of the cyborg figure that Schwarzenegger plays.

Increasingly his films featured grim one-liners – referred to by distrustful critics as 'so-called humour'. From the camp self-awareness of *Commando*, Schwarzenegger has moved into the explicit comedy of *Twins* (1988) and *Kindergarten Cop*. At an early point in *Twins* we see Schwarzenegger wandering the streets of LA with wide-eyed awe. He confronts a pumped-up advertising image of Stallone in *Rambo III*, jokingly comparing the size of the image to his own biceps. The fact of the body is central to such visual gags. The advertising slogan for *Twins* which went with an image of Schwarzenegger and Danny de Vito was 'Only their mother could tell them apart', again punning on size.

At the same time Schwarzenegger has continued to play action roles in films such as *The Running Man* (1987), *Predator* (1987) and *Total Recall* (1990). In both *The Running Man* and *Total Recall* he plays a kind of extraordinary-everyman figure, combating tyranny in future-world situations. Schwarzenegger's enactment of the Terminator in the 1991 sequel was similarly remodelled as an heroic figure. He is sent back in time to protect John Connor from a superior model of Terminator, the T1000. His role is significantly modified in *Terminator 2*, not only through the use of a parodic self-referentiality in the film, but through the gradual 'humanising' of his character. This process involves the establishment of an affectionate relationship between the Terminator and the young John Connor. Seen through Sarah Connor's eyes, the Terminator is the ideal father. The use made in *Terminator 2* of the strength of Schwarzenegger's body, his size, which seems to provoke the need for a reassuring humour in other movies, is fascinating. Schwarzenegger becomes a protective figure in this film, with his solid qualities played off against the T1000 against which he is pitted. This updated machine is made of a metal alloy which allows it to change shape at will, acquiring a terrifying fluidity. The updated Terminator is typified by a lack of the bodily definition that is so important to the image of the bodybuilder. That the T1000 is a feminised monster is evident in this fluidity and is echoed in director James Cameron's comments that he chose actor Robert Patrick for the part for his catlike qualities. Within the film Schwarzenegger's muscular solidity is played off against both the unstable qualities of the T1000 and the rather iconographically unstable figure of Linda Hamilton as Sarah Connor.[7]

SYLVESTER STALLONE: THE BODY AND THE VOICE

Sylvester Stallone achieved international fame in 1976 as the writer and star of *Rocky*, which took the Academy Award for best picture. *Rocky* is the story of a down-at-heel boxer, Rocky Balboa (Stallone) who is given, as a PR exercise, the chance to fight the champ Apollo Creed (Carl Weathers). His ambition is to 'go the distance', to prove his existence on a public stage. The sentimental story of Rocky's move from low-life to achiever is told through the progression of his relationship with his girlfriend Adrian and her brother Pauly, along with his trainer and other acquaintances. The film culminates in a vicious bout between Rocky and Creed. Rocky survives the contest and is reunited with Adrian, with the film ending in a freeze-frame, close-up, image of the two together. The couple have made their way through five *Rocky* films, with the most recent, and reputedly the last, released in 1990. Popularly, the story of Rocky has been read as Stallone's story, a reading that has been actively encouraged by the star's publicity machine. The themes of rags to riches, achievement through struggle within a white immigrant community, determination to succeed against all odds and the figure of the underdog, elements at the heart of *Rocky*, became central aspects of Stallone's star image.

Adverts for *First Blood*, the first film in the Rambo series, picked up on Stallone's image as a fighter with the tagline 'this time he's fighting for his life'. Commenting on the direction of his career after *Rambo III*, Stallone has suggested that 'I came into this business as an underdog and that's what works best. My going too far into Supermanism has become a turnoff' (*Empire*, June 1990: 38). Specifically here Stallone is commenting on the pumped-up excesses of the body seen in *Rambo III*, a film which didn't have the box-office success in the States of the previous two, despite the fact that it was a huge success on the international market.

The success of Stallone's 'Rambo' persona served to consolidate the dumb, beefcake aspects of his image. The box-office appeal of the *Rocky* and *Rambo* series have cemented the popular identification between Stallone and these two characters, whilst departures such as *Rhinestone*, a musical in which he starred with Dolly Parton, or *FIST*, in which he played a union leader, not only failed to match their commercial success, but also failed to shift that identification. Two recent attempts at comedy, *Oscar* (1991) and *Stop Or My Mom Will Shoot!* (1992) have also died at the box-office. The popular construction of Stallone's star image in a variety of media has followed the identification of his image with Rocky and Rambo, an identification which is in line with the excessive, more disturbing connotations of the muscular male hero, in contrast to the supposed 'heroic health' associated with Schwarzenegger. Stallone's films, and by extension the action cinema which came to be referred to as 'Rambo-style' films, have been dismissed by critics who point to the violence and the repetition of roles, joking about endless sequels and rejecting what was seen as typically one-dimensional performances. If Schwarzenegger has used comedy in his films to extend his appeal, humour has also been a significant element in Stallone's attempt to turn his image around. The visual jokes in *Rhinestone* centred around Stallone's shortness and his physical incompetence alongside the figure of hard-punching Dolly Parton. After such box-office disasters Stallone made a concerted effort to turn his persona around at the end of the 1980s with the release of *Tango and Cash* (1989) and *Lock Up* (1989). Whilst these are both action pictures, they attempt to reformulate Stallone's image. *Tango and Cash* uses verbal and visual comedy to achieve its effects. In a moment that is often referred to, from the early part of the film, Stallone's character asserts that 'Rambo is a pussy'. Such jibes at a character with whom Stallone was so closely identified were widely reported at the time as part of a bid for respectability, an attempt to shed the negative qualities associated with his role as Rambo. Indeed Stallone's attempt to change his image was rapidly incorporated into that image itself, providing a focus for interviews and features.

After a very public divorce from actress Brigitte Nielson, Stallone's publicity machine launched an attempt to redefine his public persona. In an interview, given at the time, the star accepts the criticism directed at his action films, adding that 'I always had it in the back of my mind that there would be a period when I felt I'd done my commercial tour of duty, and I could do something experimental. I just didn't think it would take so long'. The interview goes on with Stallone asserting that he had tried 'to break out of the Rocky mould' with '*Paradise Alley* and *FIST*, which were not action pictures' (*20/20*, April 1990). Reproduced from *American Film* the whole interview and accompanying feature centres on the need for Stallone to change his image. Stallone appears to accept the rebuke of pandering to commerce, invoking the rigours of the traditional star system which is interestingly expressed through a military metaphor, a 'commercial tour of duty' which, once over, is to be followed by a period of experiment. The opposition between art and commerce that is drawn on here is a familiar one, often deployed in cultural criticism. This opposition is further mapped onto an opposition between the mind and the body. Such a set of associations are recognisable from longstanding traditions of cultural commentary which oppose art and the mind to commerce (the popular) and the body. Thus the *Sunday Mirror* magazine announces that 'the new Stallone wants to be taken seriously', that 'at 43 he wants to be accepted for his brain as well as [his] brawn'. This short photo-feature offers a new image of the star in which, while 'the biceps may still be as firm . . . the light brown eyes are now framed by glasses'. Stallone took to wearing glasses in public, if not in pin-ups. He spoke in interviews of his art collection and his desire to make films about figures such as Poe and Puccini. Such pleas for cultural respectability evoked this suspicious response from the *Guardian*:

> So widespread is the continuing retreat from rampant masculinity that even a Neanderthal like Sylvester Stallone can't stop flashing his New Man credentials; enter the new caring, sharing, sensitive Sly, wearing spectacles and much more concerned with showing off his Picassos than his pecs.

The objection, voiced by several reviewers, to the turnabout at work in Stallone's image involves a suspicion precisely of the ways in which different masculine identities are produced through surface changes, the replacement of one image with another which serves only to emphasize the artificiality that is operating here.

The opposition of specs and pecs, sensitivity and the Neanderthal, situates Stallone's attempts to turn his image around firmly within recent shifts in images of masculinity. This process involves an attempt to reorganise the respective significance given to the body and the voice. The muscular male body, foregrounded in the star images of a range of 'physical actors', such as Stallone, Schwarzenegger and Dolph Lundgren, is played off against the voice. The verbal dimension is often played down in a cinematic tradition which is so centrally to do with the spectacle of the body. Introducing the interview cited above, the author expresses surprise as to what a talkative guy Stallone is: 'This is Rambo? Talking so *fast*? Stallone, so closely identified with Rocky and Rambo that people assume he's stupid and wooden-tongued, was clowning around in a Warner's post-production room'. The commentary continues:

> Although you think of Stallone as a heavyweight, up close he appeared more of a middleweight, with quick moves and a light, almost spritely grace. He spoke quickly, too, almost in a stream-of-consciousness style. His voice was a little higher pitched than usually heard in his movies, but often for effect he went deep into the Rocky tone. Wearing glasses and his standard outfit of dress shirt and slacks, he was well-tailored, well-barbered and very smooth of face.
>
> Stallone's tired of being considered dumb, and *Tango and Cash* is supposed to help remedy that. His character is a cop, but an erudite, glib cop. Stallone sees the movie . . . as his first step away from hard-core action pictures.

Presented as an attempt to reveal the 'real' Stallone, the interviewer addresses us with a bemused tone, deflecting attention away from the body ('more of a middleweight') to the more 'civilised' qualities associated with fashion and the voice. Stallone's voice is described as higher pitched, his body less imposing than the macho image would suggest. The 'civilised' signifiers of glasses and fashion are invoked, set against the display of the unclothed male body within the action film. This play is taken up in *Tango and Cash* in the digs made about Tango missing his wardrobe.

Reviewers have on the whole refused the attempt at a shift in Stallone's image, retaining the emphasis on the body, rather than the voice. A feature in the *Guardian*, for example, commented of *Rambo* that 'Stallone . . . substitutes oafish muttering for dialogue, making that other hero of the genre, Clint Eastwood, seem almost garrulous'. Over the last twenty years Eastwood has become respected enough as an actor and film-maker for some, though by no means all, to see his minimal style as craft. Eastwood's performance can thus be seen as the artful withholding of words, rather than an artless inability to speak. Inflections of speech and silence are central to the play of different definitions of masculinity and maleness in the action cinema.

The hysterical rambling of a character like Leo (Joe Pesci), a witness in need of protection in *Lethal Weapon 2* (1989) mark him out as weak and unthreatening. This also highlights the rather different hysteria to which Mel Gibson's character is subject in the film – the whole premise of his character is his supposed 'death wish' which allows him to perform as a cop since he is not afraid of potentially deadly situations. The term 'Rambo' is often used to denote stupid behaviour, an irrationality which is closely linked to the inarticulacy of the action hero, of the stress on the body and *cinema as spectacle*, rather than the voice.[8] In contrast to the more physical movie stars who have emerged from body culture, Eastwood's is, to an extent, an invisible body. Generally fully clothed, the power of his character is signified through characteristics such as firepower and marksmanship. The fast draw, for example, is a key icon of the three 'Dollar' films, as well as being at times played for laughs. With the advent of the 'physical actor' the male body is made startlingly visible. The action hero as returning war hero, for example, actually carries the war within himself. Conflict is literally inscribed in the hysterical (overdetermined/overdeveloped) male body.

LOOK WHO'S TALKING: THE WISE-GUY PERSONA IN THE ACTION CINEMA

Enlisting Jimmy Dix (Damon Wayans) as his partner at the end of *The Last Boy Scout*, Joe Hallenbeck (Bruce Willis) jokes that, this being the nineties, a hero can't just take out bad guys. He has also to give them a one-liner. Like 'I'll Be Back' asks Dix, with reference to Schwarzenegger's trademark line. At points, this spectacular movie seems an exercise in wordplay, with the heroes and the villains trading complex insults, challenges and comebacks as well as commenting on each other's verbal performance. I've already spoken in Chapter 3 of the uses made of Bruce Willis's star image in *Die Hard* and *Die Hard 2*. Willis's wise-cracking persona was initially derived from his role in the hit TV series *Moonlighting*. This comedy/drama/detective series centred on the Blue Moon detective agency, though little in the way of detection ever happened, and the action consisted mostly of verbal confrontations between Willis and Cybill Shepherd in a variety of guises. Whilst *Die Hard* gives the audience Willis as action hero pin-up, his persona is very much defined through the voice. He is, in this, much more wise-guy than tough-guy. *The Last Boy Scout* brings the two together in violent scenes which involve a certain black comedy, as in the memorable scene in which Willis, after being slugged, threatens to kill one of the men holding him captive if he is hit again. When the bad guy takes no notice, Hallenbeck kills him, with a single, understated blow, to the outrage of a second, rather ineffectual, bad guy who looks on. The 'joke' here revolves around the fact that Hallenbeck follows through on a threat – 'I'll kill you' – which is a common part of everyday speech, but one which is rarely meant literally. Words are very clearly deployed in the film as part of a battle, a struggle for power, behind which lurks the threat of physical violence. This verbal sparring, the challenge posed by the uses of words, echoes the complexities of the uses of language within black American culture, as well as traditions of stand-up comedy, with which Wayans is associated, and which Whoopi Goldberg also draws on in her role as a narcotics cop in *Fatal Beauty*.[9]

In mellower mode, Willis scored a huge success as the voice of baby Mikey in *Look Who's Talking* (1989). (Damon Wayans's voice was also used, along with those of Willis and Roseanne Barr, in the sequel.) Indeed the particular style of masculine identity that Willis enacts as John McClane in the two *Die Hard* films has something childlike about it, a trait shared with his role in *Moonlighting*. A perpetual adolescent, even if a knowing one, there is a sense in which he seems to be playing games (cops and robbers, cowboys and Indians). *Die Hard* has Willis/McClane cracking jokes to himself, wearing a facial expression which seems to convey his sense of surprise and confusion that he is at the centre of the explosive narrative events. McClane styles himself as the dandy cowboy Roy Rogers, keeping up a running commentary at the same time. If *The Last Boy Scout* represents one of the grimmest versions yet seen of the Willis wise-guy character, the comic aspects of his persona are played out more fully in the more fantastic *Hudson Hawk*, in which he sings old show tunes as a way of timing robberies with his partner Tommy. Further, if there is something childish about the Willis persona, a good deal of *The Last Boy Scout* centres precisely on his nightmare relationship with an unfaithful wife and foul-mouthed daughter, a focus which emphasises the difficulties of the role of father though these are ultimately 'resolved' in the film's final scene. Whilst there is an unquestioning, idealised relationship between father and daughter in Schwarzenegger's *Commando*, Hallenbeck's daughter in *The Last Boy Scout* is hostile and abusive in the extreme. Dix also functions in some senses in the role of a 'son' to Hallenbeck within the film, referred to as a kid, so that their relationship, which is based on verbal battles, functions as a testing ground for the ultimate family reunion with which the film concludes. The complexities of the figure of the 'father' in recent action films, including *The Last Boy Scout*, are taken up in later chapters.

In the framework that emerges through an analysis of these star images we can see how an emphasis on the verbal is put to work in *Tango and Cash*, a film that sets out to be humorous, using the backchat associated with the wise-guy to take swipes at Stallone's he-man image within a buddy movie format. The film can work with such a redefinition of Stallone's image, partly because of the surrounding publicity, but also because of the presence of Kurt Russell as Stallone's partner and the comic tone of the relationship between the two. *Tango and Cash* plays off two male types in its buddy pairing from the 'bad cop, worse cop' scene which serves to tell us that, despite the glasses, Tango is no softy, to the boldly (or crudely, depending on your point of view) drawn contrast between the two men's styles. Russell plays out a well-established persona, the macho slob who is sent up in Carpenter's *Big Trouble in Little China* (1986), worshipped in *Backdraft* (1991). An extraordinary but regular guy, Russell retains a tough-guy aura whilst exuding those qualities that pass for normality. The opening sequences of *Tango and Cash* are concerned to establish the differences between the two cop heroes – their offices, guns, clothes, appearance, eating habits and social graces. Both Ray Tango and Gabriel Cash are media stars, cops who get very public results and who, whilst they have never met, maintain a rivalry over their respective press coverage. Cash dismisses Tango, whose picture is featured in the newspaper, as 'Armani with a badge', and Tango's Captain paraphrases the press coverage as 'Down Town Clown versus Beverly Hills Wop' which about sums it up.

As the film progresses Tango and Cash move from rivalry to friendship, partly drawn together by the plot to frame them, and partly through the character of Kiki/Katherine, Tango's sister. They survive the ordeal of prison together, escape together and proceed to unmask the conspiracy of drug dealers orchestrated by arch-villain Perrette (Jack Palance). From the separate press photos we see at the beginning of the film they progress to the final newspaper image, a parody of *Desperately Seeking Susan*, with the two clasping raised hands. By the end of the film they are finishing each other's sentences. Russell's presence allows for repartee between the two tough guys, swapping jokes in the shower and kidding around. Giving Stallone a chance to wise-crack and dress up, it is Russell who gets his shirt off within the first few minutes of the film (a trait of the action hero). And it is also Kurt Russell who ends up in female drag, posing as the (rather butch) 'property' of Tango's sister in order to make a getaway from the club where she is a dancer. Playing upon the pleasures of dressing up and the acting out of different star images, Tango and Cash are offered as good to look at, 'two of the department's most highly decorated officers'. As in the *Lethal Weapon* films, desire between cop partners is invoked and disavowed within the framework offered by comedy. Indeed, comedy opens up a space for male and female drag, allowing a play with the 'boundaries' of gendered identity, with jokes about the male image and sexuality which are not permissible within the more earnest dramas of the action tradition.

The use of comedy represents one way of undermining the more disturbing aspects of the muscular action hero, though as in the case of *The Last Boy Scout*, this is not necessarily a substitute for the centrality of violence and explosive spectacle. Nonetheless, a key distinction emerges in the action films of recent years, between a silent (seemingly inarticulate) and an extremely verbal representation of the action hero. A dichotomy can be seen to develop in which the anxieties provoked by the physical display of the white male hero are displaced either through the use of comedy, as in many of Schwarzenegger's films, or through the deployment of images of torture and suffering, a strategy pushed to the extreme in Stallone's earnest prison drama, *Lock Up*. This last film is discussed further in the following chapters, as are the other strategies, referred to here, through which masculinities and sexualities are represented in the action cinema.

5

MASCULINITY, POLITICS AND NATIONAL IDENTITY

'Physical acting', the cinematic performance of the muscular male body that has been associated most directly with such stars as Arnold Schwarzenegger and Sylvester Stallone, achieved a new visibility during the 1980s. Stallone and Schwarzenegger vied for the position of top box-office male star, presiding over what could be seen as a renaissance of the action cinema. The revival of the action/adventure film also generated a critical unease which, as we've seen, centred on concerns about the politics of these 'heroic' narratives. Film critics such as Andrew Britton and Robin Wood expressed an unease to do with the ways in which these films were both recognisable, and yet distinctive, harking back to the cinematic past whilst articulating 'new', potentially parodic, images of masculine identity. In this context, questions over the political status of the image – whether, for example, the figure of the hero was intended as a parody or an endorsement of a tough masculinity – became crucial. The qualities of a self-reflexive knowingness, so apparent in many films of the 1980s, could be construed as a form of auto-deconstruction, or as one more ideological disguise, a comedy that pre-empts criticism since 'it's only a joke'. These questions acquired a new urgency at a time, the mid-1980s, when some forms of postmodernist discourse seemed precisely to refuse any political fixing of meaning. Yet, if political fixity is a characteristic of propaganda, it is rarely to be found in the popular cinema, particularly a popular cinema that seeks, and finds, success in international markets. Thriving on ambiguity, Hollywood cinema performs that most utopian of exercises – it has its cake and eats it too. It is with an awareness of such a context, that this chapter examines issues of politics, masculinity and national identity in the action cinema.

During the 1980s, action films such as *Indiana Jones and the Temple of Doom*, *Commando*, *Die Hard* and *Predator* paraded the bodies of their male heroes in advanced stages of both muscular development and undress. One film in particular, *Rambo: First Blood Part II*, became the over-determined reference point for a whole range of concerned media discourses, generated from both the left and right. A mini-panic was orchestrated around the film in Britain, leading to a BBC ban and a whole host of journalistic and academic speculations on 'Rambo-style' films, 'Ramboidal violence' and the resultant characterisation of the mid-1980s as the 'Age of Rambo'.[1] Thinking about the reputation of this film, perhaps the most notorious of the muscular movies, offers a useful way to open up the relationship between masculinity, politics and the action film. *Rambo* was a film whose reputation preceded it and, to an extent, engulfed the film text itself. The film, a big-budget sequel to Stallone's 1982 hit *First Blood*, was notorious well before it played British cinemas in 1985. In the context of the Beirut hijacking, within which the film got its American release, President Reagan was reported as saying 'After seeing "Rambo" last night I know what to do next time it happens'. These comments provided the most public framing device through which *Rambo* was read as Reaganite, as endorsing a hawkish foreign policy, a muscular lack of diplomacy. A visual link was made in a much-reproduced poster image of the time which featured Reagan's head superimposed onto Rambo's torso and dubbed 'Ronbo'. Reagan had already been widely linked to a revisionist re-evaluation of America's role in Vietnam. In Britain, the film was released into the aftermath of a particularly punitive campaign against 'video violence' which had led to the banning of many titles, along with increased censorship and the passing of the 1984 Video Recordings Act which legislated for the certification of all films released for video. Directed specifically at the horror film, commentators at the time conjured up a series of images of evil films invading British culture from foreign lands.[2] It is worthwhile sketching, however briefly, this context since *Rambo* was a film that was successful worldwide. The film's appeal has most often been contextualised within a specific understanding of American political history. Though this is of course important, and I discuss below the film's situation in relation to representations of Vietnam, it is not everything.

The pumped-up figure of Stallone as Rambo seemed to offer more than just a metaphor, functioning for various cultural commentators as the literal embodiment of American interventionism. Thus critics could speak, for example, of 'the presidentially approved fantasy of Rambo regeneration' (Louvre and Walsh 1988: 6). Since the mid-1980s the term 'Rambo' has become common currency, earning an entry in the updated *Oxford English Dictionary*. For the record, 'Rambo' is defined as 'a Vietnam war veteran represented as macho, self-sufficient and bent on violent retribution', a term which is 'used allusively'. As we'll see, 'Rambo' actually operated to condense a range of discourses concerning sexuality and politics. This chapter centres around the cultural significance and critical reputation of 'Rambo' as a phenomenon. The impetus for this work stems partly from a desire to pay a little more detailed attention than is usual to a set of movies which are often either characterised as monolithic, or ignored altogether. This marginalisation perhaps echoes the revulsion the films seem to provoke in the cine-literate, or at least the critical, audience.[3] Indeed the particular terms in which this group of films has been dismissed proves to be as interesting a site of inquiry as the films themselves, partly due to the extreme loathing that they have managed to provoke, but also because an examination of the terms in which that loathing has been expressed allows an address to questions of masculinity and cinematic representation. In this sense, reading the muscular cinema through the frame of ideology may not tell us much. I don't want to argue that an ideological analysis has no purchase here, since the action film offers us, amongst other things, complex ideological configurations of nationhood and masculinity. Yet the ideological analysis of narrative, as suggested in Chapter 3, often seems to lead to a loss of specificity. We find an erasure of, on the one hand the differences that exist between different stars and their films, and, on the other, the diversity of potential or actual readings available to audiences.

THE 'AGE OF RAMBO'

A series of controversies and press speculations led to the production of a phrase like the 'Age of Rambo' to describe the 1980s. This characterisation formed just one version of the frequently renewed suspicion that society is in moral decline, a decline that is measured against a mythicised past. Within a variety of journalistic and academic discourses, an operation of condensation allowed a series of critical and cultural worries to be represented, embodied perhaps, in the figure of 'Rambo'. Two aspects of the 'Rambo' persona and films have been singled out for particular critical attention. The most evident is the association that has been drawn by some critics between the muscular cinema of the 1980s and the Reaganite New Right in the United States. Here Rambo is seen to cinematically correct the national humiliation of a defeat in Vietnam. As the *Guardian* had it:

> SYLVESTER STALLONE'S Rambo II has become more than just a movie. It opened in American cinemas at the right time to profit from the Beirut hijacking. When the White House was impotent with rage, patriotic Americans could watch the muscle of Rambo destroy the Vietnamese and Russian armies as he rescued GIs from Communist prisons; he won in the cinema the war the United States lost on the ground.

This view of the film, as one which 'released the frustration of a nation', is standard and *Rambo* has, by and large, remained the low-quality reference point against which to define new Vietnam movies such as Oliver Stone's *Born On the Fourth of July* (1989).[4] *Rambo* has been repeatedly used to define the quality of other Vietnam movies, broadly along the lines of an opposition between realism and comic-book fantasy. This type of criticism emerges from a long tradition in which American narratives dealing with the war have been received with scepticism. Controversy also surrounded the release of *The Deer Hunter*, for example.[5]

It is interesting that whilst America's involvement in Vietnam defines *Rambo*, with its invocation of the figure of the Vietnam veteran, the film itself is not set during the conflict. The only scenes to directly invoke that period in the whole cycle are the flashbacks of torture in *First Blood*. In this the film is positioned to one side of the 1980s' wave of movies centred on Vietnam. More generally, *Rambo* is one of the few muscular movies to actually tell us the country in which the fiction takes place, or to offer anything more than the most basic historical reference point. Another such film is *Rambo III*, which is set in Afghanistan. This was a notorious mistake in marketing terms, since in the very week of the film's release the Soviet Union announced its troop withdrawals. It is far more usual, if the American action narrative isn't set within the USA itself, to evoke an unspecified foreign location. It is also noteworthy that whilst a film like *Commando* lists a range of global hotspots in which John Matrix/Schwarzenegger has been involved, reference to Vietnam is studiously avoided. The action takes place instead in a vague terrain. Similarly, whilst we might remark of the jungle setting of *Predator* that this is 'Vietnam', this is only to assert that it is reminiscent of the conventions of the Vietnam movie. There is a defining sense of placelessness informing both the muscular action cinema and its articulation of the heroic figure. This is partly a function of the need to sell to international markets, but also serves the mythic (that is, generalised, universal) status to which the narratives aspire.

The second set of critical concerns which inform the perception of 'Rambo' is already implicit in the *Guardian*'s assessment, cited above, with its references to muscular power (Rambo) versus impotence (the White House). Power and potency are constitutive discourses of masculinity. The figure of Rambo has often been taken to represent the (re-)emergence of a threateningly physical understanding of masculinity. *Rambo* is, within this view, seen as symptomatic of a 1980s' backlash against feminism, functioning as 'a sexist assertion of male dominance' (Louvre and Walsh 1988: 56). It has been suggested, for example, that the 'hard-edged masculinity' of Rambo 'makes a statement on behalf of every violent husband and every child-abusing male'.[6] In an overview of the period, Jonathan Rutherford postulates the existence of 'two idealised images' structuring our understanding of masculinity in the 1980s. These images, termed 'New Man and Retributive Man' he takes as corresponding 'to the repressed and the public meanings of masculinity' (Chapman and Rutherford 1988: 28). For Rutherford, images of the 'New Man' attempt, partly in a response to feminism, to articulate men's repressed emotions, revealing a 'more feminised image' (ibid.: 32). Against this, the public face of Retributive Man 'represents the struggle to reassert a traditional masculinity, a tough authority'. Perhaps unsurprisingly, he asserts that the 'classic figure is Rambo', evoking a world in which '*First Blood* is still a feature of every high street video shop and the image of Stallone with his huge machine gun adorns the t-shirts, books and toys of tens of thousands of little boys' (ibid.: 28). This ubiquitous figure:

> advertises a destructive machismo as the solution to men's problems. He is John Wayne with his gloves off, wildly lashing out at everything that threatens and disappoints him. He confronts a world gone soft, pacified by traitors and cowards, dishonourable feminised men. It is a world that has disrupted his notions of manhood and honour. It threatens his comprehension of who he is. And his attempts to recreate order, and subdue the forces that threaten him, degenerate into a series of violent actions.
>
> (ibid.: 28–9)

The invocation of threatened children is significant here, according with a more general argument that the western world has, as Jeffrey Walsh puts it, 'inflicted psychic damage on its young people through the popularization of militarist culture'.[7] We need to be aware here of the extent to which the figure of 'children under threat' has been invoked to legitimate a whole range of censorious policies, particularly in relation to representations of gay sexuality. Children and the family, that is, are often invoked as a displaced way of speaking about more general societal fears, to do with the supposed excesses of popular culture, as well as the feared behaviour of those groups constructed as marginal.[8]

In Rutherford's schema, violence 'represents a retreat into physical force whose fantasy is played out in toy shops across the country'. His sharply drawn contrast between the articulate and caring new man on the one hand and an image of Ramboidal frenzy on the other is quite familiar. A regressive retreat into fantasy, it is suggested, is not only cowardly, but *childish* (conducted in toy shops), indeed it is implicitly *unmanly*. A rhetorical strategy is in operation here, one which seeks to polemically redefine the terms through which an understanding of 'good' and 'bad' masculinities are constructed, with the exercise of physical power devalued as unmanly. Yet this strategy not only leaves unquestioned those articulate, institutional forms of power, but can be seen to represent the embrace of a patriarchal rhetoric which constructs so many other groups as childish, needing both punishment and protection. The point is worth making since the tone of Rutherford's comments echoes an already existing discourse which has framed the difficulty of the task facing men, which is that of working through 'their' masculinity. This task is expressed in terms of an opposition between a verbal man (often cast as feminised) and a physical man. I don't mean to suggest that such a dichotomy is a feature of all writings on masculinity. It is however evident in certain discourses, finding its most popular expression in the notion that men need to 'express' the 'feminine side' of themselves. Such a conception tends to preserve two polarised embodiments of masculinity, new man and action man, in Rutherford's schema.

These polarised figures, who appear at the same historical moment, need to be seen as interacting with and informing each other. Otherwise, the effect is to critically reproduce a stable binary relation between femininity and masculinity, an either/or that is mapped onto different male types. This opposition, between verbal and physical abilities and the definition of masculinity they propose, has been critically worked out in relation to muscular movies. By contrast, a model that stresses masculinit*ies*, the plurality of masculine identities, allows particular cinematic images of the male hero to be situated within a wider cultural context, in which they are seen to play off and work with each other rather than existing in some secure opposition. This may begin to tell us why the critical recognition of masculinities matters, since the representation of gender and sexuality in the action cinema involves a complex articulation of factors such as class and race. Masculinity is written in complex and diverse ways over the male and female body, the black and the white body, in the action genre. Susan Jeffords's recent book, *The Remasculinization of America*, addresses the ways in which Vietnam representation, both at the time of America's involvement and since, is concerned to reinscribe gendered relations of power. She effectively demonstrates the working of gendered discourses within a diverse range of texts, but goes further than this in an assertion that the writing of gender over-rides all other differences, so that:

> The defining feature of American war narratives is that they are a 'man's story' from which women are generally excluded. For such narratives, gender is the assumed category of interpretation, the only one that is not subject to interpretation and variation of point of view, experience, age, race and so on.
>
> (Jeffords 1989: 49)

Jeffords asserts here that gender operates, within Vietnam representation, as a unifying category which effaces all other differences. This perspective allows a fascinating insight on the oedipal adventures of the white American heroes of 1980s films, such as *Platoon* and *Full Metal Jacket*, heroes who, in their shifting attitudes towards the war and their comrades-in-arms, come to represent 'America'. Such a representation is quite explicit in *Platoon*'s rites-of-passage narrative, which features the retrospective voiceover of the hero Chris, who comments on his own war experiences as a metaphor for the nation's turmoil. Whilst such films may well assume an audience who can cohere around the male identity that is offered, different audiences may well have other concerns and investments in Vietnam representation. In the case of *Platoon*, the story that is told is very clearly that of a middle-class white man, whose difference from the 'grunts' and black Americans with whom he 'finds himself' in Vietnam, cannot be effaced by the strategies of the film text alone.[9]

If 'Rambo' operates to condense a range of discourses it also stands in for a range of films, those movies starring musclemen or featuring violent action sequences. And, just as there is a generalised notion of the persona and films, there is a generalised way in which the term is used, associated as it is with ideological reference points as diverse as Ronald Reagan and child-abuse, American cultural imperialism and a regressive masculinity. In contrast to the way in which the term cuts across such a range of discourses, reference to 'Rambo' is usually characterised by an assumption of the very *obviousness* of what is meant. To give an example. Robert Lapsley and Michael Westlake illustrate their discussion of Eco's idea of the shot as utterance with the example of a 'shot of Sylvester Stallone naked to the waist firing a rocket-launcher' which 'does not signify "Rambo" but rather "there is Rambo", or more probably "here is Rambo single-handedly defeating the Evil Empire"' (Lapsley and Westlake 1988: 44). The 'Evil Empire', a term drawn from the film series *Star Wars*, also of course refers specifically to Reagan's characterisation of the Soviet Union in another of his notorious speeches. With this reference, and with the foregrounding of action, 'Rambo' seems obvious enough to be used as an illustration. Of course the meaning of 'Rambo' is in some senses clear, precisely because it has been used so often to signify a thuggishly violent nationalistic macho. That is to say, the term has acquired a meaning through its repeated use in a variety of journalistic and political as well as cinematic contexts. It isn't possible to look at the film or think about the term without reference to the complex history of signification in which it has been involved.[10] The narrative has become inseparable from all the other narratives in which Rambo came to play a part through the 1980s, such as Reagan's public gaffes or fears about video and computer games and their effects on children.

SEMPER FI? MASCULINITY AND NATIONHOOD

A discursive link between nationhood and masculinity provides an important context for considering the muscular action cinema. Nationhood and masculinity are crucial terms within most war films, indeed combat films generally. Yet cinematic discourses of American manhood are profoundly ambiguous, certainly in the three *Rambo* films, and in many others critically designated as the texts of macho revisionism or, in its crudest version, as dumb movies for dumb people. *Rambo* and, by extension, other muscular movies have been criticised for their rewriting of history, for the erasure of, in particular, the history of America's involvement in Vietnam. Such critical concerns represent, in part, an important desire to see historical justice done. But in terms of an exploration of the films I'm talking about here, such criticisms do need to be contextualised and worked through. It is in this sense that the following comments on the war film, the action film and the muscular cinema are offered.

That Chuck Norris, as I mentioned earlier, has sought to distance his *Missing In Action* series from the anti-government populism of the *Rambo* films, is perhaps indicative of the rather ambiguous articulation of America and belonging in the *Rambo* series. Such ambiguities operate across the muscular cinema more generally. In the *Rambo* series we see the articulation of a masculinity which is *out of place*, with the films' narratives fuelled by problems of location. The films discussed here can be seen to repeatedly pose a question: is there a place for the muscular hero in America? Just as often, we find that neither America's urban nor rural society has a place for the hero. Increasingly then the powerful white hero is a figure who operates in the margins, whilst in many senses continuing to represent dominance. This is an important trait in many action pictures and is central to the pleasures of the text.

In the three *Rambo* films, problems of location can be read via the symbolic space of Vietnam and its relationship to America. In particular this imaginary geography mobilises two key terms: *home* and *hell*. In *First Blood*, home, specifically smalltown America, is defined as hellish. Rambo is arrested for vagrancy, tortured and hunted, first by the local sheriff's department and then by the National Guard. The film ends with Rambo's much-ridiculed monologue of rage against an America in which he has no place. Collapsing in tears into the arms of his military mentor, Colonel Trautman, Rambo is finally led off into captivity. *Rambo: First Blood Part II* opens with Rambo breaking rocks in jail. On the promise of a pardon, he returns to Vietnam with a secret mission to search for American POWs. An advertising slogan for the film told us that 'What you call hell, he calls home' (i.e. Vietnam). This construction of Vietnam as home, which is equated with a space where the hero can perform, is accompanied by the paradoxical narrative struggle to bring the MIAs/POWs home (back to America), to a place that is precisely defined as unwelcoming, which is far from homely. Commenting on the populist themes of the Vietnam film, it is with some surprise that Leslie Fiedler notes that 'even in *Rambo II*' the hero's 'righteous wrath is directed at an American enemy' (Fiedler 1990: 398). In the final moments of the film, Rambo, refusing an offer to return to the States and re-enlist, walks off into the sunset to live 'day by day'. This could be seen as a telling generic moment derived from the image of the western hero or, alternatively, as typifying the empty nostalgia through which some critics have categorised contemporary Hollywood.

Rambo's ending was greeted with horror by critics who objected to the speech in which Rambo, on behalf of the POWs, speaks of a desire for 'our country to love us as much as we love it'. As with many action movies, the patriotic strength of such pleas is articulated alongside a narrative rejection of America. Rambo makes his speech in response to Trautman's mistaken rebuke that, whilst the Vietnam war may have been wrong, he should not 'hate his country'. Rambo replies that he would 'die for it', before leaving the scene. He is discovered at the beginning of *Rambo III* living in a buddhist monastery in Thailand where, according to the film's publicity, 'he has gone to find the inner peace that has always eluded him'. The opening sequence of the film replays a scene from Cimino's *The Deer Hunter* (1978) with stick fighting taking the place of Russian roulette. Trautman, the sole figure in military uniform amongst a crowd of gamblers, watches Rambo fight but loses him in the chaos that follows. Here Rambo's immersion in the culture of the Orient is seen as positive, regenerating rather than self-destructive as it appears in Cimino's film. Of course the history of western representations and uses of a mythicised 'Orient' is complex in itself and too large a topic to be discussed in any great detail here. Briefly, *Rambo III* invokes the 'Orient' as a space for white men and women to discover themselves (self-discovery is a common theme of the Vietnam narrative), along with a set of counter-cultural resonances which have often been used precisely to define the otherness of the Vietnam veteran within Hollywood cinema.[11] Tom Laughlin's *Billy Jack* (1971) is an early example of the latter, a film which casts the veteran as not only a hippy with an affinity for the American Indian, but as skilled in martial arts. The all-American nationalism so much discussed in relation to the *Rambo* films – Rambo as a 'pin-up for the president' – is also strangely oppositional and absent, articulating a love of nation which is based on a complex relationship to America.[12]

In thinking about these questions, Jeffords's analysis of gender and Vietnam representation can be positioned alongside the more general concerns of the action picture. Rather than the specificity of the war movie, the action picture offers the audience a complex identification with a hero who asserts his right to belong to a nation which rejects him. Hence the importance of a non-WASP, white ethnicity in, for example, American gangster narratives. In the *Rocky* films, this emphasis on ethnicity is maintained against the construction of black Americans and an Aryan-Russian opponent. In the opening moments of *Rambo*, the muscular figure of Stallone/Rambo is imaged as imprisoned, shot from above framed by barbed wire, and seen in close-up through a wire fence. Rejection is a crucial term for a narrative which is based around the figure of those 'left behind', the POWs. The sequence in which Rambo is abandoned by the American military, with the rescue helicopter just out of reach, echoes a visual repertoire established through various Vietnam films. Such images express the powerlessness of the 'ordinary soldier' of which these narratives speak, whilst at the same time they offer, in the figure of the muscular hero, an extraordinary soldier. At a more general level, the play with a borderline of acceptance and rejection defines cinematic figures such as the heroic sergeant, the private eye and the rogue-cop, figures who are neither officers nor criminals. It is worth pointing out, in terms of the processes of identification at work here, that dispossessed groups do not necessarily reject the nation of which they are a part. In the poem 'I, Too, am America', Langston Hughes articulates the centrality of blackness to an American identity. More than this the poem asserts that once the culture realises its omission 'They'll see how beautiful I am/And be ashamed'. Hughes asserts the right not only to be part of America, but to be part of a necessarily changed understanding of that nation.[13]

Cinematic articulations of masculinity and nationhood are problematised within American cultural traditions, particularly in terms of imaging Vietnam, around the politics of 'race'. Nationalism has provided a crucial rhetorical language in a variety of anti-colonial struggles. Yet colonialist discourse also operates within nations. Vietnam representation deploys racial discourses in complex ways, from the Vietnamese, who are (un)represented as invisible Orientals, to the black Americans who are symbolically central, if marginal to the narrative, in films such as *Platoon* and *Hamburger Hill*, and the white heroes who 'find themselves' within the colonial space of Vietnam. Made during the conflict itself, the propagandistic film *The Green Berets* (1968) had been careful to feature black and Asian performers (such as Raymond St Jacques and George Takei) acting alongside John Wayne as spokesmen for American intervention. Whilst Vietnam was the first major conflict to follow the de-segregation of the American military, the disproportionate numbers of casualties amongst black soldiers has become a repeated point of protest (countered by official denials) in an all too literal demonstration of the different values placed on black and white American bodies. The war also came to a peak during a time of political upheaval in the States, with the civil-rights movement and protests against the war itself. This confluence, in the mid-1960s, was accompanied by the very public protest against the war by figures such as Muhammad Ali, who lost his title as heavyweight boxing champion for his refusal to take up arms in Vietnam. Mary Ellison, in her discussion of black music and the war, points to the clear anti-war views of prominent black American activists, as well as the voicing of such views in black popular culture. She also cites the anti-war sentiments expressed by black servicemen in Vietnam, sentiments which were expressed partly in terms of an affinity for the Vietnamese struggle against the US in terms of a shared colonial experience.[14] The grim irony of the historical moment saw the juxtaposition of the black struggle for equality in the States, with the rhetoric of democracy that supposedly legitimated the war in Vietnam.

Just as 'Vietnam' films are not concerned to address the Vietnamese, or the political issues surrounding the conflict, the contradictory experiences of black American servicemen rarely form an explicit part of mainstream American fictions. In *Platoon* a stylised black American culture (Motown and marijuana) is juxtaposed with an equally stylised view of white redneck culture (country music and beer). The film sets up two extreme spaces which are associated with these groups, and the audience follows the white hero's dilemma: which imaginary identification will he make? Chris (Charlie Sheen) is a volunteer in a drafted army, a literate middle-class figure positioned amongst the ranks of the dispossessed. As in *Hamburger Hill*, the stereotypical invisibility of the Vietnamese enemy allows a focus on the tensions within the male group. As Jeffords's analysis of the primacy of gender implies, racial difference is constructed within the world of *Platoon* as little more than a way to talk about the two different versions of masculine identity that Chris is offered. Within the different terms of *Rambo*'s fantasy narrative, we are offered the working through of a populist drama of the dispossessed. This is exaggerated, with something of a parodic edge, in *Rambo III*. Griggs, the voice of American officialdom, reels off the familiar litany that, should Rambo be caught, 'we'll deny any participation or even knowledge of your existence'. 'I'm used to it' replies Rambo, a phrase which refers to the other films in the sequence, indeed the action genre, and the ever more impossible odds the character faces, but also to Stallone's star image as an 'underdog' within a white immigrant community.

TRUTH AND VIETNAM DISCOURSE: 'TELLING IT LIKE IT IS'

Narrative confusions, as some reviewers noted at the time of its release in 1984, mark Chuck Norris's supposedly more 'positive' version of American involvement in Vietnam. Whilst some of this may be put down to the exigencies of low- to medium-budget feature film production, it is nonetheless worth taking note. The narrative premise of both *Missing In Action* and *Missing In Action 2: The Beginning* (both 1984) is that Norris, as Colonel James Braddock, is in a POW camp in Laos. Yet we find him at the beginning of *Braddock: Missing In Action 3* (1988) at the fall of Saigon, amidst the crowds of Vietnamese who are desperate to get into the American embassy. Braddock has also acquired a Vietnamese wife, Lin, who is inadvertently left behind, presumed dead, despite all the fuss made about his wife back home in the States during *MIA 2*. Twelve years later, on discovering that Lin is not dead and that they have a son, Braddock returns to Vietnam, wreaking havoc as he does so. America's role in Vietnam is rather messily expressed here through the figure of family and parental responsibility. Perhaps it could be argued that a trajectory of narrative coherence is not at issue in a cinema which is so much concerned with spectacle, particularly in this, the mid-range of the market. Yet, if the action cinema is informed by a sense of placelessness, Vietnam remains a named, if completely imaginary, space, operating as a reference point for shared experiences (for the male group), a training ground (for the individual hero) or simply acting as a generalised explanation for the hero's instability.

The title of Alf Louvre and Jeffrey Walsh's collection of writings, *Tell Me Lies About Vietnam*, indicates the defining importance of a notion of truth in the discourses around America's Vietnam with which the book is concerned. In their introduction, Louvre and Walsh emphasise the importance of uncovering and retaining the details of historical evidence in opposition to the fictions of the 'blockbusting film'. They cite the example of *Rambo*, a film which they claim is seen in unspecified 'non-English-speaking countries' with 'sub-titles that equate the Vietnamese with the Japanese, the Russians with the Nazis'. Such a transformation they take as an indication of how 'ideological war is waged', noting that even the film's 'slender historical referents' have 'been wholly replaced by myth, cliché and stereotype'. For Louvre and Walsh such an 'arrogant contempt for history is profoundly dangerous' (Louvre and Walsh 1988: 22–3). The equation between the Vietnamese and the Japanese spoken of here certainly wouldn't be at odds with the anti-Japanese flavour of many Hong Kong action films, and here the importance of international markets for the popular cinema returns. In a similar vein, Leslie Fiedler writes of his surprise on learning that 'during the recent revolution there, a reporter had found a band of Maoist guerillas in the Philippines watching *Rambo* on their Betamax' (Fiedler 1990: 398). Such a phenomenon, the fluidity of historical referents within an internationalised culture, makes sense in terms of the fictions that popular films play and replay, the pleasures that the films offer. Though these pleasures do not necessarily accord with the project of compiling a detailed ethnography of the Vietnam war, they nonetheless bear a relationship to a process of cultural accounting, in which issues of power, oppression and the struggle against it, are worked out in stylised form. It is in this sense that Leslie Fiedler sees *Rambo* as mythic, having both a specific resonance in that it provides a narrative of American involvement in Vietnam, and operating in terms of a generalised right-wing populism, directed against all forms of governmental authority.

In the many critical and personal accounts that form part of Vietnam representation, a notion of truth – 'telling it like it is' – has been vital. This partly reflects a need for those involved to tell their stories. Within such discourses it is hard to see *Rambo* as anything other than insulting. Its pleasures are those of fantasy, not those of realism. Yet it is clear from *Platoon* that fantasy is also at work in those films initially hailed as 'realistic' in their portrayal of the conflict.[15] It is not only the hotly-debated issue of realism that is put into question here, but also the issue of whose fantasy, whose story is at stake in the evaluation. The problem with *Rambo*, in this sense, is the absence of a context: the films that haven't been made (or haven't been distributed) and the stories that haven't been told. To compound this, many of those who made up the film's audience would have been more familiar with 'Vietnam' as a set of generic conventions than as an historical reference point, or perhaps as an historical reference point perceived through generic conventions.[16] The stories of personal experience that are often told about Vietnam also emerge as generic. Bruce Jackson has written of his conversations with Vietnam veterans in which, whilst a large proportion could assert that they knew of friends who had gone through the archetypal 'Nam' experiences, few could themselves testify to such experience. Jackson reports how he asked a class of veterans:

> 'How many people in this room had a buddy who was spat upon by an old lady or a hippie or something like that?'
> Maybe a third of the hands went up.
> 'How many people in this room were spat upon themselves?'
> No hands went up.
>
> (Jackson 1990: 402)

The importance of this for Jackson lies with the way in which the repetition of powerful narratives provides a way to talk about some shared experience, or indeed to make the experience one that is shared, whether it is 'true' or not.[17] Incidentally, both of the 'experiences' that are cited by the veterans in Jackson's study, are also referred to in Rambo's final monologue in *First Blood*.

Much is, necessarily, at stake for cultural critics, if not for all audiences, in Hollywood's representation of Vietnam. Yet the Hollywood cinema has never been particularly committed to, or concerned with, the 'accurate' rendition of history. In their reluctance to engage with underlying economic and political forces, films about Vietnam are little different from Hollywood films about, for example, World War II. Such factors are, by and large, not the concerns of a commercial, entertainment cinema. It is, for Walsh, no defence of Hollywood's Vietnam movies to say that other movies are just as 'bad'. But should we look to the popular cinema for an analysis it cannot provide, answers it cannot give? Through all those critical readings that see movies that are ostensibly concerned with something else as being really 'about Vietnam', the possibility that movies ostensibly 'about Vietnam' may be more concerned with, and more interesting to think about in terms of, other issues has received little consideration. Critical work in recent years has done much to challenge and redefine the supposed objectivity of 'history' as a body of knowledge, asking whose story the discipline takes as its subject. In this context, it is worth noting that when the action cinema does take war as its setting, it is often addressed through the experience of the soldier, in particular through the figure of the 'grunt' who is at the bottom of the military hierarchy. In the much cited line from *Rambo* – 'Do we get to win this time?' – it is far from clear who the 'we' refers to. This confusion may indicate something of the complexities of the populist address at work in this film. It might also allow us to think about the complexities of the populist address *per se*.

More generally, the cinematic representation of the hero is bedevilled by the need to provide a space in which he can perform, in which he can be, in Laura Mulvey's words, a dominating 'figure in a landscape' (Mulvey 1989: 20). A definition of the heroic figure emerges as one who is typically outside, if not actually opposed to, the mainstream. He is a loner who accrues an additional romanticism by being out of the ordinary. The (temporary) rejection of violence is, perhaps ironically, a common theme of the contemporary action narrative. This draws on a lengthy tradition of representation in which we see heroes who have rejected their role as soldiers or as officers of the law. The hero has often either retired from the military and gone to seek life elsewhere, or operates at the periphery of such organisations. Incidentally, I would suggest that this allows us to distinguish a group of films, such as *Top Gun* and *Platoon* (both 1986), *Full Metal Jacket* (1987) or *Wings of the Apache* (1990) which offer the military setting as a space for male rites of passage. Often it is only a personal motivation that can bring the hero out of his 'retirement'. Witness, for example, Chuck Norris's *Invasion USA* (1985) in which Matt Hunter only enters the battle to save America for the sake of pursuing an old rivalry, and after the death of a close friend.

The opening sequences of *Commando*, a tongue-in-cheek action movie in which Arnold Schwarzenegger stars as John Matrix, provide an indicative example of the ambiguous state of 'retirement' in which the action hero is often to be found. The film's pre-credit sequence shows a series of unexplained and violent assassinations carried out by an unidentified group of men. Matrix is then revealed through fragmented close-ups of the Schwarzenegger muscles, pumped-up as he carries a log over his shoulder. The tough guy is then cast as loving father in a credit montage of scenes featuring Matrix with his daughter Jenny – fishing, feeding deer, eating ice-creams and teaching her martial arts. But Jenny is kidnapped in a raid on their mountain retreat and Matrix is forced to move back into action. While Matrix complains that he and Jenny 'were going to build a normal life here', at the first sight (actually smell, since Matrix catches the odour of intruders) of action, he runs to the garden shed which is well stocked with rifles. The military paraphernalia of the soldier has not been abandoned, but exists in a sort of limbo which functions to question the possibility of the very normalcy which is sought.

A certain populist appeal has been generically associated with the figure of the hero who is outside or apart from state institutions, and who is therefore in a sense untainted by their inevitable corruption. The figure of the individual hero, pitted against the state, draws not only on pioneer rhetoric, but also on those paranoid narratives of the 1970s in which the hero finds himself enmeshed in a conspiracy that ultimately leads either to his own boss, or to the very top of the political, military or law enforcement hierarchy. Of course, such ambiguities about the position of the hero in relation to authority, his loyalties and allegiances, are now clichés expressed, for example, through the hero's ritual assertion that there 'won't be a next time'. Such clichés obviously relate in part to the refinement of the sequel as a cinematic form, so that if the hero is successful in his box-office mission then there may well be a 'next time'. This structure of repetition is mocked in *Die Hard 2* with McClane's rhetorical question, addressed to himself: 'How can the same shit happen to the same guy twice?'

'DO WE GET TO WIN THIS TIME?'

Within the muscular action cinema, images of the bodybuilder hero as self-created and as produced for display, are played off against discourses of natural strength, in which he is presented as a gifted individual. Thus Schwarzenegger's character smells the human enemy approaching in *Commando*, whilst in *Predator* he covers himself in mud to elude the alien killer. Such images mark his character out as something of a 'natural warrior', particularly when the hero's self-sufficiency is contrasted to representations of America's high-tech weaponry. The sense of being at home within a natural setting also informs the portrayal of Rambo, who employs the techniques of guerilla warfare, his habitat signalled as the jungle of Vietnam or the American forests of *First Blood*, in which he tells Sheriff Teasle, 'In town you're the law, out here it's me'. Such an identification returns us to populist themes, particularly in Rambo's ambiguous alignment with nature and against a technology that is defined as bureaucratic. Despite reference to the oft-seen image of Rambo with rocket-launcher, the bow and arrow and the knife are key weapons within the Rambo narratives. Together with Rambo's Indian/German descent, these weapons invoke the figure of the 'noble savage'. An associated atavism comes to the fore in Rambo's spectacular destruction of computer hardware at the operational base in Thailand.

Yet Rambo's bow and arrow are also high-tech, combining the image of a simple technology with spectacular explosions. As J. Hoberman points out, there is a deliberate, and quite effective, confusion at work in these films between images of conquering nature and identifying with it. His talismanic long hair locates Rambo as 'wild', associated with nature rather than culture – in *First Blood* Teasle advises him to get a haircut in order to avoid any further police harassment. 'Rambo', says Hoberman, 'is a superb icon: a hippie he-man . . . a patriotic loner . . . a sort of Apache *Übermensch* or a Prussian noble savage' (Kruger and Mariani 1989: 187). Such a collision of qualities offers a complex, and confusing, articulation of masculine identity. Of course Hollywood cinema, indeed popular culture more generally, does not operate within a simple binary system and is routinely able to bring together such sets of seemingly contradictory qualities. The physical power of figures like Rambo, a power that is marked primarily through the body, is showcased within a narrative which also offers the ritualised suffering of the male hero as spectacle.

In her analysis of the *Rocky* cycle, Valerie Walkerdine writes that boxing 'turns oppression into a struggle to master it, seen as spectacle' (Burgin *et al.* 1986: 172). She signals class as a key and somewhat neglected term through which images of fighting and the male body need to be conceptualised. The *Rocky* films point to the way in which the body of the working-class man is both subjected (to the rigours of labour) and resistant. This is made explicit in *Rocky II* with the play of different images of masculine identity. Rocky is commissioned to advertise 'Beast' aftershave, but is fired because he is unable to read the 'dummy cards' on the set. His illiteracy prevents him from getting an office job, and he is later laid off from the meat factory where he has taken a temporary manual job. These images of failure in the world of work are set against Rocky's plea to his wife, who wishes him to give up fighting, to allow him to 'be a man'. When Rocky works in the meat factory, he is isolated in the shot, clearly distinguished from the rest of the men. In such ways Rocky can be both ordinary, a representative of the group, and extraordinary, an individual able to fight for, and win, the world title. The character of Rocky is clearly constructed in terms of the Italian immigrant community to which he belongs. In turn, this is opposed to the champ, Apollo Creed, a 'flash' black American who has no clear location within an ethnic, or any other, community. Creed is only seen with his wife in a huge mansion, or with his trainer at work. Creed's articulate speech, his ability to use the media, mark him out as a stylised enemy in both class and racial terms. Creed's story of struggle cannot, it seems, be told within the *Rocky* films which offer him up as a rich and intelligent member of the boxing establishment. That this drama is played out in the boxing ring – one arena in which black men have found a space to perform within American culture – makes Rocky's triumph very much at the expense of a racially constituted other.

The contradictions of masculine identity generated in the narrative around class – the working-class man, who sells his labour, does not have the resources necessary to 'be a man' – are worked out through racial difference.

A key figure from the conspiratorial narratives of the 1970s, which feed into the anti-government feeling of the Rambo films, is that of the investigative journalist. Rambo is initially cast in this role, sent into Vietnam to take pictures of a 'deserted' prison camp, though it is ultimately revealed that the whole escapade is a cover-up and the hero is abandoned by the same government forces who dispatched him. In contrast to the figure of the heroic journalist invoked in *All The President's Men* (1976), the physical actor is constructed as inarticulate, unable to speak. In response to the suggestion that *Rambo* articulated the nation's mood, one critic retorts 'Articulate? Hardly. Stallone . . . substitutes oafish muttering for dialogue'. Rambo is dubbed 'Zombo', a figure who 'grunts' the final speech which is 'the nearest he comes to a full sentence'. Linked to the zombie, to the living dead, Rambo here becomes both a comic and a fearful figure. It was precisely this kind of rhetorical transformation which allowed the use of 'Rambo', within the British press, in an hysterical discourse about violence in the cinema. Within the terms of the film, Rambo is precisely constructed as a 'grunt', as one of the voiceless figures contemplated by Chris Taylor in *Platoon*. At the same time as Rambo is a 'grunt', he is also given a fantastic strength and a colonial stage on which to play out a fantasy of retribution.

In thinking about the political impact of these films, I want to return to the phrase 'dumb movies for dumb people', the critical characterisation of muscular cinema as retrograde entertainment for those who know no better. The popular audience emerges here as a powerful figure of the dispossessed, signalling those groups who have been effectively silenced and then designated too 'dumb' to speak. Recalling Rutherford's opposition between 'new man' and 'action man', we can see here how cultural (class) power is associated with an articulate, verbal masculinity, an identity that is played off against a masculinity defined through physicality. In constructing this opposition *as if* western culture allowed men the freedom to choose, power is simply left out of the equation. In the proliferation of critical writings that seek to explain the 'obvious' ideological project or the 'facile' pleasures of *Rambo*, the verbal dexterity of critics is brought to the fore – the film seems to bring out all manner of puns, alliteration, rhetorical flourishes and beautiful turns of phrase. Whilst critics repeatedly assert that there is nothing more to be said, more and more words are generated through a desire to *explain* the impossible (inexplicable) success of *Rambo*.

Rambo, a film in the most part distasteful to the reviewers of the liberal press, became an issue due to its popularity, signalling a concern with the response to the film rather than the film itself, a concern with the audience. For instance Derek Malcolm's *Guardian* review compared the 'simplistically reactionary' *Rambo* with the previous summer's *Red Dawn*, which was less disturbing since less successful. What was at issue for Malcolm, and others, in thinking about *Rambo* was 'a success so huge that you have to question why'. He suggests that when one does 'only a fool would not be worried that an action movie of this banality should be received with such evident satisfaction'. He writes of 'hundreds of thousands of young Americans baying in the aisles', telling us that we can learn a lesson from *Rambo*. Our 'knee-jerk liberal horror should be muted' since:

> It's much better to know what we face than not to admit it. *Rambo* is an excellent lesson in how the far right gains the support of the very people to whom it should be anathema. Perhaps, in a revolting way, the film's good for us.

Here Malcolm sets up and works through an opposition between us and them – the sophisticated liberal us and the passive victims baying in the aisles, them.

Of course the central populist discourse structuring *Rambo* draws precisely on an us/them dichotomy, however shifting and ambiguous it may be. Indeed the articulation of masculinity and national identity through the figure of the muscular anti-hero offers a more complex set of signifiers than left/liberal discourses can seem to allow. Critical responses to this film, and to the action cinema more generally, are deeply paradoxical. Rambo/Stallone is taken to signal a threatening and out-of-control masculinity, but is both disturbing and ridiculous since he looks like a woman (his 'breasts' and long hair). *Rambo* represents an all-American call to nationalism which confuses hell and home. Finally, *Rambo* is criticised for the erasure of history, for a chauvinist dehumanisation of the Vietnamese. Yet surely it is worth questioning why the critical response to this must be to draw on pathologising discourses which radically dehumanise the audience? Which is also to ask, what is at stake in the processes whereby the popular cinema becomes the object of a concerned analysis?

6

THE BODY IN CRISIS OR THE BODY TRIUMPHANT?

The success of the muscular male hero, both in the cinema and as a wider cultural icon, has been read as signifying a variety of phenomena. The title of this chapter offers a choice between two polarised understandings of the muscular hero, whose over-developed and over-determined body has been taken by some to indicate the triumphal assertion of a traditional masculinity, defined through strength, whilst for others he represents an hysterical image, a symptom of the male body (and masculine identity) in crisis. Within both critical perspectives, the figure of the muscular male hero could be considered as a site for the re-inscription of difference. The appropriation of the image of the bodybuilder into a camp repertoire which itself problematises gendered identity, indicates the extent to which this figure can be decoded in a range of ways, is positioned between and across different understandings. The analysis offered in Chapters 4 and 5 of particular star images, and of the deployment of the bodybuilder as hero, reveals a complexity of signification at work in the action film, a complexity that mitigates against the understanding of the muscular hero as a *simplistic* embodiment of a reactionary masculine identity. Whether critics view the muscular male body on the screen as triumphal or crisis-ridden, he is generally taken to represent a 'new' man, functioning as a symptomatic figure who can be read as a sign of the times. The central question for many critics has, consequently, become one of whether such images reassert, mourn or hysterically state a lost male power. An 'either/or' opposition has tended to frame critical discussion of images of masculinity. In thinking about the historical context from which these images of men emerge, as well as the extent to which they draw on and are part of discourses of class and race, it is more appropriate to frame an analysis in terms of 'both/and', a phrasing which allows for a discussion of the multiplicity and instability of meaning. Rather than understanding the muscular male hero as either a reassertion, or a parodic enactment of masculinist values, we can examine the ways in which he represents both, as well as being produced by the ongoing and unsteady relationship between these, and other, images of masculinity.

Evidenced in the proliferation of writings, films and academic conferences in the field, 'masculinity' has increasingly become a critically visible category. Equally, the work of a variety of writers on issues of sexuality has ensured that the diverse gendered identities proposed by the term 'masculinity' cannot be simply equated with a social group, men.[1] Such critical work, along with the proliferation of images of men within popular culture itself, has led to the current critical stress on the plurality of masculine identities, on masculinit*ies*. The emergence of both these critical questions, and the images they address, can be partly situated within the historical frame provided by the post-war resurgence of the women's movement. The personal definition of the political that was characteristic of the women's movement at this time found resonance in a range of arenas. Subsequently, feminist and other polemics have been dispersed into a language of choice and lifestyle in a variety of popular discourses. In tandem with this process, men have become, through the 1980s, more overtly targeted as consumers of lifestyle. The invitation extended to western men to define themselves through consumption brings with it a consequent stress on the fabrication of identity, a de-naturalising of the supposed naturalness of male identity. Just as feminist film studies have engaged in a substantial re-evaluation of images of women, which have ranged over the whole history of the cinema, the emergence of masculinity and the male image as a subject of inquiry has led to a criticism which not only looks at the images and identities to be found in contemporary popular culture, but re-examines the past, finding there images whose meanings are less simple than they might once have appeared.

Current debates over images and gendered identities have made extensive use of the terms offered by psychoanalysis, as a theory of the (unstable and incomplete) acquisition of sexual identity, and the battery of ideas and images associated with 'postmodernism'.[2] Postmodernism offers a way of speaking about the operations of a culture in which almost anything can be commodified. It addresses the flexibility and the ambiguity of popular culture. More controversially, postmodernism has been used as a framework through which to address the supposed political *potential* of popular forms. In terms of art practices, postmodernism is associated with the play of surfaces, the appropriation and recycling of popular forms within the realm of 'art', the appearance of self-reflexive, parodic texts, and the self-conscious mobilisation of 'style' within narratives that stress plurality. Such emphases have a clear appeal to those diverse social groups who find their stories excluded from mainstream culture, even from mainstream politics, a point to which I return below. Terms like 'performance' and 'masquerade', which have been crucial to recent feminist writings on the cinema and gendered identity, are also foregrounded within a postmodern discourse about contemporary culture.[3] In terms of the muscular hero, it is possible to argue that these male figures offer a parodic performance of 'masculinity', which both enacts and calls into question the qualities they embody.

In these senses, masculinity has been insistently denaturalised, rendered multiple, within both criticism and popular images. The suggestion that meaning is elusive and multiple does not, however, fit easily with the evaluative project of a political cultural criticism, particularly one committed to a radical, modernist avant-garde. The suspicion that postmodernism, and its associated buzzwords, represents a depoliticised catch-all framework for cultural analysis, emerges precisely at this point, through the work of critics who have questioned the implicit valorisation of popular cultural forms.[4] Such hostility, which is also a part of various calls for a critical 'return to the real', reacts against those versions of the postmodern which seem to erase power, in which audiences are cast as 'free, gleefully raiding the image bank' (Medhurst 1990: 19).[5] It is crucial to acknowledge that the supposed 'freedom' to make meaning, which has been both embraced and rejected by cultural critics, cannot erase the fact of unequal access to the 'means of production', or indeed the consumption, of images. Yet I would also argue that postmodernism offers a useful, both descriptive and analytic, framework for thinking about cinematic articulations of masculinities. Indeed, for those whose critical voices have only recently been heard within the academy, the harking back to an earlier critical moment in which 'things were simpler', has something of a hollow ring to it.

FILM STUDIES, TELEVISION AND THE 'PERFORMANCE OF MASCULINITY'

What is the status of the performativity that has been attributed to masculinity in the contemporary cinema? How can we account, for example, for the undoubted marketability of the male body in the 1980s? One immediate context is that offered by the changing definitions, within a shifting economy, of the roles that men and women are called on to perform, particularly in that crucial arena of gender definition, the world of work. Richard Dyer notes a recent tendency for male stars, such as Clint Eastwood and Harrison Ford, 'either to give their films a send-up or tongue-in-cheek flavour . . . or else a hard, desolate, alienated quality'. Dyer speculates that in a world 'of microchips and a large scale growth (in the USA) of women in traditionally male occupations' the adoption of such tones suggest that the 'values of masculine physicality are harder to maintain straightfacedly and unproblematically' (Dyer 1987: 12).[6] Barbara Creed's suggestion that the pin-up muscleman star can be understood within the critical frameworks of postmodernism, also picks up on the tendency of images and texts in the 1980s to 'play with the notion of manhood'. Creed suggests that Stallone and Schwarzenegger could only be described as 'performing the masculine', a performance that she speaks of in terms of the failure of the paternal signifier, a theme to which I return at the end of this chapter (Creed 1987: 65). For Creed it is the sheer physical excess of the muscular stars that indicates the performative status of the masculinity they enact. That the terms of her analysis has a wider purchase on contemporary texts can be exemplified with reference to Michael Mann's 1980s' television crime series *Miami Vice*, a show that has repeatedly functioned as a point of reference for critical discussions of both postmodernism and masculinity.

Andrew Ross locates the construction of the male body as sexual spectacle in *Miami Vice*, in terms of both the generic history from which the show evolved, and the cultural moment of the 1980s in which it became so popular. Ross identifies a 'maverick concern with sex' in *Miami Vice*, locating this within an American context in which the show is seen to make a 'contradictory response' to the operations of campaigning groups who lobbied against advertisers sponsoring programmes deemed 'indecent or obscene', effectively setting a moral agenda for the networks. Ross goes on to argue that 'in a post-censorship climate', in which 'naked male flesh is still permissible' whilst 'female is not' then 'the widespread incidence of that male flesh in *Miami Vice* has become both the medium for developing a discourse about sexuality within the show and also a primary means of selling the show as TV commodity' (Ross 1986: 150). The cultural specificity invoked in this analysis allows us to see the show within a specific production context, as well as demonstrating capital's remarkable ability to adapt. The taboos which surround the marketing of the male body as sexual object can, like any other, be broken in the relentless search for new commodities and new markets. The controversy that surrounded the show in Britain led to the BBC transmitting only selected, censored episodes. The stylishness of *Miami Vice*, in particular its bold use of colour and music video techniques, was characterised as inappropriate for a crime series. British crime series had been dominated by a realist aesthetic, a mould into which *Miami Vice* did not fit at all comfortably, leading to dismissive charges of 'designer violence' and 'MTV aesthetics'. The stylishness of the show, along with its stress on surfaces and performance in relation to men and masculinity, also situated it critically within debates about postmodernism.

The ambiguous meaning of 'America' within the world of *Miami Vice* echoes the populist themes of the action genre. Both share anti-government sentiments that are showcased within a violent narrative, that forces the hero to act. Within American culture, Miami has often been imaged as the site of potential invasion, a space for drugs and immigrants, both defined as utterly 'foreign', to infiltrate American territory. Its proximity to Cuba makes Miami the chosen site from which to launch a

Russian/Cuban invasion of America in the Chuck Norris vehicle *Invasion USA* (1985). While *Miami Vice* has been framed by a notion of 'fortress America', with the cops protecting the nation against all the others, America is always revealed to be full of crooks. By the end of the series, after a detour to Latin America, Crockett and Tubbs finally realise the extent of American involvement in the world of vice. Confronted with a corruption that goes all the way to the top, they can do nothing but leave, since their performance of masculinity and of heroism is over. The police hero giving up his or her badge, represents a familiar generic moment. Indeed the final episode of *Miami Vice* invokes countless other narratives of conspiracy and corruption with the line 'this mission never existed'. This is in a sense the epigraph of the whole series. For Crockett and Tubbs the war against drugs is able to 'explain' social unrest at home as well as 'justify' imperialism abroad and yet if, as happens in the final episode, they lose this impossible point of reference, their very identity dissolves.[7]

The over-determined figure of drugs in *Miami Vice* functions as a 'bad' system of exchange, a metaphor for the evils of capitalism which still allows for the possibility that capitalism can function simultaneously as a 'good' system, exemplified in the other forms of consumption that are celebrated in the series. And yet this escape clause cannot ultimately be made good so that, in the end, Crockett and Tubbs can only walk away. In a similar vein, all Rambo can do is to destroy (temporarily) the technology of the military bureaucracy before also walking away – into the mythicised sunset to live 'day by day'. In none of these narratives can the hero finally function effectively within America. In the narrative logic of *Miami Vice* identity is, at best, tenuous since the heroes' success depends absolutely on being mis-recognised as their own object. That is, as undercover cops, Crockett and Tubbs must masquerade as the very drug-dealers they hunt. In one famous series of episodes Crockett, suffering from amnesia, actually adopts his drug-dealer persona 'for real'. As Andrew Ross has pointed out, 'doubleness' is absolutely central to the show, even to its title – which refers to both the object of investigation (vice, particularly drugs, in Miami) and the cry with which the police identify themselves. For Ross the 'central representational problem is the difficulty of exhibiting difference at all' (Ross 1986: 152). The problem of difference identified here is echoed by the cop hero of another Michael Mann narrative, *Made in LA*, who mournfully tells his girlfriend that 'tonight I made no difference'. The city-scape of Mann's narratives are populated by figures who struggle, like this cop, to 'make a difference' but who are ultimately unable to do so. The hero of *Thief/Violent Streets* (1981) can only survive by blowing everything up, whilst the hero of *Manhunter* (1986), being unable to preserve a line between himself and the psychotic serial killer he hunts, calls his own sanity into question.

Scott Benjamin King's analysis of *Miami Vice* echoes Richard Dyer's comments on the world of work. King offers a critique of those who understood the stylised visual beauty of the show and of its male protagonists, via postmodernism, as a narrative emptiness, seeing such perspectives as, at worst, a rather alarmingly literal interpretation of the 'end of narrative'. Instead of seeing the show as pure spectacle, as a refusal of narrative, King points out that *Vice* offers the repeated re-enactment of narratives of failure, the significance of which he locates within the context of contemporary articulations of masculinity. A reorientation of the relationship between men, masculinity and consumption in the west, necessarily effects those definitions of male identity achieved through production. King surmises that 'if postmodernism is a crisis of the excess of consumption, and, further, a crisis related to shifting definitions of masculinity, it is also a crisis in the concept of work' (King 1990: 286). In particular King signals the importance, in the construction of Sonny Crockett's character, of failure within the realm of work. Crockett's work consists of getting the bad guys, work that he is unable to perform effectively, work that is carried out in a context over which he has no control. A lack of control, accompanied by a sense of placelessness, is a defining feature of the action hero in films such as *Die Hard*, in which John McClane finds himself in an impossible situation controlled by an incompetent bureaucracy. It is perhaps the failure of work, the lack of effectivity of his efforts that allows for an understanding of the cynical outlook of the populist hero who emerged in the 1960s and 1970s, and who remains central to the contemporary action picture.

For film studies, an investigation of the male body on the screen has been framed by feminist analyses of representations of the female body, developed over the last twenty years. Writing of Robert De Niro, in the role of boxer Jake La Motta, in *Raging Bull*, Pam Cook neatly sums up the concerns of this critical trajectory in a question: 'If, as feminist film theory has argued, classic Hollywood is dedicated to the playing out of male Oedipal anxieties across the woman's body, object of the "male" gaze, what does it mean to place the male body at the centre?' (Cook 1982: 42). It is this question and the critical framework it proposes, that has dominated inquiries into representations of the male body and of masculinity in the cinema. Attempts to think through an answer to this question have been made problematic by a binary opposition of active/passive, an opposition which has structured feminist commentaries on the representation and articulation of gender in the cinema. This opposition was invoked most famously by Laura Mulvey, in her assertion that both pleasure in looking and narrative structure have been organised around a split 'between active/male and passive/female' (Mulvey 1989: 19). Since, within the mainstream cinema, 'the male figure cannot bear the burden of sexual objectification' (ibid.: 20), man is a figure who looks while woman is to be looked at. Mulvey's important polemic thus confronted the mainstream cinema at two levels, though the equation between 'active/male' and 'passive/female' are central to both. Grafted onto a psychoanalytically informed account of the structures of looking involved in the cinema, is a commentary on the typical narrative structure of the Hollywood film and the roles that men and women have tended to play within these cinematic narratives. Thinking about the contemporary action cinema involves a redefinition of Mulvey's model at these two levels, in order to take account of both changes in the formal operations of Hollywood cinema, and developments in the theorisation of sexuality and spectatorship.

In his 'Masculinity as Spectacle', Steve Neale takes Mulvey's account as his point of departure, exploring issues of identification, spectacle and the representation of the male body as erotic object within the Hollywood cinema. Neale argues, in relation to action-based genres, such as the western and the epic, that an eroticism around the male body is displaced into ritualised scenes of conflict, since it cannot be explicitly acknowledged. Neale cites instances, from the musical and the melodrama, in which the male body *is* constructed as an erotic object, specifically referring to the representation of Rock Hudson in Sirk's melodramas. While there are moments, Neale argues, in which 'Hudson is presented quite explicitly as the object of an erotic look' the look is 'usually marked as female', and Hudson's 'body is *feminised*', a process that Neale takes as a demonstration 'of the strength of the conventions which dictate that only women can function as the objects of an explicitly erotic gaze' (Neale 1983: 14–15). The feminine here is assumed to equate with women in a rather unproblematic fashion, and whilst Neale's analysis is a useful one, there is an evident danger of falling into a circular logic. That is, Hudson is described as 'feminised' *because* he is eroticised in these films. That such equations are premised on a stable gender binary, which is underpinned by a heterosexual understanding of desire and difference, is indicated by Judith Butler, when she asks what would happen 'to the subject and the stability of gender categories when the epistemic regime of presumptive heterosexuality is unmasked as that which produces and reifies these ostensible categories of ontology?' (Butler 1990: x). As Butler explores in her book, whilst shifting these regimes of knowledge and classification is problematic, going along with their assumptions of coherence may be fatal. In the case of Neale's example, we find the female gaze directed at a 'feminised' Rock Hudson. Hudson's 'feminised' image in these films is then equated by Neale with *women*, through reference to the cinematic conventions which allow 'only women' to be positioned as the explicit objects of an erotic gaze.

If it is dangerous to rely on the assumed stability of a gender binary, perhaps a question needs to be asked about what it means to place the 'male gaze' at the centre of an analysis of mainstream cinema. What once may have provided an enabling critical concept, now seems almost completely disempowering in its effects, operating as a term which fixes an analysis within the restrictions of the very gendered system it seeks to question. Though masculinities are bisected and experienced through a range of differences, feminist film criticism often seems to map onto the cinema a peculiarly heightened narrative of male power and female powerlessness. It is in this sense that the eroticised male body comes to be critically spoken of as 'feminised'. While the action hero is repeatedly subject to suffering within the narrative of which he is the centre, it is his triumph over this suffering that has been critically emphasised. In the case of *Rambo*, the film is, as discussed in Chapter 5, repeatedly cited as an unproblematic enactment of male power, despite the ambiguities operating both within the film itself and in the discourses surrounding it. It may well be the case that feminist discourses have, inadvertently, informed this process, through the ways in which women are constructed as victims and men as all-powerful, as, for example, in discussions around pornography.[8] At a more specific level, an address to the transformation of film genres over time is an important area of inquiry that can be effaced by an attention to structures taken as 'universal' or 'transhistorical'. To take an example from a different context here, Kobena Mercer draws attention to the significance of authorship, and of historical and cultural contexts for thinking about the political meanings and the pleasures of Robert Mapplethorpe's black male nudes. In the context of an attack against 'obscene' gay art in the States, Mercer rethinks an earlier essay on the pictures, along with his position as spectator. This process involves thinking, and rethinking, spectator/text relations as relations of power that are nonetheless historically contingent.[9]

Whilst psychoanalysis has itself been criticised for aspiring to a universal and transhistorical status, it also provides a theory which, at least potentially, allows us to speak outside of pathologising definitions of the normal and the deviant. Simon Watney, for example, compares a psychoanalysis which 'proceeds from a radical distrust of any attempt to privilege one form of object choice over another', to the operations of gender theory, which 'tends inexorably to foreground an exclusively heterosexual model of sexual relations which is then found, as excess or as absence, in other sexualities'. His critique of gender theory centres on the problematic terms 'active/male' and 'passive/female'. Watney indicates that the 'slippage from "male" to "active" not only has profound consequences in relation to the parallel slippage "female" to "passive" but also in relation to the evaluation of all non-heterosexual desires and practices'. For Watney, the logic of gender theory conveniently functions in order to achieve the 'immediate reinforcement of the rhetorical figures of man and woman, figures who recur throughout feminist cultural theory and linguistics locked forever in post-Edenic opposition' (Watney 1986: 16–17). Whilst a certain ambivalence can be identified around the active/passive couplet in representations of the male body, critics have often tended to see this as a tension that is raised and instantly resolved within the confines of the image. As Slavoj Zizek remarks in relation to anti-Semitism, an 'ideology really succeeds when even the facts which at first sight contradict it start to function as arguments in its favour' (Zizek 1989: 49). Thus instances of the eroticised male body in the cinema can operate to confirm that only women are ever eroticised.

In her 'Afterthoughts', Laura Mulvey discusses the Hollywood western-melodrama *Duel in the Sun* (1946) as a dramatisation of the restrictive choice available to the female viewer. Like the heroine Pearl, who must choose between two men, the female viewer must choose either masculinisation or masochism. For women watching the action picture, identification with the figure of the hero involves a problematic 'masculinisation'. Mulvey argues that 'Hollywood genre films structured around masculine pleasure' offer 'an identification with the *active* point of view' and thus 'allow a woman spectator to rediscover that lost aspect of her sexual identity, the never fully-repressed bed-rock of feminine neurosis' (Mulvey 1989: 31). For the female protagonist to make such an active identification has generally meant narrative death, as in *Thelma and Louise*, though that same film is interesting in its presentation of death *as an active choice* which is made by the film's two central protagonists. Though Mulvey suggests that 'the female spectator's fantasy of masculinisation' is 'at cross-purposes with itself, restless in its transvestite clothes', I would argue for a positioning of this transgressive fantasy within the more general pleasures of the cinema (ibid.: 37). That is, to return to the point at which this chapter began, the cinema offers one of the few social spaces in which we can make seemingly perverse identifications, structured by a utopian both/and rather than a repressive gendered binary.

The processes of shifting identifications within the action cinema involve the play of both 'passive' and 'active' identifications. The action scenario is not simply a narrative of empowerment, in which we identify with an heroic figure who triumphs over all obstacles, but is also a dramatisation of the social limits of power. Such scenarios are complex in that they invite an acknowledgement, and a working through, of the position of the audience in relation to the hierarchies sketched in the drama. In a paper on men and masculinity Lynne Segal, author of *Slow Motion: Changing Masculinities*, has argued that, as part of a contemporary process of redefining established, 'tough' masculine identities, men should begin to explore the 'pleasures of passivity' – an exploration that conjures up the figure of the 'new man'.[10] Segal's point raises a question here as to the pleasures of the insistent images of powerlessness and suffering that are offered in the action cinema. The 'pleasures of passivity', however, are very differently available to different groups, experienced as they are in relation to the limits of power. For marginalised groups, constituted through 'race' and class, screen images of either sexual passivity or a fearful violence represent the stereotypical limits of cinematic discourse. In this context, it is striking that *Duel in the Sun*, the western-melodrama to which Mulvey refers, articulates its themes of sexual identity through images of racial difference. Pearl must choose between the cultured world of wealth and restraint represented by Jesse, and the wild, outlaw figure of Lewt. The tension within the narrative comes from Pearl's own rebelliousness, her resistance to and desire for the conventions of the social world. In the opening sequences of the film this tension is figured through Pearl's 'mixed' racial descent. Her white father is represented as a noble, long-suffering, loving man, whilst her Mexican mother, who is shot for her adultery, is portrayed as sexual and treacherous. The mother is seen only through an extended sequence in which she dances inside a bar-cum-gambling hall, whilst the father shares an extended, sentimental scene with Pearl before he dies. Though the two are differentiated, Pearl mimics her mother's dancing, situated on the street outside the gambling house. The different constructions of whiteness and blackness inform the understanding of desire that is offered in the film, partially legitimating Lewt's treatment of Pearl, through myths of black sexuality. Pearl's own restlessness, her active desire for more than either of the choices offered, is mediated through the fact that she does not clearly 'fit' in either space. In such ways we can see that the Hollywood cinema mobilises the terms of activity/passivity not only in relation to gender, but through the construction of 'race' as a category, which is in turn often expressed through images of sexuality.

THE BODYBUILDER: MASCULINITY IN CRISIS?

Following on from this discussion of activity and passivity, we can recall the complex iconography which surrounds the practice of bodybuilding and the image of the bodybuilder. As Richard Dyer comments, in his discussion of male pin-ups, the requirements of active definitions of masculinity generate a need to compensate for the display of the eroticised male body. Thus 'when not actually caught in an act, the male image still promises activity by the way the body is posed' since 'images of men must disavow . . . passivity if they are to be kept in line with dominant ideas of masculinity-as-activity' (Dyer 1982: 66–7). Neale's comments on the fight as a site of displaced eroticism within Hollywood's action genres, can clearly be seen in this context. Thus, it is perhaps inevitable that it is the *action* cinema which provides a showcase for the display of the muscular male body.

As signifiers of masculinity, muscles present a paradox since they bring together the terms of naturalness and performance. Dyer has characterised this in terms of the way in which muscles can function as both a naturalisation of 'male power and domination' and as evidence precisely of the *labour* that has gone into the production of that effect (Dyer 1982: 71). The 'strain' that Dyer identifies in the male pin-up stems from this paradox, from the self-conscious performance of qualities assumed to be natural. The performance of a muscular masculinity within the cinema draws attention to both the restraint and the excess involved in 'being a man', the work put into the male body. As we saw in Chapter 5, bodybuilding has been associated with a narcissism considered culturally inappropriate for men, betraying a supposedly feminised concern with appearance. Thus, whilst Schwarzenegger's mega-stardom has done much to redefine the image of the bodybuilder, in terms of 'heroism and health', the other aspect of the persona identified by Alan Richman, that of an excessive narcissism, remains.[11] Negative reviews of *Rambo*, for example, cast the figure of the bodybuilder as womanly – the display of his upper body generates a comparison with Jane Russell. Though this has been most often discussed in terms of women's involvement in the sport, there is a sense in which bodybuilding does trouble the categories through which sex, as well as gender, is designated in our culture. The pumped-up male and female bodies found in action movies and on the bodybuilding circuit, are physically similar. Against, for example, a slim, languid image of adolescent androgyny, which is familiar from fashion pages, the mature (overdeveloped) body itself is very much emphasised in the world of the bodybuilder. The extent to which the bodybuilder troubles the categories of both sex and gender are visually evident, even celebrated, in the display of the body that defines the sport.

If there is an ambivalence located around the masculinity of the male bodybuilder whose body is offered for pleasure and display, this ambivalence is also present, though less forcefully, in other images of the male body. Representations of men and women, masculinity and femininity are shot through with such ambivalence. This is because neither masculinity nor femininity operate as clear sets of qualities that can be fixed in relation to the body. Such instability indicates the problems involved in reading contemporary images of masculine identity in a search for the signs of 'crisis'. To speculate about the recent emergence of a crisis in masculinity implies that masculinity represented, say until the 1960s, a stable category. Against this stands, to take just one example, critical work which has explored the complex constitution of masculinity and sexuality in relation to colonial discourse in the nineteenth century.[12] We might more usefully think about representations in terms of the particular ways in which the insecurities of masculine identities are made manifest at any given point. The figure of Rambo has been seen, for example, as signifying a masculinity in crisis, representing the limit case of the American tough guy. As we have seen, it is not only the box-office popularity of this figure, but the critical responses which sought to read him as symptomatic, that produced this reading, at a particular historical moment. Rowena Chapman understands the relationship between the 'new man' and the male action hero in these terms:

> The Macho is representative of traditional armour-plated masculinity from Bogart to Bronson, a whole panoply of atomised and paranoid manhood wreaking order through destruction; its apotheosis is the figure of Rambo, bare-chested and alone, wading through the Vietcong swamp, with not even a tube of insect repellent for comfort. Given this hard-nosed agenda, the new man was an attempt to resolve some of the obvious contradictions of the Classic Macho, to recognise and make peace with the feminine within itself, in response to feminist critiques.
>
> (Chapman and Rutherford 1988: 227)

I have already suggested that the 'new man' and the 'action man' are complexly inter-related. In terms of Chapman's comparison between the two, it is important to appreciate that the 1980s' redefinition of the action man/hero also responds to feminism in complex ways, and not just as part of a 'backlash'. Any 'tradition' of representation involves both continuity and change, so that the figures Chapman invokes – Bogart, Bronson and Rambo – all represent distinct articulations of heroic male identities that have changed over time.

The 'contradictions of the Classic Macho', to which Chapman refers, also emerge from the specific historical contexts in which these identities have developed. Macho culture represents one, complex, response to oppression – an attempt to assert a power which has precisely been denied. Isaac Julien and Kobena Mercer suggest, in the same volume of essays, that 'black men have incorporated a code of "macho" behaviour in order to recuperate some degree of power over the condition of powerlessness and dependency in relation to the white slave-master' (ibid.: 136). They also discuss how the complex interaction of stereotypical representations and actual behaviour, which is forged in cultural history, produces particular identities that are both 'true' and 'fictional' at the same time. Such an interaction is crucial to the location of a white, male, Italian ethnicity in the *Rocky* films.[13] Returning to Chapman's 'new man', it is no surprise that the figure to which she refers has tended to be associated with the white, middle class. This does not mean that black, or white working-class, male cultures have simply not responded to feminist issues. Many writers have pointed, for example, to the ambiguities of both gendered and racial identities at work in black popular music.[14] To take an example specific to the action cinema, we can recall here Stallone's attempts, discussed in Chapter 4, to qualify a macho persona through the increasingly explicit mobilisation of conventional signifiers of femininity. Alongside this process we have seen how several critics have described the figure of Rambo as demonstrating a *failed masculinity*, particularly in terms of his inability to speak, but also centred on his physical appearance – breasts, hair, eyes. These understandings emphasise the need to situate an analysis within the diversity of images of masculine identity in cultural circulation at any one point, and to acknowledge the histories that have produced them.

In *Heartbreak Ridge* (1986) Clint Eastwood, as Gunnery Sergeant Tom Highway, wrestles with his own military toughness in an attempt to achieve a reconciliation with his wife, a reconciliation which is finally brought about by the conflict in Grenada. As the publicity for the film had it, Highway is 'a hard-drinking loner but he's trying to reorganise his life and understand the woman he loves'. In order to 'understand' Highway stumbles his way through women's magazines, struggling with the language of relationships in which they deal. He painfully asks his ex-wife 'did we mutually nurture each other . . . did we communicate in a meaningful way in our relationship?' The existence of feminism and the problems of a tough-guy masculinity, which both formed an essential part of Eastwood's role as Wes Block in *Tightrope*, becomes a structuring joke in *Heartbreak Ridge*. The language of nurturing and relationships is placed in a context that makes it seem comical. This is the context of the training-camp movie, a sub-genre of the war film, in which young male rebels are made into marines, instructed in masculinity. In such a setting individuality and choice are necessarily relegated to the background. Stanley Kubrick's *Full Metal Jacket* (1987) is perhaps the most extreme version of this formula, subjecting the audience to an analogous experience through its relentless use of abusive language and images.[15] The joke in *Heartbreak Ridge* is not at the expense of women or feminism as such. Rather, and particularly when taken alongside the incessant verbal references to homosexuality in the film, it demonstrates a certain awareness of the cultural context within which the cinema operates, and in which the film will be received. *Heartbreak Ridge* struggles to maintain an unproblematic, heterosexual male group, with Eastwood's character barking out reminders to his charges that he didn't join the army to take long showers with his men. Featured across a range of recent action movies, such as *Lethal Weapon* and *Tango and Cash*, this repeated insistence threatens to draw attention to the very fact of homosexual desire that it seeks to deny.

Hollywood mythology thrives on paradox. It generates a multitude of stories of excess, one of which revolves around the star's rise from rags to riches, obscurity to fame. The world of bodybuilding similarly offers men the promise of moving from wimp to Mr Universe. We can recall here the mode of address used by the muscle magazines referred to in Chapter 4.

At an explicit level the reader is invited to emulate the figures depicted, to work out and develop their own body. Admiring descriptions of the male body are firmly positioned within the context of the workout, encouraging the reader to become an active consumer within bodybuilding culture. The bodybuilder as movie star combines then, two potent narratives of male success within western culture. Well aware of this formula, stories of the lucky breaks and hard work through which the star achieves his or her position, also form the basis for many of the narratives of the action cinema, which follow the struggles of the hero to succeed. Whilst the pleasures of a narcissistic identification with a powerful figure are clearly on offer in an audience's relationship to the action movie, the action narrative also, as we've seen in relation to *Miami Vice*, acknowledges repeated failures, pointing out the frustrations of the hero's position. Now, this play of success and failure is also found in the stories which circulate around the stars, forming part of the ongoing star melodrama which is played out in magazines and in the popular press. The typical repertoire of the star melodrama includes not only political involvement but marriages, divorces, children, assertions and denials of homosexuality, alcohol, pills and so on.

Bearing in mind the complexity of the circulation of meanings at stake in the star system, we can consider the specificity of the stories surrounding the muscular star. The publication of an unauthorised biography of Schwarzenegger, Wendy Leigh's *Arnold*, whilst it alleged past associations with right-wing politics, and extreme arrogance, quickly contributed to and became part of the star's image. Such political rumours, and the party politics of Schwarzenegger's campaigning for George Bush, which place him in the public realm, are situated alongside stories of a commodified private life, as with, for example, stories about his daughter's illness. The combination of such elements has the effect of producing the star's life as melodrama. The muscular star is, in effect, brought down to size, rendered almost ordinary. One biography of Stallone, released in Britain after the success of *Rambo*, features an anecdote which works through this process in terms of bodybuilding and the performance of a masculine identity. Stallone is described as an underdeveloped child, suffering from a variety of physical disabilities and teased for his *girlish* name. The narrative that is set up here is, in common with that frequently elaborated around Schwarzenegger, a 'before and after' story in which bodybuilding provides the key to the successful achievement of a masculine identity.

As part of its rhetoric of advertising self-improvement, *Muscle and Fitness* magazine cites an anecdote of Sylvester Stallone seeing Steve Reeves in *Hercules Unchained*. 'When he walked out of the theatre afterwards, Sly remembers an unremitting inner voice demanding, "Do you want to be a bum, or do you want to be like Steve Reeves?"'. In this instance, fantasised cinema images are recycled and offered, second-hand, as a possibility to the reader. The pin-up which displays the star's body alongside the interview, functions as 'proof' for the reader that the enactment of this fantasy identification is possible. Bodybuilding is offered as a form of protection which speaks to insecurity. Within this discourse, the body itself functions as a sort of armour against the world. The discourse of bodybuilding aspires to make the body signify a physical invulnerability, but the fact of vulnerability always remains a key part of the bodybuilding narrative. The best-selling workout videos and books produced by men such as Schwarzenegger and Dolph Lundgren offer a how-to guide for the body.[17] The title of Chuck Norris's autobiography *The Secret of Inner Strength* is self-explanatory in this context, with Norris offering his own code of ethics and advice on 'How to Make Your Life Better'.

The project of a book like *Stallone! A Hero's Story* is to explore the familiar star-biography terms emblazoned on the cover: 'A Fighter, A Lover, A Superstar'. As a part of the publicity machine the book seeks to give its readers a picture of the 'real' Stallone, who is cast as both powerful and vulnerable, the same doubleness operating in discourses of bodybuilding. The book frames this dichotomy in terms of Stallone's two most famous personas, so that he is described as wearing a 'cool, confident, almost Rambo-like face' in public whilst in private he is 'adoring and Rocky-like' (Rovin 1985: 204). This doubling further mirrors the two personas of the hero that Valerie Walkerdine finds in *Rocky II*. The interior sets for the film, Walkerdine comments, 'are made especially small so that he looks giant-size and yet remains a 'small man' in the outside world: a man who has to fight and to struggle therefore "to be" the big man at home' (Burgin *et al.* 1986: 173). This is a specifically domestic version of the play which structures the action movie, between the hero as a powerful figure, with whom we can identify, and the hero as a threatened figure, in need of the protection that only the developed body can offer.

Performance as a constituting quality of masculinity involves not just physical potency but a sense of acting the part, playing out a male persona on a public stage. Chuck Norris came to his career in movies from an involvement in karate as both a teacher and, of course, as world champion. He appears as Bruce Lee's opponent in the grand finale battle, set in Rome's Colosseum, in *Way of the Dragon* (US: *Return of the Dragon*). In his autobiography, Norris talks of the challenge that acting posed to him. This challenge is expressed in terms of performance, the different skills involved in performing karate and performing for the camera. 'In karate', he tells us, 'you are never to reveal anger or fear to your opponent. For years I taught myself to control my emotions and not to show them. When I began to act, I suddenly had to learn to bring all these guarded feelings to the surface' (Norris 1990: 144). Here control of the emotions forms an additional layer of protection for the fighter. The need for protection can, in turn, be linked to a fear of contamination and to more general fears about the body and its relation to technology which have been addressed by critics under the rubric of 'body horror'.[18] In the cinema of the 1980s Frankenstein's monster has been transformed into a cyborg, like Schwarzenegger as the Terminator or RoboCop. Even in Schwarzenegger's comedy picture, *Twins*, he is cast as the result of genetic engineering, manufactured to be both physically stronger and intellectually superior to the rest of humanity.

The fact of the performance of the tough-guy persona, that it is part of a ritualised conflict enacted around the social control of space, is often an explicit part of the contemporary action picture, as in the intricate verbal play that is worked through in *The Last Boy Scout*. Stallone's *Cobra* (1986), which was something of a flop at the box-office, sends up certain aspects of the tough-guy persona, with Marion Cobretti/Stallone joking that he really wanted to be called Alice. That 'Marion' was John Wayne's 'real' name is indicative here of a nervous play around the performance of a (cinematic) tough male identity. Cobretti is pitted against a villainous gang who seem at points to be engaged in some form of pagan worship and whose members speak hysterically of a new world order. The figure of Cobretti is, like Rambo, detached from the world of officialdom, relegated to work on the 'zombie squad'. In terms of the film's relative failure, we might speculate that he is not 'outside' enough, operating as he does as an agent of the state. Cobretti is an efficient killing machine, who is called in to 'off the bad guys' when all else has failed. There is little separation between him and his job, with his home visualised as an extension of the office, complete with surveillance equipment and files. Unlike Rambo though, he is a representative and not a victim of the state. And unlike Harry Callahan in the *Dirty Harry* films, or Travis Bickle in *Taxi Driver*, two heroes dedicated to the eradication of impurity, Cobretti is not pathologised. Rather he is *hidden*, beneath his gloves, his dark glasses and the protection offered by the built body.

In *Cobra* the body of the hero has no space in which to operate except as an over-determined version of the state. This is precisely the role played by Schwarzenegger in *The Terminator*, a film in which he is ultimately revealed to be literally a machine, operating in the service of computers from the future, who have taken over the world and are trying to wipe out the impurity that is humanity. Schwarzenegger achieved cult status with the film, yet we are put in the position of identifying with Sarah Connor, the heroine who takes on, and destroys, the Terminator. Whilst Schwarzenegger's Terminator masquerades in cultish shades and black leather, his opponent in the sequel, the more sophisticated T1000, assumes the form of a uniformed Los Angeles police officer. Institutions are always problematic in muscular movies, generally corrupt and not worth defending, so that a personal quest must motivate the hero. The hero may be a policeman or a soldier, but he more often than not acts unofficially, against the rules and often in a reactive way, responding to attacks rather than initiating them. The action hero recognises that he is, as Rambo puts it, 'expendable'. Representatives of the state utter a myriad variants on the line, 'this mission never existed'. Temporarily reinstated in the forces and sent back to Vietnam in *Rambo*, the hero cuts away most of the high-tech equipment that has been issued to him before he even lands. His final frustrated gesture at the end of the film is to destroy the government's computer hardware at the operational base in Thailand, screaming as cartridges are sprayed everywhere. The confusions of nature and technology, in for example the characterisation of Rambo as a sort of high-tech 'noble savage', perhaps indicate a need to see the muscular body as more than a machine, as self-created rather than state-created, as it seems to be in *Cobra*.

This tension is made explicit in the training montage from *Rocky IV*. In this film Rocky is to fight the Russian champion Ivan Drago (Dolph Lundgren). Rocky journeys to Russia to take on Drago after the death of his mentor Apollo Creed in the ring, back in the States. Rocky goes to train in a remote house surrounded by snow, ice, mountains and the KGB. The montage cuts between parallel images of Drago and Rocky training. Drago is seen surrounded by officials, monitored by numerous machines, images of mechanisation and control which culminate in a close-up of him being injected with steroids. Rocky meanwhile is supported only by the small team made up of Paulie, Adrian and his trainer. The two men's exercises dynamically mirror each other, but are contrasted as Rocky's training includes images of him chopping logs, helping peasants and so forth. His training culminates in the triumphal ascent of a mountain which a revolving camera celebrates from above. This sentimental opposition of a populist, self-created muscular strength and an artificial, mechanical tool of the state is a crucial one, restating the hero's control over his body.

The action cinema's play with figures of power and powerlessness incorporates the setpiece revelation of the body of the hero. Within this structure, suffering, and torture in particular, operates as both a set of narrative hurdles to be overcome (tests that the hero must survive) and as a set of aestheticised images to be lovingly dwelt on. Relatively few studies seem to comment in any depth on the figure of the male hero in this context, pursued and punished as he so often is. Pam Cook's analysis of *Raging Bull* sees the film as working through 'the loss of male power' which follows from the presentation of 'the powerful male body as an object of desire and identification', a loss which, since we mourn it, centres yet again on 'the founding image of male power, the phallus' (Cook 1982: 43). *Raging Bull* tells the tragic story of Jake La Motta succumbing to his own position of powerlessness, losing the 'animal violence' which had stood for 'a resistance to exploitation, a desire for freedom' (ibid.: 46). Such struggles and desires are central themes of the boxing narrative, and they also, as we have seen, form an important part of the mythological narratives surrounding the Hollywood star. Boxing brings together the display of the male body with images of male power and powerlessness. In the ring and outside it the male body is both subjected and resistant. A space of spectacle and struggle, the boxing ring 'becomes an enclosed arena of masculine performance, a site of contest between two skimpily-clad contenders who enact a ritualistic and idealised fantasy of masculine potency' (Krutnik 1991: 190). In the *Rocky* films, both the hero and his opponents are subject to an excessive punishment that is pictured in the carefully choreographed fights. These fights are lovingly shot in slow-motion, providing a counterpoint to the rapid montage of the training sequences. The boxer is also subject to the mobsters and promoters who live off the fighter. He is resistant then to both the physical blows – surviving, going the distance – and to the machinations of those who 'want a piece'.

Such physical struggles for self-control and for control over one's body provide a powerful set of associations in the boxing narrative. In the original *Rocky* there is an exchange between Rocky and Adrian which voices these themes. The couple's first date takes place on Thanksgiving, in a deserted ice-rink. Rocky talks of how he became a fighter and his father's advice that 'you weren't born with much of a brain, so you'd better start using your body'. To this Adrian replies that her mother had told her the reverse: 'you weren't born with much of a body so you'd better develop your brain'. These two options succinctly outline the possible escape routes for both the working-class man and woman. Valerie Walkerdine's analysis, discussed above, locates class as a key factor in thinking through the ways in which fighting, violence and the male body are conceptualised in the boxing narrative, suggesting an understanding of the films 'as a counterpoint to the experience of oppression and powerlessness' (Burgin *et al.* 1986: 172). Fanon's comments on the powerlessness of a colonised people, in *The Wretched of the Earth*, can serve to highlight here the relationship between a physical fantasy and relations of power:

> The first thing which the native learns is to stay in his place, and not go beyond certain limits. This is why the dreams of the native are always of muscular prowess; his dreams are of action and of aggression. I dream I am jumping, swimming, running, climbing; I dream that I burst out laughing, that I span a river in one stride, or that I am followed by a flood of motor-cars which never catch up with me. During the period of colonization, the native never stops achieving his freedom from nine in the evening until six in the morning.
>
> (Fanon 1985: 40)

These nocturnal fantasies emphasise the ways in which images of a physical power function as a counterpoint to an experience of the world defined by restrictive limits. Fanon describes a situation in which these limits are enacted over the body through colonial discourse – it is these limits that generate the fantasy of physical activity. This analysis can be extended in thinking about the operation of other kinds of limits, since 'the body is not a "being", but a variable boundary, a surface whose permeability is politically regulated' (Butler 1990: 139). If *Rocky* offers the boxing narrative as a drama of limits this is, however, as I've already discussed, at the expense of a black opponent constituted as other. This is to say that within these fictions we can identify the operation of different kinds of limits.

Rocky's (Italian) whiteness has a quite specific set of meanings when placed within the context of boxing. He represents the Great White Hope, taking on the black champion, Apollo Creed.[19] Since the scenarios of the *Rocky* films are some way removed from the concerns of professional boxing, this question also needs to be framed within a more general set of questions to do with activity, passivity and the male body as it is constructed through 'race'. The black male body has been represented in terms of extremes within Hollywood's symbolic – either radically sexualised, active, or passive and desexualised. The jokey but tough use of the 'buck' as a stereotype in *Shaft*, plays off against the various 'castrated', passive figures who operate as buddy to the white hero. Within the action cinema, the white male body, in a move that combines these two poles, is defined as both powerful and suffering. Whilst the body of the white hero is cut up and penetrated within the action narrative, he also survives. The assertion of a powerful body is framed by either images of suffering or a humour which is centred on the performance of gendered identity. The two modes are brought together in the final fight between Vernon Wells and Arnold Schwarzenegger in *Commando*. The two men trade comic insults and sexualised compliments on their performance, whilst slashing, stabbing and punching each other. In the first film of the series, Rocky's eye must be cut open before he can continue the final fight. In both *First Blood* and *Rambo III* Rambo repairs his own wounds, literally sewing himself up in one instance. The violence inflicted on the body is so extreme in *Lock Up* that critic Sheila Johnstone dubbed Stallone's character the 'Saint Sebastian of the maximum security cells'. These images serve as metonymic representations of castration, marking the limits within which the hero must operate.[20] The reference to Saint Sebastian points to the homoerotic associations of the images of bodily penetration that are so common in the action genre. This homoeroticism, which is consciously mobilised in *Commando*, for instance, can be further discussed in terms of a refusal, or a failure, of the role of the father.

ACTION MEN, FATHERS AND FIGURES OF AUTHORITY

In a recent interview Jean-Claude Van Damme, asked about his gay male following, muses that perhaps 'they miss affection and that's why they like to have a father figure'. He adds that his gay fans may also 'like the physique I have', at which point interviewer Jim McClellan notes in an aside to the reader, 'it's a possibility' (*The Face*, March 1992: 44). Given the knowing homoeroticism of recent Van Damme films, such as *A.W.O.L.* and *Death Warrant*, the production team at work seems well aware of the star's appeal. The 'explanations' offered by Van Damme highlight the fact that the cinematic hero is in the business of performing manliness not only at the level of physique, incorporating as well a desire to embody authority, to play the figure of the father. Yet it is precisely this performance, and the patriarchal authority it involves, that eludes the action hero, indeed is sometimes actively refused by him. Action movies here insistently work through a set of motifs related to sexuality and authority, motifs which are mapped onto both narrative structure and the body of the male hero. Linking the questions of the male hero's effectivity at work within a postmodern context, the embodiment of an excessive physical performance and an anxious narrative of male sexuality, is the 'crisis of the paternal signifier', to which Barbara Creed refers. Creed posits this failure as a way to contextualise the muscular hero as 'simulacra of an exaggerated masculinity, the original completely lost to sight' (Creed 1987: 65). It is ironic, in this context, that Sarah Connor/Linda Hamilton sees the Schwarzenegger cyborg as the perfect father for her son in *Terminator 2*. His knowledge, physical power and the fact that he follows orders without question, having no desires of his own, mark him out from the series of inadequate humans with which we learn she has been involved. The failure to produce *things* within the world of finance, is linked to both a failure of masculinity, and a failed relationship to the father for the heroes of 1980s' films such as *Wall Street* (1987) and *Pretty Woman* (1990). And while both these films effect a reconciliation of sorts, the problem of the paternal position haunts the action narrative with its corrupt and untrustworthy figures of authority.

The psychoanalytic notion of homeovestism, which is defined as 'a perverse behaviour involving wearing clothes of the same sex' proves useful in this context (Zavitzianos 1977: 489). Referring to various case histories, Zavitzianos describes how the use of garments associated with paternal authority, and most particularly uniforms associated with sports and the military, provides a way to stabilise body image, to relieve anxiety and to raise self-esteem. Of course Zavitzianos, in an all too familiar clinical tone, tells us that with treatment 'the homeovestite may evolve from a homosexual object to a heterosexual one'. It is indicative of the uncertainty at stake here that it is precisely at such points, when the boundaries between different categories become blurred – as in the performance of an exaggerated version of a socially expected identity – that a reassuring talk of 'improvement' emerges. The value of this concept is that the paraphernalia of masculine uniforms and identities, which are often taken as 'normal' and 'natural' is, as much as any other form of behaviour, seen as part of a fantasy structure which is *invented*, in which the terms of the natural lose any purchase.

A less pathologising version of this notion is to be found in Lacan's concept of 'male parade', in which the accoutrements of phallic power, the finery of authority, belies the very lack that it displays.[21] In a similar way the muscular male body can be seen to function as a powerful symbol of both desire and lack. Here heroism functions as an element of costume. Within the narratives which I have discussed here, the position of the father, a position of authority, lacks credibility in various ways. This lack of credibility is part of a denaturalisation of masculinity and its relation to power, a shift that can be seen to be enacted in the virtually woman-free zone of the action narrative. Within the action cinema of the 1980s, anxieties to do with difference and sexuality increasingly seem to be worked out over the body of the male hero – an economy in which the woman has little space or function. In *Die Hard 2* Holly McClane (Bonnie Bedelia) is literally suspended in the air until the final minutes of the film, trapped in a stranded plane which circles the airport where the action takes place. Whilst it is played out on a huge stage, McClane's despairing drama is also a small drama, a family romance. Both *Die Hard* and *Die Hard 2* draw to a close with McClane searching for his wife amongst the debris, covered in blood and crying out her name, seeming like nothing so much as a child. Indeed while Holly McClane provides the term which holds the narrative together (since neither the job of cop nor patriotism provide the hero's motivation) she and John McClane are rarely together, with the moment of reunion constantly postponed. Only once, in the first film, do we see the family together, with McClane as a father – glimpsed as an image, a framed photograph in Holly's office, which she has turned face down in disgust.

Fatherhood is an important theme within many films of the 1980s in comedies such as *Three Men and A Baby*, *Parenthood*, *Kindergarten Cop* and *Look Who's Talking*. The opening sequences of *Backdraft* feature Kurt Russell's character as a child who looks on as his fireman father gets blown up. This loss leaves Russell to face the impossible task of filling the paternal shoes, though he ultimately dies, like his father, 'in the line of duty'. This example indicates something of the terms of the action cinema's involvement with themes of fatherhood and authority. In the *Lethal Weapon* films, it is significantly the black family that provides a point of security and paternal authority, with Danny Glover's fatherly stability clearly distinguished from the unsettled, hysterical, persona that Mel Gibson adopts in the film. In part this designation of the black buddy as father figure is in line with the ways in which black characters, cast in a subordinate role, frequently offer a point of security for the white male hero – functioning as the reliable friend, or the good informant. However, in terms of the complex history of black representation in Hollywood, referred to in Chapter 2, the casting of the black hero as a fatherly figure also provides a way to avoid the authoritarian connotations which accompany the white hero when he is cast in that role. That is, to assign symbolic power, which is associated with the position of the father, to the black hero who emerges from a sterotypically passive history of representation, sidesteps an evident failure to make that paternal position work in relation to the white hero. A disturbing assertion of fatherly authority does take place in *The Last Boy Scout*, a film which presents us with a white, suburban family in crisis, upon which Bruce Willis manages to impose some kind of order, ultimately getting his sassy daughter to show some respect and call him 'Sir'. The film itself is populated with failed figures of authority. In an astonishing opening sequence Billy Cole, a black football player told he must win at any cost, guns down opposing players before blowing his own brains out on a rain-sodden field.

Postmodernity, whatever else it is taken to designate, can also be seen to signal significant redefinitions of work and the masculine identity that it proposes. This helps us to situate and historicise the shifts in Hollywood's representation of the male hero. In turn, though, Andy Medhurst has characterised postmodernism as the heterosexual version of camp, a discourse in which both the play of multiple identities and acts of appropriation are fundamental. Sincerity, says Medhurst, is 'the ultimate swear-word in the camp vocabulary' since while it 'implies truth; camp knows that life is composed of different types of lie' (Medhurst 1990: 19). To say, for example, that the enactments of masculinity seen in the action cinema seem like nothing so much as a series of exercises in male drag raises a question of sincerity, since it is the awareness of performance that distinguishes the masquerade from sociological conceptions of social roles. Yet, within the cinema, whose awareness are we speaking about – the producers, the stars, the audience? When Rae Dawn Chong, watching Arnold Schwarzenegger and Bill Duke fight it out in *Commando*, sighs 'I don't believe this macho bullshit', who is she speaking to, or for? There are a whole range of experiences and identities – those of lesbian and gay audiences, of black and Asian audiences, of all the margins that make up the centre – that are rarely addressed directly by the Hollywood cinema in the way that those of white men seem to be. Yet the enactment of a drama of power and powerlessness, a drama which has a special resonance for marginalised groups, is intrinsic to the anxieties about masculine identity and authority that are embodied in the figure of the struggling white hero. The problems of authority which surround this figure have had an impact on the representation of black heroes and action heroines within recent action cinema. Indeed, it is the terms of this physical drama, of power and powerlessness, that has been carried over through the end of the 1980s and into the 1990s in the production of the muscular action heroine who is discussed in the next chapter.

7

ACTION HEROINES IN THE 1980s

The limits of 'musculinity'

It would be possible to see the centrality of action heroines in recent Hollywood film as posing a challenge to women's social role, and to her representation within the cinema's symbolic order. This is the terrain over which a developing debate is currently being conducted, within feminist film criticism, as to the significance of the action heroine. Cinematic images of women who wield guns, and who take control of cars, computers and the other technologies that have symbolised both power and freedom within Hollywood's world, mobilise a symbolically transgressive iconography. At the most fundamental level, images of the active heroine disrupt the conventional notion – often significantly present as an assumption within feminist film criticism – that women either are, or should be, represented exclusively through the codes of femininity. The critical suggestion that the action heroine is 'really a man', a suggestion that is addressed further below, stems from this assumption and represents an attempt to secure the logic of a gendered binary in which the terms 'male' and 'masculine', 'female' and 'feminine' are locked together. As the earlier discussion of action heroines of the 1970s indicates, the female protagonists of contemporary action films emerge from a long cinematic and literary tradition. However, the action heroine has also, in the last twenty years, undergone a significant redefinition in western films. Thus, although she is not a product solely of the 1980s, there is a specificity to the appearance of recent action heroines. I characterised this in Chapter 1, in terms of the heroine's move from her position as a subsidiary character within the action narrative, to the central role of *action heroine*, a figure who commands the narrative. A more specific phenomenon associated with recent cinema is the appearance of a *muscular* action heroine, a figure who is discussed below in relation to the growth in women's involvement in bodybuilding as a sport and what this means for the development of shifting, 'masculine' identities for women.

Frantz Fanon's analysis of the symbolic and actual limits imposed by colonialism, cited earlier, provides a useful perspective through which to think about the operation of class and race within the muscular fantasies of empowerment that structure the action cinema. Fanon's work also makes clear the extent to which colonial discourse positions its subject within a sexualised rhetoric. Following on from this, Kobena Mercer has made the salient point that for critics to talk about stereotypical representations of blackness-as-passivity in terms of the figure of 'castration', operates to once more recentre sexuality (which is fantasised as either excessive or absent) as the trope through which blackness can most usefully be spoken about and understood.[1] In criticism, as in aesthetic practice, these stereotypes cannot be simply sidestepped – this much is evident from the action films, such as *Shaft* and *Predator 2*, discussed in Chapter 2. The incorporation and working through of these stereotypes, within both contemporary criticism and the film text, makes clear the extent to which the constitution of the body as sexed and as gendered intersects with its constitution as a subject of class and racial discourse. The fantasies of a muscular physical power that Fanon speaks of – expressed in dreams of jumping, running, swimming and climbing – are also bound into images of a masculine (though not, necessarily, male) strength, that is constructed as both an expression of freedom and a form of protection. Thus he suggests that 'the native's muscles are always tensed' (Fanon 1985: 41). These images, which speak of both bodily invincibility and vulnerability, clearly accord with the kinds of operation through which the male body is constructed in the action cinema.

Metaphors of constriction and freedom, which draw from the actual limits through which lives are lived, have also been central to women's fiction. Such metaphors have been strategically mobilised by feminist writers. Maxine Hong Kingston's *The Woman Warrior* works through such an opposition in her fantastic portraits of Chinese-American womanhood thus:

> When we Chinese girls listened to the adults' talking-story, we learned that we failed if we grew up to be but wives or slaves. We could be heroines, swordswomen. Even if she had to rage across all China, a swordswoman got even with anybody who hurt her family. Perhaps women were once so dangerous that they had to have their feet bound.
>
> (Hong Kingston 1977: 25)

Here images of a fabulous power and freedom are defined against images of extreme constriction. And whilst Hong Kingston clearly refers here to a female experience, and to male experience in *China Men*, her work effectively blurs the boundaries between categories of masculinity and femininity.[2] This is a literature concerned with the history and experience of limitation and constriction as it constitutes both women and men. Both oppression and fantasised escape are, however *imaginary* they may be, in effect inscribed *over the body*. To return to the contemporary cinema, we can take the controversial film *Thelma and Louise* as a narrative of criminal women, centred on heroines who seem to delight in their transgression of both the law and of the constraints within which they have lived their lives. The film enacts a drama which is about the transgression of limits – the opening up of the American landscape of the road invokes, for example, a pioneer rhetoric. The equally controversial *Basic Instinct* orchestrates a rather different narrative of sexual investigation. The female protagonist, Catherine Tramell (Sharon Stone), is both an aggressively sexual woman and a serial killer – a criminal woman who transgresses both the law and Hollywood's conventions of female behaviour. This chapter addresses some of the issues which are posed by such films, as well as the debates which have framed their reception. What is the significance of the appearance of the female action heroine in the mainstream of Hollywood cinema production? How does this figure relate to the established Hollywood codes for representing both authority, and the populist hero's refusal of that authority? Debates concerning the political status of the active/action heroine are explored specifically in relation to *Thelma and Louise* and *Basic Instinct*. Following on from the question of 'masculinisation', raised within feminist evaluations of the action heroine, the impact of women's involvement in bodybuilding is considered in terms of the transgression of bodily limits.

SEXUALITY, FEMINISM AND FILM: THE CONTROVERSY OVER *THELMA AND LOUISE* AND *BASIC INSTINCT*

'This film is a con'. Thus ran the opening of *Spare Rib*'s review of Ridley Scott's *Alien* on its initial release back in 1979. With the exception of this film, in which Sigourney Weaver stars as Ripley, when feminist writers have addressed the action cinema at all during the 1980s, it has only been to dismiss the genre as macho and reactionary in familiar terms. However, the emergence of a series of diverse action-based films centred on female protagonists has begun to generate a debate as to the political status of these films and their heroines. *Thelma and Louise*, a road movie also directed by Ridley Scott, was the surprise hit of the summer of 1991, both in America and in European countries such as Britain and France.[3] The success of the film generated a series of articles, reviews and other commentaries which diversely praised, expressed concern or fascination at its 'gun-toting' heroines. Some saw *Thelma and Louise* as a feminist reworking of a male genre, the road movie, with women taking the place of the male buddies familiar to viewers of popular Hollywood cinema. For others, the film represented an interrogation of male myths about female sexuality, an admirable commentary on rape and sexual violence. I've already spoken of the way in which *Thelma and Louise* has been appropriated by some women as a 'lesbian film'. Elsewhere *Thelma and Louise* has been characterised as a betrayal, a narrative that cannot follow through on its own logic. Far from being about empowering women, in this view the image of women-with-guns is considered to be one which renders the protagonists *symbolically male*. Whatever view we take, *Thelma and Louise* and associated female heroines have generated, at the beginning of the 1990s, an academic and journalistic debate analogous to that sparked by the muscular male stars of the 1980s.[4] The film has also been consumed in an historical moment marked by the public re-emergence of familiar questions to do with sexuality, violence and relations of power between men and women, in the publicity surrounding the nomination of judge Clarence Thomas to the Supreme Court and the Kennedy rape case in the United States.[5]

Thelma and Louise follows the adventures of two white southern women in the United States who take off for a weekend of fun and end up on the run from the law. After an attempted rape leads to a fatal shooting and flight from the police, the theft of Louise's savings leads Thelma to armed robbery. With its outlaw heroines pushed beyond the point of no return, *Thelma and Louise* takes its place with a group of recent movies which put female protagonists at the centre of those action-based genres often reserved for men. A series of talked-about film performances from a variety of action sub-genres, all invoked the figure of the independent woman as heroine. Whilst films such as *Aliens* and *The Silence of the Lambs* and the performances of their female stars have caused much critical interest, an attendant suspicion can be detected that this type of role, indeed the appearance of women in the action cinema at all, is somehow inappropriate. Critical responses are never univocal, of course, but feminist critics have responded to these films with various combinations of pleasure and disgust, enthusiasm and suspicion. These films, it seems, whilst praised and enjoyed for their centring of women, are for some potentially tainted by exploitation. Such a sense of critical unease is certainly worth exploring. For if action movies centred on men have drawn condemnation for their supposed endorsement of a hyper-masculinity, how can the negative reaction to the emergence of female action heroines be contextualised and understood? The films themselves may well prove easier to understand when placed within the context of the popular cinema, and the tradition of the American action movie in particular, rather than in the context of a tradition of feminist film-making against which they are sometimes judged and, inevitably, found wanting.

Laura Mulvey concluded her well-known polemic essay of the 1970s, 'Visual Pleasure and Narrative Cinema', with the suggestion that women would have little or nothing to mourn in the passing of the Hollywood cinema.[6] While recognising that the popular cinema of today is, in many ways, different from the popular cinema that Mulvey addresses, I want to raise a set of questions about the pleasure that both female and feminist spectators *do* take from mainstream movies, pleasures which are not dictated by any rules of same-sex identification or by heterosexual understandings of desire. The best way to express this might be in terms of a contradiction between what 'we' know and what 'we' enjoy, since the kinds of fantasy investments at work in the pleasures taken from the cinema cannot be controlled by conscious political positions in the way that some criticism seems to imply.[7] A tension between the project of legitimating women's pleasures and the desire to assess representations politically informs a good deal of feminist criticism. It is ironic then that a critical disapproval of the 1980s' and 1990s' action heroine may stem in part from a feminist cultural criticism which has, in seeking to legitimise various pleasures and pastimes, classified popular forms and genres into male and female. The notion that some forms of activity and entertainment are more appropriate to men and some to women, that some genres can be called 'masculine' whilst others are labelled 'feminine', has a long history. Such a notion has its roots in commonsense understandings of appropriate male and female behaviour as well as in the categories set up by those who produce images and fictions – such as the 'woman's film'. Ironically a designation of 'inappropriate' images derived from a feminist critical tradition, coincides here with a more conventional sense of feminine decorum, a sense of knowing one's place within a gendered hierarchy. As much as anything, this critical trajectory reveals the operation within feminist criticism of a class-based, high-cultural, attitude towards the popular cinema, an attitude familiar from other forms of criticism. This is an important point since, as we have seen in previous chapters, class is a central term in the narratives of the popular action cinema.

Thelma and Louise charts the development of its two heroines as they move from the routines and confinement of everyday life to the freedom of the open road. In the process they move from the supposedly female space of the home to the freedom of the supposedly 'male' space that is the great outdoors. The martial-arts movie *China O'Brien* also follows this trajectory, with China resigning her job as a city cop to return to her home town, where she ultimately becomes sheriff. A montage sequence shows her driving through the countryside in an open-top car, images of her face in close-up intercut with her surroundings. Whilst there is nothing particularly unusual in this, cinematically speaking, Rothrock here occupies the role of a 'figure in a landscape', the phrase Mulvey uses to describe the narrative control assigned to the male protagonist (Mulvey 1989: 20). The film seems to coyly acknowledge this shift, including a shot of a male gas-pump attendant, his chest exposed and hair blowing in the wind. The construction of this secondary male figure as spectacle provides a counterpoint to China's position as a dominating figure within the film. The road comes to signal a certain mythicised freedom.

At the outset of *Thelma and Louise*, Thelma (Geena Davies) is a shy, childlike woman, playing the role of meek housewife to husband Darryl's macho self-centredness. Louise (Susan Sarandon) is a waitress, capable and in control, balancing the demands of customers and workmates. The two set off for the weekend, Thelma's inability to decide *anything* resulting in a jokey sequence in which she packs just about everything she owns. This confusion is intercut with the neatness of Louise's apartment, everything cleaned and in its place. These images conjure up two recognisable extremes of an inability to cope, set against a calm efficiency. These comic extremes in turn set up the terms within which these characters will change and develop through the course of the narrative. I've already spoken of the ways in which a rites-of-passage narrative is a key feature of the Vietnam movie, a narrative in which the (white) hero 'finds himself' in the other space of Vietnam. These narratives build on a tradition of imperialist fictions within film and literature, in which Asia and Africa are constituted as exotic spaces for adventure. This structure is seen most explicitly in *Platoon* and is parodically, if rather viciously, drawn on in the 'Asia' of *Indiana Jones and the Temple of Doom*.[8] The heroine of women's fiction is centred in a rather different rites-of-passage narrative, though one which nonetheless represents a coming to knowledge. Maria La Place discusses the operation of such a narrative trajectory in many women's novels and stories which 'centre on the heroine's process of self-discovery, on her progression from ignorance about herself (and about the world in general) to knowledge and some kind of strength' (Gledhill 1987: 152). Specifically referring to the 1940s' film and novel *Now Voyager*, La Place outlines the extent to which this transformation is both signalled and partly achieved through changes in the heroine's appearance – weight loss, new clothes, hairstyle and so on. This transformation is reminiscent of the narratives constructed around the male bodybuilder, whose physical transformation supposedly signals his changed status in the world. The rites-of-passage narrative that situates women in relation to health or body culture defines the heroine's transformation through the body. Such a transformation is enacted over the protagonists of *Thelma and Louise*, with their changing appearance seen by Kathleen Murphy as a literal shedding of skin when, in the final moments of the film, 'the Polaroid of two smiling girls on vacation that Louise shot so many miles ago blows away in the wind, as insubstantial as a snake's outgrown skin' (Murphy 1991: 29). The end credit sequence continues this theme with a series of images of the two women, taken from different points in the narrative, which trace their transformation.

There is though a further sense in which the film's drama is enacted over the bodies of the two heroines. A drunken sexual assault on Thelma propels the two women on the road. Initially it is Louise who takes control, who rebukes and then shoots Harlan dead. Thelma's response is hysteria.

'What kind of world are you living in?' cries Louise on hearing Thelma's suggestion that they hand themselves over to the police. Later, when Louise's life savings have been stolen by JD (Brad Pitt), a young man Thelma has taken a liking to, it is Thelma who begins to take charge. She robs a convenience store, a performance we see through the flickering images, filmed by the store's surveillance video, as they are replayed by the police to an astounded Darryl. By the end of the movie both Thelma and Louise are armed, literally with a gun stolen from a state trooper, and metaphorically with a powerful sense of self and of the impossibility of a return to their earlier lives. They decide to head for Mexico since, as Thelma puts it, 'Something's crossed over in me. I can't go back – I just couldn't live'. Through these later scenes, the women are no longer just running, but enjoying the journey. The film offers a series of spectacular images, visual echoes of the women's changed perception. The two women shoot up a tanker, after its driver, who has plagued them at various points along the road, has refused to apologise for his behaviour. The truck explodes in a mass of flame. Driving through the desert landscape at night, their car is lit up from within – a surreal beacon. In this quiet moment they contemplate the night sky. Exhilarating and frustrating, the now notorious final image of the film has the two women driving off a precipice rather than give themselves up.

The narrative of transformation which structures *Thelma and Louise* is analogous to the developments in Linda Hamilton's character, Sarah Connor, in *The Terminator*. Like Louise, Sarah begins the film as a harassed waitress. Told by her lover and protector, Kyle Reese, that she is destined to become a legend to the rebels of a future society, she moans that she can't even balance a cheque book. By the end of the film she has acquired military discipline, becoming well-armed and self-sufficient. The militaristic iconography is continued in the sequel, *Terminator 2*, extended and literally embodied through Hamilton's muscular frame. A turning-point for Sarah Connor in *The Terminator* comes when Kyle is wounded and she must take control. At the very moment that he looks like giving up the fight, she screams at him to move. Addressing him as 'Soldier', she takes up the role of a commanding officer who harangues a tired platoon in order to save them, a role familiar from many Hollywood war movies. It is after this proof of her transformation, and Kyle's death which follows soon after, that Sarah finally terminates the Terminator. Kyle must die since, like the male hero, it seems that the action heroine cannot be in control of an adult sexuality. At the beginning of *Aliens* Ripley refuses the offer to accompany the military on an Alien-hunting mission, telling company man Carter Burke – 'I'm not a soldier'. She finally agrees to accompany the military platoon as an observer. Once there, however, despite her protestations, Ripley effectively takes control from the inexperienced military leader – like Sarah Connor she is transformed into a soldier.

It is perhaps the centrality of images of women with guns in all the films I've referred to thus far, that has caused the most concern amongst feminist critics. The phallic woman, that characters like Sarah Connor and Ripley represent, is seen as a male ruse, and a film like *Thelma and Louise* as 'little more than a masculine revenge fantasy' whose 'effect is perversely to reinforce the message that women cannot win'.[9] Here we can see the obverse process of that critical move by which the suffering of the hero has been read as a testament to his, and consequently patriarchy's, invincibility. In turn the struggles of the female protagonist seem only to reinforce her passivity and secure her ultimate failure. Disruptive narrative or representational elements exist, within such a critical view, as little more than precursors to their ultimate hegemonic incorporation. Hence these images are taken to represent a double betrayal, holding out a promise that can never be fulfilled ('This film is a con'). Though it is not the project of this book, it might well be worth exploring further the kinds of masochistic fantasies at work in such critical moves. Alternatively, situating a film like *Thelma and Louise* within the tradition of popular cinema might, as I've argued, allow us to see it differently. Within many Hollywood action narratives, access to technologies such as cars and guns (traditional symbols of power) represents a means of empowerment. These technologies are also intimately bound up with images of the masculine. The female protagonists of the films discussed above operate within an image-world in which questions of gender identity are played out through, in particular, the masculinisation of the female body. Within *Thelma and Louise* the possession of guns and the possession of self are inextricably linked through the dilemmas that the film poses about freedom and self-respect. Drawing on a long history of representations of male self-sufficiency, the film traces the women's increasing ability to 'handle themselves', a tracing that follows their ability to handle a gun. Thelma can barely bring herself to handle her gun, a gift from husband Darryl, at the start of the film – picking it up with an expression of distaste, in a rather 'girlish' fashion. As the narrative progresses, she acquires both physical coordination, which denotes self-possession, and the ability to shoot straight. When the two women shoot out the tanker, they happily compliment each other on their aim.

Thelma and Louise is for the most part comic in tone. It is for this reason that, despite all the gunplay, the women only once shoot anybody, the killing which sends them on the run, through the entire course of the film – in order to keep the heroines as sympathetic figures they cannot be constructed as wantonly violent, so there is no final shootout. The carefully contained criminality represented in the figures of Thelma and Louise can be contrasted to the figure of Catherine Tramell in *Basic*

Instinct, an intensely controversial film which has provoked protests in the United States against its 'negative' representation of a 'lesbian' heroine. *Basic Instinct* is, by contrast to *Thelma and Louise*, a thriller, and the heroine is a monstrous but fascinating figure. We are positioned with an equally monstrous detective hero, Nick, played by Michael Douglas, who investigates a series of murders associated with Tramell. The publicity images for the film showed the two in an embrace, Douglas in profile with his back to us, Stone staring out of the image at the viewer. Because Tramell is the villain of the piece, her transgressions can be of quite a different order to the heroic women who learn about themselves, and each other, on the road in *Thelma and Louise*. The most obvious antecedent for both the narrative and characterisation that *Basic Instinct* mobilises, as well as critical models for thinking about its articulation of sexuality, is the *film noir* of the 1940s. Several critics have pointed to the power and potency of the image of the deadly *femme fatale* who is found in these films. Such critical models often direct our attention not only to the ideological implications of a narrative progression, in which the strong woman inevitably dies or is punished, but to the lasting impression that her figure leaves us with. Thus Janey Place remarks that *film noir* is 'one of the few periods of film in which women are active, not static symbols, are intelligent and powerful, if destructively so, and derive power, not weakness, from their sexuality' (Kaplan 1980: 35). Here the *femme fatale* is seen to turn around the terms within which 'woman' is defined, so that both her power, and the power against which she might be seen to resist, is constituted through the terms of sexuality.

Catherine Tramell is certainly cast as a *femme fatale*, a deadly woman who uses her sexuality against men. Tramell is a wealthy, sexually aggressive, woman who becomes involved with various men who are destined to become characters in her books, and ultimately to be killed off once they have outlived their usefulness. More controversially, Catherine is cast as bisexual – or rather polymorphously perverse. Critics who attacked the portrayal of Catherine as a lesbian, either ignored the fact that she spends a good part of the film sexually involved with men, or constructed this as a pathologising narrative in which she is 'cured' of her lesbianism. Whilst this is certainly what Douglas's character seems to believe within the film, as he brags about his sexual performance to Catherine's girlfriend, for instance, there is also a clear sense in which the audience cannot fully accept this version of events. Indeed a sustained narrative tension stems from the ambiguity which surrounds Tramell's attitude to Douglas, particularly an uncertainty as to whether or not he will become her next victim. In the publicity poster from which Sharon Stone stares out at the viewer, her mouth (and hence her expression) remains hidden, rendering her a mysterious figure. The final image of the film itself echoes this sense, so that the ending is left deliberately sinister and uncertain. Filling the frame is the murder weapon, an ice pick, which is hidden beneath the bed that Tramell shares with Nick/Douglas. Such an ambiguity may indicate that the 'active' heroine who is associated with the figure of the *femme fatale*, as Place defines her, is quite distinct from the action heroine, who is rarely an ambiguous figure for the audience. In thinking about recent action cinema we need to pay attention not only to the ambiguity which is at stake in the gendered identity of the *active heroine*, but the redefinition of the sexed body that is worked out over the muscular female body of the *action heroine*.

WOMEN, BODYBUILDING AND BODY CULTURE

Women are becoming increasingly involved in bodybuilding as a competitive sport. It is now also a commonplace part of the exercise programmes recommended in women's magazines, no longer perceived, as it once was, as a marginal activity associated with only a few 'fanatical' sportswomen. This involvement has led to the rapid growth of the bodybuilding industry and, as Laurie Schulze points out, shifts in the 'ideal' female body – as it is offered to women through fashion magazines, models, beauty culture and so on. The soft curves presented as defining the ideal female form in the 1950s, has shifted to an emphasis on muscle tone in images of the 1980s and early 1990s. At the same time, of course, the market for men's cosmetics has expanded, championed by several successful men's style magazines.[10] Some bodybuilding magazines now extend their promise-cum-challenge to 'build yourself a better body', to women as well as to men. Both beauty and body culture have responded then, though perhaps in contradictory ways, to the successes of the women's movement, most particularly in the repeated invocation within advertising of the figure of the (sexually) independent woman. The advent of the female bodybuilder represents a distinct part of this response. Schulze argues that the female bodybuilder 'threatens not only current socially constructed definitions of femininity and masculinity, but the system of sexual difference itself' (Gaines and Herzog 1990: 59). Bodybuilding, that is, makes explicit the extent to which both sex and gender constitute the body within culture, problematising the boundaries of what constitutes drag (see Butler 1990; Epstein and Straub 1991). Yet Schulze is also concerned to demonstrate that the threat posed by the female bodybuilder is almost instantly allayed within dominant culture. Her analysis thus seeks to show how the 'domestication of a potential challenge to dominant definitions of a feminine body is accomplished' (Gaines and Herzog 1990: 61). Despite this assertion of failed potential, the final pages of Schulze's essay are tentatively given over to thinking about the consumption of these images by specific audiences and within the subculture of female bodybuilding itself. Here bodybuilding is admitted as a space where the meanings attached to the sexed body are increasingly uncertain and shifting.

Given the extent to which 'woman' has been equated with nature – within both feminist and other more mainstream discourses – the muscular female body raises a different, if related, set of issues than those touched on in my discussion of the muscular male hero. Whilst the muscleman produces himself as an exaggerated version of what is conventionally taken to be masculine, the female bodybuilder takes on supposedly 'masculine' characteristics. Muscles as a signifier of *manual* labour become appropriated for the decoration of the *female* body. Both figures draw attention to and redefine a bodily understanding of gendered identity. Some of the rich connotative qualities of the muscular female body are brought out by Robert Mapplethorpe in his photographs of bodybuilder Lisa Lyons in his book *Lady: Lisa Lyons*. Published in 1983, Mapplethorpe's black and white images were the result of a sustained collaboration between the two. The photographs play with the conventional associations of the sexed body. They feature the clash of a range of 'masculine' and 'feminine' connotations, which stem not only from the presentation of the body as substance, but the ways in which it is decorated, posed and presented to the world. 'Feminine' fabrics such as lace are juxtaposed with the hard 'masculine' texture of Lyons's muscular body. At other points Lyons is dressed in fetishistic garb which is both qualified and further sexualised by her physique. This contrast is also expressed through the nudes, many of which echo classical poses associated almost exclusively with the male nude. One image focuses on a fragment on Lyons's body, isolating her arm, which is flexed to reveal biceps, and one breast. Other images frame her striking muscular poses against a natural landscape, playing off the associations of woman-as-nature against these images of woman-in-nature. Far from rendering her manly through her muscularity, these photographs emphasise both the hardness of female muscles and the softer flesh of the breasts.

Women's participation in *health* culture, bodybuilding in particular, as opposed to beauty culture, sets unconventional (for women) standards of attainment, and consequently has a series of implications for ideals of both femininity and masculinity. If the muscles of the male movie star or bodybuilder can seem either parodic or dysfunctional, then the muscles of the female bodybuilder only serve to emphasise the arbitrary qualities of these symbols of manual labour and of physical power. Conversely, the hardness of the muscles goes against a history of representation – visual and verbal – in which the female body is imagined as soft and curvaceous. The sport of bodybuilding is thus the arena for yet another manifestation of a contradiction between the naturalised and the manufactured body, specifically in debates about what a female bodybuilder should look like, and how she should be *judged*. In the cinema the muscular physique of

Linda Hamilton as Sarah Connor in *Terminator 2* offers a distinctive visualisation of the heroine. Both her physique and her tough performance is in addition to the array of weaponry with which she is endowed, making her a formidable figure. By way of contrast to her role in the earlier film, in which she needs to be taught by the male characters how to function heroically, she is determined to be prepared for her second battle with the Terminator. She works out in a gym she has improvised from the iron bed in the mental institution in which she has been incarcerated following the events of the first film. This persona juxtaposes traditionally masculine and feminine characteristics – she is a butch-*femme*.

I want to discuss here the implications of the iconographic transgression at stake in recent characterisations of the action heroine generally, and the muscular female body specifically. A discussion of three quite different films may help to follow up some of these points. In *Getting Physical*, a 1984 television movie which deals with female bodybuilding, and in which Lisa Lyons herself appears, we see the protagonist discover a sense of self through bodybuilding. The semi-documentary *Pumping Iron II: The Women* (1984) follows a female bodybuilders' contest. It also received some considerable commentary from feminist critics on its release. *Perfect* (1985) casts Jamie Lee Curtis as an aerobics instructor in a California health club. Though none of these three films is an action narrative, all deal with women's position within health and body culture, and all are taken from the same moment, the mid-1980s, in which the muscular male star was becoming a significant box-office phenomenon.

In *Getting Physical* we see women's bodybuilding through the eyes of a new recruit to the sport. The film is, on some levels, a classic makeover story in which the female protagonist, initially lacking any confidence or motivation, becomes, through physical change, a confident individual in her own right who is accepted by her family, her boyfriend and the world in general as she poses on the stage of a bodybuilding contest. Kendal comes to bodybuilding by accident, has to be persuaded into it. In the film's first sequence we see her rushing to an audition for an acting role. She is clumsy and over-weight, with a tedious office job. Kendal smokes, eats a lot without any real enjoyment and does not feel comfortable with her family. Her father complains that she cannot 'get serious' about anything. After she is unable to defend herself from being assaulted in a parking lot Kendal goes to the police station where she meets Mickey, the man who becomes her boyfriend. He suggests she takes self-defence classes, giving her the address of a gym. On arrival at the gym Kendal is introduced to the spectacular world of bodybuilding. We see the muscular bodies of women working out from Kendal's point of view. Close-ups of flexing legs and arms are intercut with her admiring face. For the first time she aspires to something, determining to look the same. Kendal is physically challenged. *Getting Physical* traces Kendal's increasing commitment to bodybuilding which ultimately leads to her decision to leave her office job and to abandon her aspirations to be an actor. Instead she enters a bodybuilding contest as a way to succeed on a public stage. Taken under the wing of a professional bodybuilder, Nadine (Sandahl Bergman), and her husband/trainer, Kendal leaves home in order to train. Kendal's bodybuilding is opposed by both her boyfriend and her father, who see it as disturbing and unfeminine. Finally though they both come round, applauding her performance in the contest with which the film ends.

Whilst not a particularly sophisticated drama, *Getting Physical* poses in new terms a basic narrative that has long been a staple of women's and teenage magazines – that of acquiring confidence, independence and social/familial acceptance. The makeover is expressed through images of physical strength, which clash with a traditionally 'feminine' passivity. In the opening sequences of the film such passivity is pathologised, with Kendal presented as listless and uninterested in life. The drive for physical perfection seen in *Perfect* is, by way of contrast, constructed as pathetic and humiliating. The world of health culture is depicted through the cynical eyes of John Travolta as Adam Lawrence, a *Rolling Stone* journalist. He is interested in another, 'serious' story and follows up a piece on California health culture only as a fall-back. *Perfect* deals with aerobics rather than bodybuilding. Though the film is, like *Getting Physical*, set in a gym, the connotations of aerobics emerge here as remarkably different from those of bodybuilding. Lawrence's story, which is centred on health clubs as the 'singles bars of the 1980s', is to run under the title 'Looking for Mr Goodbody'. Lawrence pretends to Jamie Lee Curtis that he is writing an in-depth piece on the club, whilst actually penning an exploitative article which mocks both the women and the men who attend the club. Their concern with the body is pathologised whilst, at the same time, Sally and Linda, two of the film's female health-club goers, are found physically wanting, photographed in 'unflattering' angles and lighting. Ironically the sexualised display of the body is one of the film's key pleasures, and was certainly central to the way in which it was marketed. Schulze criticises *Getting Physical* for its construction of Kendal's bodybuilding as a way to 'facilitate (heterosexual) romance', despite the fact that at one point in the narrative her refusal to give up training causes her to break up with her boyfriend (Schulze 1986: 39). Further, the bodybuilding narrative of that film contrasts starkly with the obsessive reference to sexuality and the body that typifies *Perfect*, released at roughly the same time. Perhaps because of its newness, or because of the uncertainty that it seems to generate, the image of the female bodybuilder is not representable within the terms of sexualised display.

Since it is concerned exclusively with competitive bodybuilding, *Pumping Iron II: The Women* takes on much more centrally the problems of definition that are necessarily an issue for the female bodybuilder. As various critics pointed out at the time of the film's release, its terrain is in part that of the cultural definition of femininity with which feminism has also been concerned. Here though, as with *Getting Physical*, the film has been characterised as failing to do justice to the transgressive potential of the built female body. Thus Christine Holmlund argues that:

> Far from abolishing stereotypes based on visible difference, *Pumping Iron II*, and *Pumping Iron* as well, visibly position the body as spectacle, then sell it as big business. In both films, the threat of visible difference and the threat of the abolition of visible difference are contained and marketed – as flex appeal.
>
> (Holmlund 1989: 49)

The potential of the film lies for Holmlund, as it does for most critics, in its rendering of the sexed body as artificial, self-created rather than natural. As with commentaries on the sexual politics of the muscular male stars, such an overlap between high theory and popular culture could only be a 'coincidence'. Jane Root's review picks out, for example, the moment at which 'the elderly and predominantly male judges get together to discuss the purpose of the event. Their allotted task for the evening? To "agree on a definition of femininity"'. Root suggests that this 'unselfconscious and unintentionally hilarious comment provides a neat example of the pleasures afforded by this documentary, which seems to have stumbled on some of the hottest issues around for feminism and cultural politics' (*Monthly Film Bulletin*, November 1985: 346). Root's suggestion that the film-makers and participants in female bodybuilding have 'stumbled' on a knowledge forged within feminist cultural politics is indicative of a certain intellectual arrogance in relation to popular culture. Against this we might consider that both the debates with which feminist cultural politics is engaged, and the particular forms of popular culture considered here, emerge from the same historical moment. This would involve criticism recognising its own historical location, instead of conceptualising ideas as emerging from nowhere and then being surprised that the concerns elaborated within the realm of theory might also be found in the popular.

Holmlund sees *Pumping Iron II* as voyeuristic, commercial and shallow. In a particularly telling passage, she argues, in relation to Bev Francis, the woman with the most massively built body in the film, that:

> the association of muscularity, masculinity, and lesbianism invokes these fears of a loss of love for spectators of both sexes, though in different ways. If heterosexual men see Bev as a lesbian, she is threatening: lesbians incarnate sexual indifference to men. If heterosexual women see Bev as a lesbian they must reject her: to like her would mean admitting that they might themselves be lesbian, which

> would in turn entail the abnegation of traditionally feminine powers and privileges.
>
> (Holmlund 1989: 43)

Apart from the construction of the audience for the film as exclusively heterosexual, we can note here how the pleasure of looking at these bodies – what Root calls the film's 'uninviting subject matter' – is erased by a feminist analysis which takes on the role of looking at and pronouncing judgement on popular culture. Holmlund's analysis depends on a clear distinction between the interdependent categories of heterosexual and homosexual. Yet might not part of the pleasure of the film be the dissolution of such rigid categories within the imaginary space of the cinema? Laurie Schulze, who initially sets out the deconstructive aspects of the female bodybuilder, produces a similar analysis in which this figure is complexly incorporated back into a patriarchal heterosexual mainstream due to an insistence on her femininity. Schulze argues that the female bodybuilder 'must be anchored to heterosexuality; if she is not, she may slip through the cracks in the hegemonic system into an oppositional sexuality that would be irrecuperable' (Gaines and Herzog 1990: 61). Yet, in terms of the problematising of borders and boundaries, it is precisely the femininity of the female bodybuilder that destabilises her relationship to the supposedly secure categories of sex, sexuality and gender. By existing across supposedly opposed categories, the female bodybuilder reveals the artifice of that opposition. Casting lesbianism as an irrecuperable, or even an oppositional, sexuality attempts instead to secure a binary logic. Judith Butler makes the same point when she signals the ways in which a notion of homosexuality supports and structures, is in fact necessary to, heterosexuality (Butler 1990). Indeed Schulze finds in the interviews she conducts with lesbians on the subject of female bodybuilding, a conservatism about gendered and sexed bodily identity. Schulze reports rather than analyses the responses she received, though she makes clear the extent to which the muscular-yet-feminine female body is found to be disturbing because it falls between conventional categories of sexed and gendered identity, categories which are as important to lesbian identities as they are to straight identities.[11] It is in such a way that the polymorphous perversity, which characterises Catherine Tramell in *Basic Instinct*, necessarily fails the political demands of a homosexuality defined in opposition to heterosexuality.

'MUSCULINITY' AND THE ACTION HEROINE

In thinking about the contemporary action heroine it would be a mistake to rely exclusively on the critical models associated with the *femme fatale* which are useful in thinking about *Basic Instinct*, since the heroines of other successful films of this period, such as *Silence of the Lambs* and *Aliens*, as well as *Fatal Beauty* or the *China O'Brien* films discussed in Chapter 1, are neither outlaws nor criminal. Their behaviour – going against the rules, going out on a limb – operates as a variant on that of the populist action hero who must break the law in order to secure some kind of justice in the world. Thus in the two *Aliens* films Ripley finds herself doing battle not only with the Alien, but with a conspiratorial company which has a ruthless disregard for human life. In *Silence of the Lambs*, trainee Clarice Starling is invited to participate in the FBI's investigation of serial killer 'Buffalo Bill' only to be systematically excluded from it. An early image frames Starling, at the FBI training centre, as the only woman in an elevator car full of men. Most of the group tower over her, whilst the pale blue of her sweatshirt contrasts to the red in which the men are dressed, emphasising her relative isolation. She ultimately aligns herself with a serial killer, Hannibal Lecter, who can provide her with clues as to the killer's identity and motivation, scraps of evidence withheld by Jack Crawford and his team. Finally it is Starling's perception that leads her to the killer's house – her quiet arrival intercut with all the blasting of Crawford and company bursting noisily into an empty house, armed to the teeth.

The position of the action heroine in relation to the institutions of the state is often as problematic as that of the hero, though this is necessarily represented in different ways. A key film in this respect is Kathryn Bigelow's *Blue Steel*, which stars Jamie Lee Curtis as a rookie New York cop. *Blue Steel* is a complex, psychological thriller which attempts to explore the role of women in the action cinema. The film both invokes and teases out the implications of the sexualised gloss that is often played out over the figure of the action heroine. Working through a sustained cinematic weapons fetish, *Blue Steel* follows through the difficult institutional location of Curtis's character, Megan Turner. At three moments, spread through the course of the narrative, Turner is asked why she became a cop. That this is insistently an issue is crucial to the rather eerie tone of the film, which has Turner play with the answers that it might be possible to give to this question: that she wanted to shoot people, or that she loves violence. Finally, she simply murmurs, 'him'. This last explanation is the most ambiguous – does 'him' refer to her father, with whom she is in conflict throughout the film, the serial killer Eugene with whom she is involved, or a more generalised 'he'? Yet an uncertainty also significantly surrounds the 'joke' explanations that Turner gives. Her deadpan assertions that she became a cop for the violence are given in response to the different attitudes, contemptuous, incredulous, fearful or patronising, that the men she meets take towards her role. Questions of status and authority are further worked through in Turner's relationship to her father and her attitude to his violent treatment of her mother. Ultimately she arrests him, cuffing him and dragging him to the car, though she can't finally turn him in.

The films discussed above all work with a variety of types of femininity, defined and redefined through the body and through the invocation and transgression of the kinds of behaviour considered appropriate for women. In *Alien*, Sigourney Weaver's Ripley is defined against a series of other female types, such as Lambert, who is weak and hysterical and, at a more metaphoric level, the ship's computer Mother. Barbara Creed has demonstrated the many ways in which the film works through monstrous images of femininity, in particular through the characterisation of the Alien (Creed 1986; 1987). The spaceship, as a science-fiction microcosm of humanity, includes women within its world. The inclusion of women in both the civilian crew of the Nostromo in *Alien* and the military team of *Aliens* signals both the metaphoric status of the drama that they enact, and the fact that it is set in the future. Yet, despite her rank, the narrative makes certain that Ripley should still be seen to struggle to establish her authority with Ash in *Alien*, a struggle that reprises an earlier scene, in which Parker and Brett drown out her words with steam. These hierarchical conflicts effectively position Ripley as an outsider action heroine. As we have seen, such a marginality is crucial to the characterisation of the action hero within Hollywood cinema. Similarly, as the marines in *Aliens* emerge from their 'hyper-sleep', they are reassembled into a military team of which Ripley is clearly not a part. Although Ripley is initially separated from the 'grunts' and associated with the military command, her populist allegiance to the troops quickly becomes clear.

The military coding of *Aliens* redefines the premise of the original to some extent since, as with other sequels, it must deal with the fact that the audience may already be familiar with the source of the film's horror and threat. At first Ripley is positioned on the top table with the lieutenant who, as one of the soldiers puts it, 'think's he's too good to eat with the rest of the grunts'. The hostility in *Aliens*, between an experienced crew and an inexperienced and bureaucratic officer, is familiar from a range of war and action movies. Whilst the military are in uniform and Burke, the company representative on the mission, is in civvies, Ripley's dress, with leather flying jacket and fatigues, is iconographically somewhere between the two. Early on she tells Burke that she is 'not a soldier' but as previously noted, despite being initially jumpy, Ripley is ultimately able to take command. As with any populist hero, the turning point comes when the military team find themselves defenceless against an Alien attack and the ineffectual lieutenant hesitates about pulling them out. Ripley seizes the controls of the armoured car from which they are monitoring the massacre, driving into the complex to rescue the troops. When it is revealed that the company has betrayed them all, as in the first film, it is clear whose interests Ripley defends, and she gradually emerges as the 'natural leader' of the platoon. When most of the military have been either killed or lie unconscious, Ripley suggests that Corporal Hicks take command. At this point Burke gives away his company allegiance, and his contempt for the platoon by calling Hicks a 'grunt'. We can contrast Ripley's incorporation into the military team with the isolation of Whoopi Goldberg's character in *Fatal Beauty*, discussed in Chapter 1. Goldberg/Rizzoli is repeatedly attacked by both cop colleagues and villains, assailed with verbal insults and physical violence. The film offers no supportive team to back her up, so that Goldberg is isolated within both the film frame and the narrative. Which is to say, to be a team player involves being admitted to the team in the first place.

Aliens further presents us with the striking figure of Jenette Goldstein as Private Vasquez, a muscular woman with cropped hair. Gesturing at Ripley in an early scene, Vasquez asks a fellow soldier 'Who's Snow White?', establishing something of a distance between the two, though they ultimately find themselves on the same side. Butch but not boyish, Vasquez is an iconic tough action heroine. Since Vasquez is a team player, not an outsider, she is ultimately allied with Ripley against the company and the military authorities. On waking from hyper-sleep she immediately starts doing pull-ups in front of the screen, and in a notorious scene responds to a male colleague's question 'Ever been mistaken for a man?' with the reply 'No, have you?' before slapping the hands of her buddy within the unit. Vasquez enacts the female action persona of the 'ball-busting' woman. Leona, played by Maria Conchita Alonso in *Predator 2* has a similar role, literally grabbing an annoying male cop's crotch. Later in a bar she asks him 'How are your balls?' to which he responds 'Fine – How are yours?' All this posing and verbal horseplay dwells on, and comically works over, the problems of the figure of the tough woman in the male team. In order to function effectively within the threatening, macho world of the action picture, the action heroine must be masculinised. The masculinisation of the female body, which is effected most visibly through her muscles, can be understood in terms of a notion of 'musculinity'. That is, some of the qualities associated with masculinity are written over the muscular female body. 'Musculinity' indicates the way in which the signifiers of strength are not limited to male characters. These action heroines though, are still marked as women, despite the arguments advanced by some critics that figures like Ripley are merely men in drag.

In *Terminator 2* Linda Hamilton's tough physique is played off against the strength-in-fluidity of the monstrous T1000 which pursues her and her son John. The T1000 can take on any form and imitate any voice, though he spends most of the film cast as an LA cop. At times we see him turn into a mercurial liquid, reconstituting himself when damaged. His limbs can also be transformed into sharp metallic tools. I argued earlier that the T1000's fluid ability to transform his body constructs him as a feminised monster, in contrast to the solidity of Schwarzenegger as the protective cyborg, the good Terminator. The terror of the T1000 lies partly in its ability to transform its body from fluidity to a sharp metallic hardness, as when it tortures Sarah Connor by stabbing her with an arm transformed into a blade. Whilst such images obviously draw on figures of penetration, they also bring up once more themes of the vulnerability and invulnerability of the body already discussed in relation to the male hero. The significance of this motif in relation to the action heroine is discussed below.

POWER AND POWERLESSNESS: THE BODY OF THE HEROINE

Whilst Sigourney Weaver's persona as Ripley has been a firm favourite with audiences, an inordinate amount of debate has been given over to the political implications of the final scenes in which, thinking she has destroyed the Alien, she undresses in preparation for sleep. Ripley's near-nakedness, her vulnerability in this sequence is not an insignificant narrative moment, but neither is it the only image in the film, or a moment only for male viewers as some critics have suggested. This much-discussed moment of the film can also be understood in terms of the extreme images of bodily vulnerability and invulnerability that are mobilised in the action cinema. As with much of the Hollywood cinema, action films operate in part to dramatise transgression – a transgression that may take the form of the breaking of official codes of the law as in *Thelma and Louise*. These codes can often be taken to stand in for symbolic codes of social behaviour. Transgression is a term resonant for feminism, implying the crossing of boundaries and the breaking of taboos. Feminist film studies has paid much attention, for example, to the figure of the *femme fatale*, a woman who destroys the hero, and ultimately herself, with her monstrous desires. Crime cinema is concerned with the delineation of normality and perversion at the obvious level of narrative content. But the cinema is also concerned to explore the exciting and often sexualised border that it thus calls into being, articulating the heroism of the gangster and his tragic demise, the sleaziness of law enforcement and the horrors of feeling trapped by the law. The establishment and transgression of limits is the stuff of Hollywood cinema rather than an occasional by-product. Thus, a politicised understanding of the image and of narrative content, such as that offered by feminism, needs to be supplemented by a sense of the image at play within a narrative dynamic which produces the cinematic experience as sensuous, rather than simply cerebral.

In James Cameron's sequel, *Aliens*, Ripley is again both a vulnerable and a powerful figure. The tension between power and powerlessness, which is that generated by the law, is also explored and exploited in action/science-fiction films such as *RoboCop* and *Total Recall* which centre on men.

The body of the hero or heroine, though it may be damaged, represents almost the last certain territory of the action narrative. In *RoboCop* and *Total Recall* neither the body nor the mind is certain, both being subject to state control within a science-fiction dystopia. In *RoboCop* the figure of the cyborg plays off the metallic shell of the hero with its seeming invulnerability, against the glimpses of human flesh and the memories of a human past maintained beneath. *Total Recall* plays off the body of Schwarzenegger, famous as Mr Universe, within a narrative in which his mind has been stolen – again the hero finds himself powerless, mentally manipulated by a ruthless government agency. Similar problems of identity afflict Murphy/RoboCop, who has flashbacks of his former life, images which seem to be taken from home video since they are transmitted to us through his mechanical 'eyes'. Such images draw on the generic currency of conspiratorial science-fiction. When all else fails, the body of the hero, and not his voice, or his capacity to make a rational argument, is the place of last resort. That the body of the hero is the sole narrative space that is safe, that even this space is constantly under attack, is a theme repeatedly returned to within the action cinema.

In *Aliens* Ripley is positioned as out of place in a future world of which she knows little (she has been in hyper-sleep for fifty-seven years). Feeling like a 'fifth wheel' amongst the military team, Ripley boosts her status with the grunts by offering to take on a manual task at which she is proficient, donning a kind of mechanical skin – the loader, used to transport stores – which gives her a physical power that she is later to use in tackling the film's monstrous mother Alien. The sheer bulk of the loader gives Ripley physical stature. In this striking image the heroine directly enacts a fantasy of physical empowerment, one which is usually reserved for the hero. Her relative powerlessness, her physical vulnerability, is played with so that Weaver's femaleness additionally eroticises this fantasy of power through the transgression of gender boundaries. A much-reproduced publicity image of Weaver showed her clutching a child in one arm, weapon in another. In her confrontation with the alien the loader provides only partial protection as the monster extends its teeth inside its frame, snapping at Ripley's face.

The casting of women as the protagonists in the cop movie, the road movie, the science-fiction film and so on shifts and inflects the traditional vulnerability of the hero in such films. This is a set of genres, after all, in which the hero is constantly subject to physical violence. For women this physical vulnerability is easily mapped onto the sexualised violence of rape. The possibility of violent rape which threatens the action hero is generally only implied – though images of bodily penetration abound. Perhaps this serves to flesh out Ridley Scott's statement that *Thelma and Louise* is 'not about rape' but about 'choices and freedom'.[12] For a narrative centred on a female protagonist, rape offers one powerful way to articulate issues of freedom and choice. These issues are the substance of the road movie, as much as is the conflict between the responsibilities of home and family on the one hand, the delights of adventures and same-sex friendship on the other. Similarly, the maternal bond that is invoked in films such as *Aliens* and *Terminator 2* both strengthens and weakens the heroine in ways that draw on the complex history of 'woman' as a term within representation.

There is a whole range of determinants informing the production of the woman as action heroine in recent cinema. Her appearance can be seen to signal, amongst other factors, a response to feminism and the exhaustion of previous formulae. But as we have seen in relation to the problems which have surrounded the typecasting of Whoopi Goldberg as a black woman within Hollywood action pictures, images do not operate on some blank page but within cultural contexts which are crowded with competing images and stereotypes. The figure of the action hero is relentlessly pursued and punished, both mentally and physically. Beatings in back alleys and in boxing rings abound. The climactic moment of many action pictures is the final fight between the hero and the opponent who is physically stronger. The triumphal conquest over physical punishment is saturated with a different kind of coding when we are dealing with a heroine and the (almost always) already sexualised female body on the screen. Drawing on codes of chivalry, male violence against women has typically functioned within the Hollywood cinema as a signifier of evil. Feminism has proposed a rather different understanding of violence against women in relation to institutionalised male power, often expressed through metaphors of physical strength versus weakness. In thinking about women in the action film more specifically, we should consider that if women on the screen are excessively sexualised then so is the violence to which they are subject. This returns us to the frequent repetition of images and narratives associated with rape. The rape-revenge narrative is often used to provide a justification (since one is generally needed) for female violence in movies such as *I Spit on Your Grave*, *Ms 45/Angel of Vengeance* and the psychological thriller *Mortal Thoughts*. Seen against such a history, for the action heroine as much as the action hero, the development of muscles as a sort of body armour signifies physical vulnerability as well as strength.

8

THE CINEMA AS EXPERIENCE

Kathryn Bigelow and the cinema of spectacle

> Action movies have a capacity to be pure cinema, in that you can't recreate their kinetic, visual quality in any other medium.
>
> Kathryn Bigelow[1]

The American action cinema is defined by the spectacular visual display that it offers to its audiences, a display within which the body of the hero or heroine functions as a central term. In recent years the action cinema has generated a series of striking, and culturally resonant, visual images, from that of Rambo, which functioned as a metaphor for journalists and critics in the mid-1980s, to the diverse and challenging images of the action heroine seen in films like *Fatal Beauty* and *Terminator 2*. A stark image of Sigourney Weaver as Ripley, sporting military colours and a shaved head, has been widely used to advertise the third instalment in the saga, *Alien.*[3] The bulk of Arnold Schwarzenegger as the relentless cyborg in *The Terminator*, Sigourney Weaver in the metallic skin of the power loader in *Aliens*, the final image of *Thelma and Louise* when the screen fades to white after the women have driven their car into the Grand Canyon: these intense images allow the heroes and heroines to embody the themes of the action cinema. The dramas that are enacted over the bodies of both heroes and heroines work through the terms of power and powerlessness in a very physical sense. Though we may 'know', generically speaking, that the hero or heroine will survive the dangers of the narrative, we are also involved in a dynamic that encompasses both success and failure. The moments that are remembered, the images which an audience may take from from the cinematic experience, cannot be summed up within the terms of narrative resolution.

A criticism which focuses on the development of narrative at the expense of images is in many ways incompatible with an understanding of the cinema as fantasy, as sensuous experience. An example can be found in the critical tradition which read *Thelma and Louise* as a realist film, protesting that audiences were denied a final vision of the shattered bodies of its two heroines. Given the limitations of women's lives, the argument went, *Thelma and Louise* ought to have made clear to the audience the consequences of the heroines' actions, thus revealing the operation of patriarchal logic. Thus, in order to depict the reality of women's lives, the protagonists of this film should be definitely *seen* to be killed off. This same critical tradition has also characterised the repeated death of transgressive female figures, within the cinema, as symptomatic of patriarchal logic. As a fantasy which works through a drama about limits and transgression, however, *Thelma and Louise* operates within a different set of terms, which we might think of as utopian. In effect, a comic action film found itself judged by the standards of feminist documentary film-making, rather than those of the popular cinema. Positioning the film within the context of other contemporary narratives and images, for example, *Thelma and Louise*'s refusal to offer up the two women's dead bodies might be seen in contrast to the fetishistic use of the dead female body found in such films as *River's Edge* and *Barton Fink*, or in David Lynch's cult television series *Twin Peaks*.[2]

The products of popular cinema can rarely match up to the standards set by high culture – since they are operating within different institutional spaces, and often mobilising different aesthetic practices. For cultural critics to dismiss the products of the popular cinema, or to assert that its appeal is *obvious*, reveals little of its significance. In the rigorous decoding of what images mean politically, criticism can end up unable to speak about why these images still matter to audiences. The low critical esteem of the action cinema, indeed much of the popular cinema, can be attributed in part to the emphasis it places on spectacle over dialogue. An emphasis on the visual at the expense of the verbal in Stallone's 1989 prison drama, *Lock Up*, for example, creates a world of images through which to enact the film's intensified emotional drama, which concerns relationships between men. The body of the hero and the prison environment are rendered in dramatic lighting, bright and artificial or filtering through from the world outside, with rapid editing, extreme close-ups and long lingering shots. One reviewer smirked over Stallone's 'fatal fondness for naff montage', referring to the central section in which the cons fix up an old motor car, and the scene in which it is destroyed, both of which are rendered through music and montage.[3] It is only within the montage that prison buddies Leone (Stallone) and 'First Base' get to touch each other, playing goonish games and spraying each other with water or paint as they work on the car. It is tempting to suggest that such a sequence, which allows an intense, and sentimental, closeness between male buddies, is rendered within montage since gay desire must remain unspoken within Hollywood's world. Yet homoeroticism is central to the male action movie, and while gay desire may be unspoken within dialogue, it is very much present within the frame.[4] Indeed it is within the spaces offered by 'naff montage', and by looks exchanged between characters and so on, that the popular cinema orchestrates a variety of desires and looks. This particular example reveals a more general, and rather basic, point about the ways in which the popular cinema is a visual medium, one which uses images to tell stories, and to generate meanings.

It is also very clear though, that the play of ideologies is crucial in constructing the power of images. In the action cinema, as such diverse films as *Thelma and Louise*, *Fatal Beauty* and *Predator 2* show, the inclusion of those who have so often been excluded from the cinematic space – in that the audience's representatives on the action screen have tended to be white men – poses iconographic problems which are intimately related to ideology. A political analysis of both the ideological work, and the pleasures of the popular cinema, needs to avoid either the blanket dismissals that are so often made, or resort to what Valerie Walkerdine has called a 'populist defence of Hollywood' (Burgin *et al.* 1986: 196). If, as I argued earlier, blackness is both marginal and yet symbolically central to the action narrative, iconographic disturbances are involved in casting black performers at the centre of the action narrative. In responding to such an accumulated history of representation, film-makers have needed to experiment with the codes and conventions of the action genre. The failures and disappointments of a film like *Fatal Beauty* stem partly from a reluctance to experiment in such a way. The film-makers seem unsure of what to do with Whoopi Goldberg, so that she is often filmed in isolation from other characters, as if she was delivering a stage routine. By contrast, *Predator 2* works hard, and in complex ways, to produce Danny Glover as a black action hero. The film both draws on, modifies and to an extent reproduces, a stereotypical history of representations of blackness. In related ways, *Thelma and Louise* appropriates and redefines, for its female protagonists, the themes and form of the road movie and the buddy movie – two forms that are most familiar as a showcase for male friendship.

In this final chapter, an analysis of three films by Kathryn Bigelow, *Near Dark* (1987), *Blue Steel* (1990) and *Point Break* (1991), serves to bring together some key themes of the action cinema. I have already referred to *Blue Steel* at various points, a film whose 'gun-toting' heroine caused some controversy amongst feminist critics. Bigelow's work provides a useful point of reference for thinking about the visual aspects of the action cinema, since her work as a director is most often described as 'painterly'. These three films work through a series of striking visual images. They also reveal an acute sense of the operation of genre, complexly drawing on and redefining the horror genre, the cop thriller and the buddy action movie.

NEAR DARK AND THE 'UNCANNY'

In his essay on the uncanny, Freud comments on the distinctive operation of art and literature as a realm for the production and experience of uncanny effects. Comparing the space of fiction and fantasy to that of 'real life', he suggests that:

> the realm of phantasy depends for its effect on the fact that its content is not submitted to reality-testing. The somewhat paradoxical result is that *in the first place a great deal that is not uncanny in fiction would be so if it happened in real life; and in the second place that there are many more ways of creating uncanny effects in fiction than there are in real life*.
>
> (Freud 1919: 373; original emphases)

To extend the point, fiction, indeed art of all kinds, operates as a space for the play of fantasy, uncanny effects, comedy and other emotions. That this space is not usefully judged by the same standards as 'reality' or experienced in the same way, becomes significant when thinking about popular cinema as a space of fantasy – as in the case of *Thelma and Louise*, cited above.[5] Part of the stock in trade of narrative representations, a feature which is characteristic of many forms of both high art and popular culture, is the revelation of perversity behind a supposed normality. Such revelations may be dramatic or relatively banal, simply observing the deceptive nature of appearances. From the ambiguity necessary to sustain some kind of suspense, to complex psychological narratives of doubles and identity, this commonplace narrative device provides a way into thinking about the politics of representation in terms of the construction and dissolution of categories for identification within the cinema.

Many American horror narratives have centred around the portrayal of a perverse, often flesh-eating, family. The shock of such images plays off a contrast between the cosy connotations of home and family, and the nightmare images of cannibalism and destruction found in such films. This type of narrative also typically draws on a tension between the diverse meanings of the family within representation, as a safe, but also monstrous, restrictive space. As in *Near Dark*, Kathryn Bigelow's stylish vampire film set in the American mid-West, a common strategy of the horror narrative is a kind of doubling, in which monstrous characters or creatures echo and parody the heroes and heroines with which we are called on to identify. Thus in *Near Dark* the motherless hero Caleb finds himself involved with a perverse vampire family, which is at the same time more complete than his own, providing him with two 'mothers' – Mae who feeds him blood from her own veins to nourish him, and Silverback (Jenette Goldstein) who is referred to as 'Mother' at several points through the film. When Caleb is abducted by the vampire family, his own family are seen through the rear window of a camper-van, receding into the distance as one set of blood ties are abandoned for another. There is an acute sense of the play of genre in the film as a whole, and in the characterisation of the vampire family. Bigelow has said of her films that:

> I'm interested in playing with genre, mixing it up a bit to create a hybrid. *Near Dark* is a sort of vampire Western, and *The Loveless* is sort of biker-*noir*. It enables you to invest the genre with new material, seeing where the edges of the envelope are, so to speak.[6]

The all-American cowboy image of youth culture, invoked by Caleb in *Near Dark*, is played off against the post-apocalyptic look of the vampires. The tradition of the western is brought together with the more contemporary reference of Severen's biker gear, the traditionally European vampire situated firmly within an American landscape. The vampire family is constituted through recognisable types that are rendered disturbing. The figure of Homer is, for example, styled as the fusion of an old man and a young boy's body. Adult and childish desires are brought together, to disturbing effect.

One of the film's central scenes concerns a meeting between Caleb's two 'families'. Caleb appeals for the safety of his father and little sister, saying 'They're my family'. This scene follows directly on from the creepy masquerade which the vampires conduct in order to fool Caleb's sister, Sarah. They mimic the behaviour of an archetypal television family, Homer shifting from his adult to his child persona, shy in his introduction of Sarah to the rest of the group, Silverback reprimanding him in a motherly fashion. There is a play here around the ways in which we are encouraged to read off character traits and qualities from physical appearance. The shock of the image stems partly from a recognition of the conventional, or cultural, aspects of our knowledge about the world, the movie world in particular. The mock family appears 'uncanny' in this scene precisely because they are so recognisable – they offer an unsettling masquerade of those 'family values' with which movie audiences are familiar. Such an uncanny effect is distinct from the feelings of revulsion which the images of blood-letting and physical destruction in *Near Dark* might induce, images which the film accompanies by the sort of reassuring black comedy provided by Severen's one-liners, visual puns and so on. Indeed, the specificity of the uncanny stems from the chill recognition of something perceived as quite other, since 'the uncanny is that class of the frightening which leads back to what is known of old and long familiar' (Freud 1919: 340). The kind of doubling devices, of the two families, of Caleb's vampiric and cowboy persona, of Homer as an adult–child, that are at work in *Near Dark*, are identified by Freud as a key device associated with the uncanny in fiction. We return to the figure of the double in both *Blue Steel* and *Point Break*. Briefly though, the double functions to draw attention to the similarity between *two apparently different*, even opposed, characters or terms within a fiction. In this process, the instability of supposedly secure categories of classification becomes absolutely central.

Further exemplifying this instability of categories, Freud's analysis of the 'uncanny' begins with a lengthy etymological exposition of the relationship between two German words, *heimlich* (homely) and *unheimlich* (the uncanny). At a certain point in the uses of the word *heimlich*, which connotes homely, cosy, familiar, known qualities, the meaning of the term bizarrely shifts, acquiring the connotations of its opposite! But, as Freud points out, this is not an inversion. Rather, some too familiar qualities have become the subject of repression, so that their very sense of familiarity renders these qualities uncanny. Thus:

> the word *heimlich* is not unambiguous . . . on the one hand it means what is familiar and agreeable, and on the other, what is concealed and kept out of sight. [. . .] Thus *heimlich* is a word the meaning of which develops in the direction of ambivalence, until it finally coincides with its opposite, *unheimlich. Unheimlich* is in some way or other a sub-species of *heimlich*.
>
> (ibid.: 345–7)

Freud further develops his analysis of the uncanny in relationship to the deployment of the familiar device of doubling – the *doppelgänger* – in horror and uncanny fiction. This device is seen as initially stemming from primary narcissism functioning as, in effect, a doubling of the ego which guards against death.[7] Though the double may begin as a narcissistic assertion of self, it is ultimately, through repression, transformed into a site of negative qualities. This type of narcissism, the reinforcement of identity through the production of a double with which to identify, bears a close relationship to the narcissism we have seen at work in our relationship to the cinematic image. Yet the double here is also a potentially troubling figure who, in various fictions, comes to threaten the hero's identity.[8] In *Near Dark* Caleb loses and finds himself once more. The exchanges of blood between Caleb, Mae and Caleb's father – it is through blood transfusions that the two are rescued from their vampiric existence – signify both the instability and the reassertion of bodily boundaries. Both the device of the double and the instance of the *heimlich–unheimlich* relation evidence the close relationship between terms, within language, fiction and fantasy, that seem to be opposed. The operation of this kind of narrative dynamic within all kinds of fictions is indicative of the repeated establishment and erasure of the boundaries between supposedly clear categories of classification, processes central to the pleasures of the popular cinema.

BLUE STEEL AND WOMEN IN THE ACTION PICTURE

The psychological thriller *Blue Steel* positions rookie cop Megan Turner (Jamie Lee Curtis) at the centre of the police narrative. When Turner shoots a robber at a grocery store, she is suspended on her first night out, forced to hand over the badge and gun that she has only just acquired. No gun is found at the scene, and while we have seen Eugene Hunt (Ron Silver) take the gun used in the hold-up, the police investigators assume that Turner was at fault, that she has killed an unarmed man. Eugene becomes obsessed with Turner, carving her name on the bullets he uses to kill people on the street. He further contrives to meet Megan and they develop a relationship. Turner's usefulness as a *victim* leads to her re-instatement on the force, as a detective-cum-decoy. *Blue Steel* does not shy away from an exploration of the sexualised aspects of the position of women in the action picture. Deploying an elaborate weapons fetish, the film puts into play a conventional set of associations between guns and images of a specifically masculine power. Bigelow comments that for her 'films are most successful when they're provocative, when they challenge your thinking'. What some critics found disturbing was the fact that *Blue Steel* not only explores the relationship between sexuality, gender and the imagery surrounding guns in the Hollywood cinema, but that the film takes an obvious pleasure in the images that this generates. Thus, the disturbing implications of a fetishism surrounding women and guns are drawn out, at the same time as we are invited to share in it.

The credit sequence plays soft, ghostly music over images that move slowly in close-up around a police handgun, emphasising the different textures of the metal, the bullets and the grip. After the gun is slipped into her holster we see fragmented images of Megan Turner dressing in her police uniform of blue shirt over lacy bra, patent lace-up shoes, black tie, white gloves and a shiny cap. A close-up of Turner's face looks straight at us. She adjusts her cap and smiles – possibly at a mirror, though we don't see one, possibly at us, possibly to herself. After the graduating ceremony, during which massed ranks of uniformed figures officially become cops, a brief musical sequence shows Turner strutting down the street in her uniform. She is grinning and swaggering as two women, who have just walked past her, turn back to look in admiration. As she goes up the steps to her building a neighbour is taken back by her appearance, saying 'look at you – you look . . .', though he doesn't quite have the words to describe quite what it is that she looks like. There is a strong sense of change here – Turner has acquired a confident control of space through the act of dressing up. This sequence, of Turner dressing in her police uniform, is reprised at the end of the film. Though she has been raped by Eugene and hospitalised by the cops, Turner refuses to be rendered passive, knocking out a male uniformed cop, stealing his clothes and going after Eugene to finally dispatch him in a surreal shoot-out sequence.

In the film's pre-credit sequence we follow Turner/Curtis, gun drawn, through a corridor which resounds with the sounds of a violent domestic quarrel. This incident of domestic violence turns out to be a training exercise for Turner, an exercise in which she fails. She shoots the 'husband' but the 'wife' shoots her. 'In the field, you've gotta have eyes in the back of your head' the instructor tells Turner. More significantly in terms of the film's repertoire of images of women-with-guns, the figure of the 'wife' cannot be relied upon to play the part that Turner expects of her in the domestic scenario – someone who wants her help. Indeed, *Blue Steel* might be said to enact a conventional scenario which punishes the female character's transgressive desire to become a powerful figure. Some critics saw the film as conservative in this way, and *Blue Steel* certainly attempts to be unsettling in its uncovering of Turner's complex involvement in the weapons fetishism in which both Eugene and the film indulges. However, this interpretation of the film neglects the very power of the images it puts to work, and the pleasures those images of transgression may offer to us, pleasures to which the film itself rather self-consciously draws our attention.

Within the pared-down narrative world of *Blue Steel*, Turner is an isolated figure. Interrogated as to who could be killing in her name she insists that she doesn't know *anybody*, listing 'my mum, my dad, my friend Tracy, her husband John' as the extent of her social world. *Blue Steel* knits together a family drama with its police drama. The story of Megan's relationship with her mother and father is juxtaposed with her conflict with Eugene and with the police department. These narratives and relationships are brought together around the enigma of Megan Turner as a woman-in-uniform-with-a-gun. Her image and her role as policewoman make Turner the object of admiration, surprise, shock and disgust. These emotions and responses, presented so forcefully in the film, were replicated in critical reactions to *Blue Steel* and its subject matter. At various points in the film, characters comment on and inquire about Turner's decision to become a cop. After the graduation ceremony, she embraces her best friend Tracy who is the first to say 'I can't believe it – you're a fucking cop. You're on the right side of the law'. Megan smiles when asked how it feels, saying 'like I need a cigarette'. Megan's father, by way of contrast, will hardly speak to her, spitting out 'I've got a goddamn cop for a daughter'. Similarly, interviews with director Kathryn Bigelow repeatedly inquire as to *why* a woman is directing action pictures. Bigelow, like Turner, is often called on to explain herself.[9]

The question of Megan's motivation recurs repeatedly in *Blue Steel*. Her desire to play with the signifiers of power distances her from her family and from the 'normal' social world of marriage and family. Instead, she attracts the attentions of the psychopathic Eugene. On her first night out as a cop, Megan is asked why she is there at all. She gives a jokey answer that she always 'wanted to shoot people' though her partner isn't sure whether she's joking or not, particularly since she promptly shoots and kills a man holding-up a grocery store. Later she tells a credulous guy, who her friend Tracy has set her up with, that she likes to 'slam people's faces up against the wall'. Finally when Detective Nick Mann asks her 'why' once more, while they are on a stake-out together, she simply murmurs 'him', an ambiguous and open response which could refer to a range of characters or qualities within the world of the film. This ambiguous reference to a 'him' motivating Megan, represents a distinctive inflection of the series of dead, or threatened, women who function as motivation for the hero's alienated quest in so many action pictures. The repeated questioning of Megan's motivation serves to emphasise the generic unease of her position. Her desires are placed alongside Eugene's fantasies, in which he imagines that they are the same. Pam Cook describes *Blue Steel* as an exploration of 'a spectrum of emotions generated by gun worship, from Megan's desire for justice to Eugene's fantasies of omnipotence' (*Monthly Film Bulletin* vol. 58, 1991: 312). Megan's desire for justice is also, though, bound up in her own fantasies of omnipotence. As discussed in earlier chapters, a play around such fantasies of empowerment can be identified as one of the key pleasures offered by the action cinema.

Megan's final appeal to 'him', as a justification for her decision to become a cop, operates with reference to the men in the film, her father in particular, but also through them to a generalised 'him', a figure or a place of power to which she aspires. *Blue Steel* draws on the device of the 'double', in order to problematise those fantasies of omnipotence, drawing the parallels between Megan and Eugene that will ultimately lead to their final confrontation. Megan's father is a pivotal figure, linking the domestic and the police dramas, the familial space and the space of the law. His violence towards her mother further links Megan's father to the first sequence of the film, with its set-up images of domestic violence, a set-up which deceives Megan. A central confrontation comes when Megan finally attempts to take control of this situation, actually arresting her father. She cuffs him and bundles him into the car, though when his disbelieving laughter turns to tears as Megan *asks him* 'why', she cannot go through with it.

The problems and the pleasures of *Blue Steel* lie with the instability of Megan's position of power. As Pam Cook puts it, Megan's gun, both 'endows her with power, yet simultaneously transforms her into a fetish object'. There is no doubt though, that the film-makers are aware of this, attempting to both use and explore this fetishism. Whilst there is a specificity to this film's use of the woman as cop, particularly in its playful use of a popularised psychoanalysis, Megan is situated generically, put in a similar position to the heroes and heroines of other action narratives. The suffering that the body of the white male hero is subject to in the action picture is rewritten for a female protagonist in *Blue Steel*. As *Thelma and Louise* was to do, the film employs the ideological figure of rape to signify the violation that the central character undergoes. But the film also makes use of the boyish aspects of Curtis's star image to transgress the boundaries of sex/gender that it has to work within. Indeed the use made of Curtis's androgynous image in *Blue Steel* – the self-conscious play with guns as signifiers of masculinity and phallic power, her being dressed in a man's uniform for the final shoot-out – serves to explicitly sexualise the type of 'masculinised' female body found in many contemporary action pictures. More disturbing in this context is the film's use of grotesque anti-semitic stereotypes around the figure of Eugene, a figure against whom Megan's authority can then be defined.

POINT BREAK, MASCULINE IDENTITIES AND MALE BONDING

Point Break is a spectacular surfing movie, centring on the tense and powerful relationship that develops between FBI agent Johnny Utah (Keanu Reeves) and the charismatic leader of a group of surfing bank robbers, Bodhi (Patrick Swayze). The film brings together action, comedy and an exploration of the sexualised relationship between the two protagonists: all aspects familiar from the Hollywood buddy movie format. Like *Predator 2*, *Point Break* conducts itself at a hectic pace, with breathtaking underwater and ariel photography for the surfing and skydiving sequences. A hectic chase sequence has the camera following close-in on Johnny Utah's heady pursuit of Bodhi through a series of suburban houses, yards and alleys. Finally Utah fires his gun into the air rather than kill Bodhi, a recognition of the extent of their closeness. *Point Break* also has fun with the sillier aspects of its narrative construction, echoing the chaotic, laid-back Californian surfing philosophy espoused by Bodhi. Utah and the older FBI man Pappas (Gary Busey) with whom he is teamed, are set to investigate a series of bank robberies committed by a gang calling themselves the ex-presidents. Wearing smart suits and face-masks of LBJ, Nixon, Carter and Reagan, the gang conduct lightning bank raids, always eluding capture. Pappas is convinced that the gang are surfers since not only do the robberies coincide with the surf season, but a surveillance video of one of the bank raids shows one of the ex-presidents dropping his pants to the camera, an image that reveals a distinctive tan-line. Utah goes undercover as a surfer, getting bound up in the pleasures of the adrenalin-thrills sought and worshipped by the surfers who surround Bodhi. Utah's way into Bodhi's world is through his involvement with a boyish young woman, Tyler, who first teaches him how to surf.

Like Clarice Starling in *The Silence of the Lambs* Johnny Utah is a rookie FBI agent out to make a reputation for himself. The similarity between the two characters ends there, since they are both cast in very different terms. Starling's desperate struggle for acceptance as a woman within the FBI – her ambition – is remarked upon by serial killer and therapist, Dr

Hannibal Lecter, on their very first meeting. This intense, and thwarted, ambition marks Starling out as a very different protagonist from the easy-mannered Johnny Utah in Bigelow's film – a 'hot shot' who is deliberately surly with his FBI superior. *Point Break* is also very much concerned with different images of masculinity, diverse masculine identities. The psychological challenge that develops between Bodhi and Utah infuriates Tyler, who walks off in disgust at one point, commenting on the excess of testosterone at work. As do many action pictures already discussed, *Point Break* delights in the bodies of its male protagonists. Bigelow has described the film as a sort of 'wet western', a phrase which indicates a distinctive, and very contemporary, combination. Themes and images drawn from the male contests of classic westerns of the past, which are also noticeably put to work in *Near Dark*'s invocation of cowboy and mid-Western references, are intertwined with the need for contemporary films to present their heroes either nearly naked, or in a series of clinging costumes that display the body. The context of the surfing movie then, provides an ideal situation for the production of the body in action as visual display. Shifts in masculine identities and definitions of maleness that are articulated in the cinema, shifts which, as I argued earlier, have evolved partly through the commodification of the male body, are evident in a film like *Point Break*, which makes the most of the pin-up good looks of its stars. Bigelow argues that *Point Break* isn't a surfing movie since the 'surfing is a state of mind, a metaphor for something else. This is about personal challenge and a flirtation with death'.[10] These comments are indicative of the extent to which the spectacle of physicality offered in the surfing sequences drives the narrative onwards, as much as the surfing also clearly serves to showcase the star bodies that were one of the film's major selling points.

In Utah's pursuit of the ex-presidents, the male body becomes a central term. It is on seeing one of the surfers drop his pants that Utah, matching tan-lines with the image on the bank's surveillance video, realises that the ex-presidents are also his surfing buddies. That a surfer's ass is the only real clue Utah ever manages to come up with is indicative, not only of the rather chaotic narrative structure of *Point Break*, but also of the maverick way in which the film addresses its concerns of physicality and the spectacle of masculinity. Rather than being centred on any traditional detection or investigation, the film is visually given over to the spectacle of the male body engaged in physical feats such as surfing and skydiving. An investigative narrative evolves through Bodhi and Utah's exploration of each other. In this drama of 'doubles', in which Utah and Bodhi recognise themselves in each other, a sexualised competition between the two men takes them, literally, to new heights. The pleasures and the perils of this competition are inseparable from the film's spectacular action sequences. For instance, Utah pursues Bodhi by jumping out of a plane with no parachute. He lands on Bodhi's back and the two descend together, echoing their earlier jump through which they clutched hands. Partly through its use of breathtaking cinematic devices, *Point Break* seeks to involve the audience in its emotional drama and to bring out some of the more sinister aspects of the male-bonding narratives on which it draws. The ex-presidents' bank raids, initially a source of humour and excitement in the film, turn into a deadly game for the protagonists, ultimately resulting in Pappas's death. Similarly, the surfing and skydiving, which function as shared pleasurable experiences at first, become life-threatening for the characters as the film progresses. The final confrontation between Utah and Bodhi does not come until the film's epilogue, a relatively downbeat sequence set some months later, in a downpour on a windswept Australian beach where Bodhi has gone to find the ultimate wave. Utah agrees to Bodhi's final request, letting him walk into the sea for one final surfing experience.

One reviewer mournfully asserted that, with *Point Break*, Bigelow had 'stepped aside from the fascinatingly ambiguous feminism of *Blue Steel* to deliver a dose of macho claptrap such as to leave John Milius and Walter Hill pale with envy' (*Sight and Sound*, December 1991: 48). As with many of the other action movies discussed through the course of this book, it seems rather too simplistic to designate the operation of the male buddy movie as 'macho claptrap', though ideas of the 'macho' form part of its subject. In particular, *Point Break* draws out the implications of Utah and Bodhi's flirtation with death, which is intimately bound up with their flirtation with each other, a relationship in which the woman, Tyler, represents a token object of exchange. This exchange is also revealed to be bound up with danger, as Tyler is almost killed – caught between the two men's struggle with each other. We are invited to experience the exhilaration that the spectacle produces, but also to see its implications, as in *Blue Steel*. In an interview given to publicise the film, Patrick Swayze contrasted *Point Break* to other buddy movies, saying '[R]arely do you get a film about two guys . . . that isn't just slap-ass, macho, jokey crap. And the dynamics were very interesting because I wanted to play it like a love story between two men', which is exactly how it does play.[11]

Swayze's star image and movie successes have been largely constructed within the very different terms of the romance and the action movie, with *Point Break* bringing the two modes together. His persona draws on a series of negotiations conducted around notions of a 'sensitive' style of masculine identity, and routed through a vague hippy, or New Age spiritualism. His physical grace as a dancer, as well as his physical strength as a fighter, is emphasised in his action movies. Swayze's body, his physicality, is equally central to romantic roles, as in *Dirty Dancing* and the hugely successful *Ghost* (1991). One enthusiastic feature writer suggested that such roles, taken from genres that are often opposed along gendered lines, represent Swayze's own polarised persona. In this way, it is suggested that 'the Texas-born star has managed to exorcise the two extreme sides of his personality – the sensitive romantic ballet dancer and the rough, thrill-seeking cowhand – through his movies'.[12] If this characterisation of Swayze is reminiscent of the distinction between 'new man' and 'action man' discussed earlier, it is clear that, while both types are written through gender and defined by the body, they cannot be understood within a simple gendered *binary* that opposes female/feminine to male/masculine. This serves to remind us that the meaning of the body on the screen is not secure, but shifting, inscribed with meaning in different ways at different points.

SPECTACULAR BODIES: REPRESENTATION, IDENTITY AND IDENTIFICATION

The meanings of the different bodies displayed, paraded and commodified in the contemporary action cinema are complex. The images that the form has generated are very far from being the transparent signifiers of a simplistic sexual and racial hierarchy that some critics take them to be. As Judith Butler has argued, the body 'is not a "being", but a variable boundary, a surface whose permeability is politically regulated, a signifying practice within a cultural field of gender hierarchy and compulsory heterosexuality' (Butler 1990: 139). Identities are constituted through identification, and not essence, a process which Freud's model of the development of sexual identity allows for, though he unhelpfully limits the identifications made to the rather restricted range of the immediate family. The examination of processes of identification and the constitution of identities, which take place across a far broader set of cultural spaces than the family, demonstrates the extent to which identifications are made across such supposedly secure, and essentialised, categories as sexuality, sex, gender and race. Recent work by writers such as Judith Butler, Diana Fuss, Kobena Mercer and Eve Sedgwick, amongst others, has emphasised the provisional nature of the identifications through which different identities are constructed. Similarly the ideas and images and ideas generated by film-makers such as Isaac Julien in the independent sector, or Kathryn Bigelow in the mainstream sector, have provided an evolving context in which to speak about and develop the arguments presented here.

In the constitution of identity through complex, shifting, identifications, the popular cinema forms one space in which identities can be affirmed, dissolved and redefined within a fantasy space. This space affirms a range of identities at the same time as it mobilises identifications and desires which undermine the stability of such categories. It would be a negation of the operation of power either to argue that all audiences are free to make any identifications they wish, or to ignore the significance of political affiliations constituted out of such identifications as 'sex', 'object choice' or 'race'.[13] This book has attempted to discuss some of the specificities involved in the ways in which the action cinema, centred over the body as it is, orchestrates ideologies and identification. My argument that the range of images and experiences on offer within this form, which have been characterised by many critics and commentators as both *simple* and *obvious*, are both rich and ambiguous, stems from a desire to think about, rather than dismiss, or pathologise, the pleasures of the popular cinema. As the editors of a recent collection of writings on the work of nationalisms and sexualities have pointed out, while 'it is the lived crises endured by national and sexual bodies that form our most urgent priorities':

> These crises are not simply opportunities for the state to activate its strategies of containment and to reimpose its normativities. They also offer dissenting subjects the possibility of producing contestory practices, narratives of resistance that may reconfigure the horizons of what counts globally today as 'the political'.
>
> (Parker *et al.* 1992: 13–14)

In such a way, to construct the popular cinema as little more than the space for the operation of dominant ideologies, as an industry geared to the production of 'dumb movies for dumb people', is to critically erase the activities, identifications and desires of many audiences. If the narratives and images of the popular action cinema rarely address the specificity of particular struggles, they nonetheless powerfully dramatise the fact of struggle. These narratives of power and powerlessness, exclusion and belonging, are elaborately performed through the spectacular bodies of the action cinema.

NOTES

INTRODUCTION: Gender and the action cinema

1 Joseph Bristow (1988), for example, discusses the fragmentation and questioning of masculine and racial identity at work in popular forms such as music and music video.
2 Richard Dyer's work on the Italian 'peplum' situates these films within their national and historical context of Italy in the 1950s. See Dyer's article in Stecopoulos and Uebel (forthcoming).
3 A brief summary of the movie careers of several African-American sports stars is given in Bogle (1991: 243–5).
4 See Laurie Schulze in Gaines and Herzog (1990) for a discussion of the newly acquired cultural 'acceptability' of female bodybuilding. The drive for such acceptance is clearly part of the project informing George Butler's film *Pumping Iron II: The Women*. The original film, produced in the 1970s and starring Arnold Schwarzenegger, had done much to shift the image of male bodybuilders from the margins into the mainstream.
5 See Willemen (1981), Dyer (1982) and Neale (1983). Both Dyer and Neale usefully discuss the negotiations involved in the sexual commodification of the male body.
6 Linda Hamilton has also achieved a straight following within the cultish world of science-fiction fans. See the tone of letters published in the science-fiction film magazine *Starburst*, which idolise the Hamilton persona, often in an explicitly fetishistic fashion.
7 My discussion does not address recent black urban action films such as *New Jack City* (1991). These films represent a distinct development of blaxsploitation crime cinema which, while providing a space for black actors and directors, nonetheless still operates within a framework which draws on the ideological links forged within Hollywood between images of blackness, criminality and drugs.
8 See my 'Fists of Fury: Discourses of Race and Masculinity', in Stecopoulos and Uebel (forthcoming).
9 There is a great deal of valuable literature which deals with women readers' engagement with romance fiction in particular, and I do not want to suggest that this work is invalid. Contributions to the field such as Janice Radway (1987) offer a fascinating analysis of the pleasures available to readers of romance fiction. More problematic, though, is the widespread notion that romance readers should be weaned off their pleasures and onto something more politically acceptable.

10 See my 'Dumb Movies for Dumb People: Masculinity, The Body and the Voice in the Contemporary Action Cinema', in Cohen and Hark (1993).

11 I have explored this specifically in relation to feminist criticism in an essay in Lury, Franklin and Stacey (1991). This is not, however, a tendency that is limited to feminist analyses.

12 In Laura Mulvey's oft-cited article, 'Visual Pleasure and Narrative Cinema' (Mulvey 1989) it is the political implications of the aesthetics of mainstream cinema that she seeks to tease out. Whilst such a project is fraught with difficulties, it is also fundamental to a political analysis of culture.

In terms of an analysis of entertainment, Richard Dyer's 'Entertainment and Utopia' (1977) offers a valuable understanding of the sensibilities and the emotions, rather than any explicit political solutions, that are on offer in the popular cinema.

13 A projected fourth film in the Rambo series has been the subject of speculation in various interviews with Stallone, though it has not, as yet, taken any more material form.

14 Duncan Webster (1988) discusses the complex confluence of factors involved in Reagan's success. It is important to note that the young male audience for *Rambo*, an audience of which many commentators spoke, was largely assumed.

15 Leslie Fiedler (1990) discusses three films in this article: *The Deer Hunter*, *Apocalypse Now* and *Rambo*.

16 See Barbara Creed (1987) for a discussion which locates the figure of the muscleman star in relation to feminism and postmodernity. This essay is taken up further in later chapters.

17 See Martin Barker (1984). Horror cinema has repeatedly been the target of 'moral panics', orchestrated campaigns by the national press and groups such as the National Viewers' and Listeners' Association who have argued that children could be contaminated by horror material.

18 Duncan Webster (1989) has produced a detailed analysis of the complex, contradictory, and panic-stricken responses that the British press made to the film *Rambo*.

19 Richard Dyer (1982) talks of the 'strain' inherent in male pin-ups, a quality he also identifies as a central element in western definitions of masculinity.

20 Rosalind Coward (1984), Gaines and Herzog (1990) and Epstein and Straub (1991) offer a variety of useful essays on the cultural and sexual politics surrounding the body, sexuality and fashion.

21 Laurie Schulze discusses the specificity of female bodybuilding, as distinct from forms like aerobics, in Gaines and Herzog (1990).

22 For a brief discussion of Cindy Sherman's work and images of women see Judith Williamson (1983). The incorporation of images from popular culture into forms usually associated with high art represents one of the most discussed aspects of a postmodern visual culture. A pertinent example is Su Friedrich's 1987 film, *Damned If You Don't*, which includes a commentary on the British film *Black Narcissus*, a commentary that rewrites that narrative in the process. The film both takes pleasure in and criticises the popular images that it works with.

23 Madonna has generated extensive commentaries from feminist and other writers, with furious debates taking place in feminist magazines like *Spare Rib*. For an analysis of the differing forms of address at work in a range of women's magazines see Janice Winship (1987).

1 WOMEN WARRIORS: Gender, sexuality and Hollywood's fighting heroines

1 Star marriages and relationships are food for the publicity machine that both feeds off and supports the star system. When Stallone and Nielson were married and divorced, he was at the height of his box-office success. Pictures of the two working out together regularly appeared in movie, women's, bodybuilding and gossip magazines, a process that raised Nielson's profile immeasurably.

2 The images used to publicise *Alien*³ feature Ripley with shaved head, in an image which develops the already rather butch aspects of her persona in the first two films.

3 Several of the essays in Kuhn (1990) discuss *Alien* in some detail.

4 The configurations worked out here are discussed further in later chapters. See also my essay in Stecopoulos and Uebel (forthcoming). A comic, but accurate, commentary on Van Damme's films is found in an interview feature in the March 1992 issue of *The Face*.

5 See Mulvey (1989: 20).

6 Mulvey (ibid.: 32) discusses this legend in terms of the positioning of the spectator within a specifically gendered narrative logic.

7 Klaus Theweleit (1987) offers a well-known account of images of the male body as armour within the warrior rhetoric of military culture, though he tends towards a pathologisation of the processes through which identity is formed through the designation of bodily boundaries. The work of anthropologist Mary Douglas in *Natural Symbols* (1970) and *Purity and Danger* (1972) provides an interesting counterpoint in this instance.

8 Charlotte Brunsdon (1982) offers a discussion of such films in terms of Hollywood's response to the women's movement. See also Tessa Perkins's discussion of the shifting radical aspects of Jane Fonda's star image in Gledhill (1991).

9 Julie D'Acci provides an extensive discussion of *Cagney and Lacey*'s production history in Baehr and Dyer (1987).

The pilot movie was made in 1980 with Tyne Daley and Lorretta Swit. A TV series was finally commissioned by CBS in 1982.

10 For a discussion of *I Spit on Your Grave* as a rape/revenge movie see Barker (1984). Movies dealing with these themes often, perhaps indicatively, shade into the horror genre. For a fascinating discussion of the woman as avenger in the horror film see Carol Clover's essay in Donald (1989).

11 The sexual threat that is posed to the protagonist of the action narrative is much more heavily veiled in relation to men. The repeated narrative device of the western hero who seeks to avenge a father or brother, who has been shot dishonourably 'in the back' can be interpreted in terms of such sexualised fears.

12 Paul Verhoeven's *Basic Instinct* has generated a huge controversy amongst gay activists in America due to its casting of a 'lesbian' villain. Whilst the protests undoubtedly provided a rallying point, the perversity and ambiguities of the central character were neglected in the protests about positive and negative images.

13 The event was a women-only 'Easter Chicks and Bunny Girls' evening at the Scala Cinema in London (Easter 1992). The adverts for this event offered 'Lesbian Films including *Thelma and Louise* and *Blonde Fist*'.

14 In the context of sexual politics, the use of a term like 'perverse' is always problematic. The term is not used here in a judgemental sense, but to indicate

a turning away from the father, a refusal of the 'normal' development of (hetero)sexuality and the restrictive roles that it involves.

15 I am thinking here of, for example, Dick Hebdige's (1979) work on youth culture. Critical work around camp also stresses the appropriation of popular cultural images for and by a group excluded from representation, as in Medhurst (1990). See also Richard Dyer's comments on the significance of the star and the possibilities of reading in 'Resistance through Charisma' in Kaplan (1980) as well as his discussion of Judy Garland and gay male audiences in *Heavenly Bodies* (1987).

16 See Kobena Mercer on the fetishistic representation of the black male body in Bad Object Choices (1991).

17 Mary Ann Doane expands on the significance of this point for a feminist film criticism which seems to assume whiteness. Referring to bell hooks's work, she notes that 'there is no other of the black woman' (1991: 231). Whilst this schema has some explanatory purchase, it nonetheless retains categories of 'race' and 'sex' as essence and as unambiguous. By contrast, the value of Doane's essay more generally lies in the recognition that 'race' cannot simply be added to the agenda of feminist film criticism, but must inevitably challenge that agenda. If the (black) woman does not exist, black women do.

2 BLACK BUDDIES AND WHITE HEROES: Racial discourse in the action cinema

1 Mercer locates the ambivalence surrounding Mapplethorpe's black nudes through a potentially 'subversive deconstruction of the hidden racial and gendered axioms of the nude in dominant traditions of representation' (Bad Object Choices 1991: 181).

2 Western constructions of Asian masculinity emerge from a complex, and distinct, history. In terms of the action cinema, a discussion of dominant articulations of Asian masculinity needs to be situated alongside the huge Hong Kong action movie industry. My essay in Stecopoulos and Uebel (forthcoming) discusses the figure of Bruce Lee in this context. Richard Fung, in Bad Object Choices (1991), discusses images of Asian men within the world of gay pornography and the western-centred fantasies at work. See also King-Kok Cheung's discussion of gendered identity in the Chinese-American community in Hirsch and Keller (1990).

Perhaps more significant in the American context is the current emergence of a set of anxieties around American masculinity and the relationship to Japan, anxieties seen in a film like *Showdown in Little Tokyo*. See Dave Morley and Kevin Robins (1992) for a discussion of current American fears around 'Japan'.

3 *Predator 2*, whilst a box-office disappointment at the cinema, is having a success, like Bruce Willis's *Hudson Hawk*, through the video market.

4 For a brief discussion of *Starsky and Hutch* within the context of the development of the crime series, see David Buxton (1989).

5 See Andrew Ross (1986) and Scott Benjamin King (1990) for a discussion of masculinity, sexual spectacle and *Miami Vice*. The show, and the critical debates in which it has figured, is discussed further in Chapter 6.

6 Donald Bogle (1991) and Daniel J. Leab (1975) provide some commentary on these films within surveys of black American cinema. At a more general cultural level, *Time* magazine reported on a new visibility for black female models during the early 1970s. The terms within which this visibility operated remained very much those of the 'exotic' woman (*Time*, 16 July 1973).

7 Kobena Mercer draws on the work of Fanon to describe the fantasies of black sexuality as excess at work in western imagery and colonial culture. Fetishism functions as a key term in the analysis, indicating the processes of disavowal at work in such images (in Bad Object Choices 1991: 177).
8 In his essay 'The Uncanny' (1914) Freud discusses Hoffman's tale of 'The Sandman', in which the Sandman is an horrific figure who comes to tear out children's eyes if they will not sleep. Freud also makes clear the link between fears around the eyes and fears of castration (in Freud 1988: 352).
9 James R. Nesteby (1982) characterises Tarzan movies as the 'invisible genre' in terms of their absence from discussions of representations of blackness within an American film culture to which they are central.

3 NEW HOLLYWOOD, GENRE AND THE ACTION CINEMA

1 Dick Hebdige usefully discusses *bricolage* in relation to the practices of youth culture (1979) and theories of postmodernism (1988). I am not using the term 'high art' here in any particular aesthetic sense. Rather the phrase serves to delineate the distinct, if provisional, institutional spaces within which 'high' and 'popular' culture operates. A recognition of the changes, and similarities between the two realms in formal terms – indeed, the fact that it is increasingly difficult to tell them apart – should not obscure the different cultural value and spaces of operation that the two have.
2 I am thinking here of Fredric Jameson's (1984) well-known analysis of postmodern culture. Noel Carroll (1982) has discussed such contemporary films under a rubric of allusionism which considers referentiality as an aesthetic device.
3 Steve Neale's (1980) work on genre, in which he emphasises the mobility and transformation of generic convention, has provided an important model in this respect.
4 Douglas Gomery (1983) points to an economic stasis operating in 'New Hollywood' with the same major companies continuing to dominate production. Nonetheless, these companies could also be seen to function as publishing houses for production – independent producers thus relied on but were also to a certain extent separate from the majors in the 1970s.
5 Of course the production of series dates back well into the 1930s. It is the big-budget visibility of the contemporary sequels and series that marks their difference to, say, the Tarzan films.
6 See Bruce A. Austin, 'Home Video: The Second-Run "Theater" of the 1990s', in Tino Balio (1990).
7 See Sean Cubitt (1988). Valerie Walkerdine's essay in Victor Burgin *et al.* (1986) also takes into account the importance of video technology in thinking about the contemporary audience's relationship to film images. See also Morley (1987) for a discussion of the operation of domestic television and video technologies. It is important to note that in referring to the domestic context of these technologies, I do not necessarily mean *familial*.
8 I discuss the question of aesthetic strategies and political evaluation in 'Having It All', in Lury *et al.* (1991).
9 Tom Ryall (1975/6) points to the need for a genre theory that will take account of the specificity of popular cultural production as distinct from theorisations of high art.
10 Though in *Rambo III* (1988) the hero has, as the narrative commences, found a secure place to live in a buddhist monastery in Thailand. He also has something of an affinity for the Afghan people with whom, or on whose behalf, he

fights. Significantly, though, America cannot provide the supportive community that he needs.

11 Chuck Norris's observation is cited by Gilbert Adair (1989: 215).

12 David Buxton (1989) discusses the development of the American television series during the 1960s and 1970s in the context of the presence of the Vietnam war as a series of television images.

13 See my discussion of Bruce Lee and representations of Chinese masculinity in Stecopoulos and Uebel (forthcoming).

I am referring here to Edward Said's *Orientalism* which, although it has little to say that is specifically about China, is invaluable in thinking through the imaginary geographies through which the west has mapped the east as Other.

14 Dustin Hoffman was lauded for his performance as an Indian in *Little Big Man* during the 1970s (see for example Tom Milne's *Focus on Film* review, no. 6, 1971). For a contemporary account of Hollywood's representation of American Indians see Larkins (1970).

15 Such criticisms, it should be noted, emerged at an historical moment marked by the highly visible violence of rioting in American cities.

16 See Ron Burnett (1985), and Judith Mayne in Jardine and Smith (1987) for discussions of *Tightrope* in relation to feminist discourses and the politics of the women's movement.

17 See Richard Dyer (1977). This essay draws attention to non-representational elements in the Hollywood film.

4 TOUGH GUYS AND WISE-GUYS: Masculinities and star images in the action cinema

1 For a variety of critical essays that discuss *Blade Runner* see Annette Kuhn (1990).

2 There is a wealth of new writing on the discourses of sexuality which underpin the colonial encounter. See in particular Frantz Fanon (1986), Homi K. Bhabha (1984; 1985; 1990) and Gail Ching-Liang Low (1989).

3 For a brief discussion of John Wayne's star image see Dyer (1979).

4 Various critics of the western have drawn attention to the contradictory position in which the hero is placed. He is a figure who brings order to a community from which he is then excluded. See Laura Mulvey's discussion of this in her 'Afterthoughts on Visual Pleasure and Narrative Cinema' (1989) and also Steve Neale (1980).

5 See, for example, Ann Kaplan's paradigmatic discussion of *Blonde Venus* (1983).

6 Recent critical work has, for example, drawn attention to the operation of this equation between physical and moral health in relation to HIV, AIDS and homosexuality. See Watney (1987) and Rick Meyer's analysis of representations surrounding Rock Hudson in Diana Fuss (1991).

7 See interview with James Cameron in *The Making of T2*, a promotional video released before the film itself (an increasingly common strategy in relation to big-budget ventures).

8 'Dollar does a Rambo' read a headline in the financial pages of one British newspaper (the *Guardian*), referring to the erratic behaviour of the American currency.

9 These elements are briefly discussed by Philip Strick in his excellent *Sight and Sound* review of *The Last Boy Scout* (March 1992: 49).

5 MASCULINITY, POLITICS AND NATIONAL IDENTITY

1 See Duncan Webster (1989) for a discussion of the hysterical tone of British press responses to *Rambo*.
2 Martin Barker (1984) provides a series of essays which discuss the panic over video nasties. See also Julian Petley (1984).
3 Gilbert Adair describes *Rambo* thus:

> With its lovingly, lingeringly filmed violence, its oily sadomasochism, its pornography of blood and biceps, the red meat pornography of Stallone's naked torso and the white meat pornography of young, delicately olive-complexioned, gun-toting beauties in coolie hats and Thai silk pyjamas, with its pidgin-English dialogue and crudely racist Chinoiserie (or Chinese restaurant Chinkoiserie) *First Blood II: Rambo* is a nauseating artefact, the kind of movie one is tempted to think only the 'public' could enjoy.
>
> (Adair 1989: 142–3)

See also Jeffrey Walsh in Louvre and Walsh (1988), Adi Wimmer in Walsh and Aulich (1989). Leslie Fiedler's (1990) analysis is one of the few to express anything other than contempt for the film.
4 Suzanne Moore's review of Stone's film was symptomatic, running under the banner headline 'Scotching the Rambo myth' (*New Statesman and Society*, 9 March 1990: 44).
5 See Anthony Easthope in Louvre and Walsh (1988) for a situation of such debates within an understanding of the ideological work of cinematic realism.
6 Joseph Bristow (1988). In this useful review of recent writings on masculinity, the figure of 'Rambo' functions to summarise a series of trends in the representation of men.
7 Louvre and Walsh (1988: 56). Rosalind Coward, along with a multitude of journalists and campaigners from both left and right, have also sought to make this equation.
8 See Simon Watney's (1987) discussion of these issues in relation to representation, sexuality and AIDS.
9 Jeffords's is a complex and in-depth study which offers some fascinating comments on the representation of Vietnam within both American film and political culture.
10 Adi Wimmer bizarrely suggests that 'President Reagan, by his own account, was inspired by *Rambo* to use tougher methods with certain "Mad dogs of the Middle East"' (Walsh and Aulich 1989: 184). See also Duncan Webster's (1988) comments on how this type of association – in which popular culture is 'blamed' for foreign policy – works to obscure a political analysis.
11 *Kung Fu*, the 1970s' television series starring David Carradine, drew on exactly this confluence of elements. The East functions to signify a certain mysticism.
12 Some reviewers, such as Thomas Doherty (1986), for example, picked up on these qualities in *Rambo* (1985).
13 The poem, originally published in 1926, appears in Helen Vendler (1990: 41–2).
14 See Mary Ellison, 'Black Music and the Vietnam War', in Walsh and Aulich (1989).
15 See Katrina Porteous, 'History Lessons: *Platoon*' (Walsh and Aulich 1989), and Clyde Taylor, 'The Colonialist Subtext in *Platoon*' (Ditmar and Michaud 1990).
16 Obviously this is partly to do with the British perspective from which I am writing, but nearly twenty years on the youthful audience to which the action

cinema in the States is primarily directed may well see the war as historically distant.

17 In addition to papers like Jackson's there is a vast range of therapeutic literature around Vietnam veterans. See, for example, Robert Jay Lifton (1974).

6 THE BODY IN CRISIS OR THE BODY TRIUMPHANT?

1 See, for example, Judith Butler (1990), Diana Fuss (1989; 1991).

2 Dick Hebdige provides an exhaustive list of the many phenomena that the term 'postmodernism' has been used to designate (1988: 181–2).

3 Joan Rivere's oft-referred-to essay, 'Womanliness as a Masquerade' is crucial here (Burgin *et al.* 1986). Mary Ann Doane's (1991) work on women and the cinema exemplifies a more recent use of these concepts.

4 The arguments offered in Judith Williamson's (1986) polemic essay 'The Problems of Being Popular' are, in many respects, paradigmatic.

5 Christopher Norris, speaking at the Association for Cultural Studies Conference, Staffordshire, September 1991, talked of a need for a return to the real. Various papers at the Screen Studies Conference, Glasgow, June 1992, also made this argument, with particular reference to the Gulf War.

6 Dyer's comments provide an interesting insight on the point of production, which is contained within western culture. It is important to note though that the action movies which I discuss in this book are popular on the international market, and thus consumed within a variety of contexts.

7 See Valerie Hill and Yvonne Tasker (1992) for a discussion of Michael Mann's work.

8 Feminist debates around the issue of pornography have generated much writing, which cannot be summarised here. However, whilst organisations like Feminists Against Censorship have provided a challenge to the assumption that feminists will inevitably oppose pornography and support censorship, there is something of an orthodoxy in operation. Simon Watney (1987) provides a useful discussion of the relationship between feminist campaigns against pornography, with the passive (and normative) construction of the 'public' this involves, and state censorship.

9 Kobena Mercer's essay appears in Bad Object Choices (1991).

10 Lynne Segal was speaking at the Teaching Media in London Conference on Masculinity, January 1992.

11 Alan Richman's feature article on Arnold Schwarzenegger is discussed in Chapter 4 and appears in the American edition of *GQ*, May 1990.

12 See, for example, Homi K. Bhabha (1984; 1985), Gail Ching-Liang Low (1989) and essays in Andrew Parker *et al.* (1992).

13 Chris Holmlund offers some interesting comments on the significance of an Italian ethnicity in Stallone's films in her essay in Cohen and Hark (1993).

14 See Kobena Mercer (1988) on Michael Jackson, and Suzanne Moore's discussion of Prince in relation to postmodernism in Chapman and Rutherford (1988).

15 Gilbert Adair (1989) discusses the use of obscene language in *Full Metal Jacket*. Also see Jeanine Basinger (1986) for a detailed discussion of the many subgenres of the war film, including the training-camp movie.

16 Under the headline 'The star who terminated his past', the *Daily Mail* (12 July 1991) ran a story reporting Schwarzenegger's hosting of a Gala evening at the Simon Wiesenthal Center (along with rumours of a large donation to the Center). The story explicitly locates the event in terms of the star's image and

the work that is put into it – here how he 'killed off the Nazi smear'. The 'smear' itself, as well as Schwarzenegger's public attempts to distance himself from it can, like any other element, be incorporated into the star image.

17 These workout videos also offer the stars as sexual spectacle. Dolph Lundgren's *Maximum Potential* seems deliberately filmed to bring out the homoerotic aspects of the muscleman star persona.

18 See the essays by Philip Brophy and Pete Boss in the 'Body Horror' issue of *Screen* (1986) as well as the essays in Annette Kuhn (1990).

19 Joe Flaherty (1982) discusses this aspect of the films, pointing to an intended association between Carl Weathers/Apollo Creed and Ali, Mr T/Clubber Lang and Spinks.

An equally bizarre set of white fantasies about the black boxer are enacted in Norman Mailer's portrait of Ali in *The Fight* (1973).

20 See Steve Neale (1983: 10) for a discussion of the wounded hero and his relationship to images of castration in the context of the western.

21 Male 'parade' is discussed, in the context of the masquerade, by Stephen Heath in Burgin *et al.* (1986).

7 ACTION HEROINES IN THE 1980s: The limits of 'musculinity'

1 Kobena Mercer was speaking on 'I Want Your Sex', a documentary on images of black sexuality (broadcast on Channel 4, 12 November 1991).

2 See King-Kok Cheung's article in Marianne Hirsch and Evelyn Fox Keller (1990) for a discussion of gender, race and the critical reception of Maxine Hong Kingston's work in America.

3 Part of the discussion of *Thelma and Louise* presented in this chapter is taken from my contribution to a forthcoming volume edited by Berenice Reynaud and Ginette Vincendeau, *20 Ans De Theories Feministes Du Cinema*, Paris: CinemAction Editions du Cent.

4 See, for example, Botcherby and Garland (1991); Botcherby (1991); Murphy (1991); Dargis (1991).

My discussion also draws on a paper given by Jane Arthurs, 'Thelma and Louise: On the Road to Feminism?', at a conference on Feminist Methodology (January 1992).

5 A videotape of the Kennedy-Smith rape case is now available in stores, a point which indicates both the visibility and saleability of this case in particular and rape in general.

6 Laura Mulvey (1989: 26).

7 For example, Janice Radway has suggested, in relation to the project of ethnographic research on the romance, that 'our' political project is 'one of convincing those very real people to see how their situation intersects with our own and why it will be fruitful for them to see it as we do' (1986: 107). This project, in which nothing can be taken from the popular since 'we' know best, involves the suggestion that 'fantasies can be used as a site for political intervention', a suggestion which fails to recognise the importance of a structure (to which shifting signifiers may be attached) within fantasy (ibid.: 120).

By way of contrast we could consider the arguments made by Jacqueline Bobo in relation to *The Color Purple* in which the responses that readers make to a particular film are given a critical validity. Bobo does not approach her subject matter with the assumption that she can correct deviant readings (in Pribram 1988).

8 Jackie Chan's *The Armour of God* (Hong Kong, 1986) turns this formula around somewhat. For much of the film the Chinese adventurer heroes explore an exotic European landscape.
9 This quotation, from Joan Smith in the *Guardian*, is cited by Jane Arthurs (ibid.).
10 These comments on the form and operation of men's style magazines, draw from a paper on the subject given by Andy Medhurst at the Association for Cultural Studies Conference, Staffordshire, September 1991.
11 Similarly one of Schulze's respondents describes the image of the female bodybuilder as too 'working class', like 'Tammy Wynette with muscles' (Gaines and Herzog 1990: 77). Such a commentary makes apparent the rather obvious point that the responses made by lesbian audiences are also structured through discourses of class. To construct a lesbian audience as necessarily oppositional erases the differences existing within that supposedly simple category.
12 Interview with Ridley Scott in *Sight and Sound* (July 1991: 18–19).

8 THE CINEMA AS EXPERIENCE: Kathryn Bigelow and the cinema of spectacle

1 Interview with Kathryn Bigelow, *Monthly Film Bulletin*, vol. 58 (November 1991: 313).
2 These comments relate not only to critical articles and reviews of *Thelma and Louise*, but to some of the responses generated by papers I have both given and attended on the film. In general, responses to the film on these occasions have been positive, but with distinct reservations along the lines I have indicated in this section of my argument.
3. Sheila Johnstone, review of *Lock Up*, *The Independent* (1 February 1990: 13).
4 Hollywood is also a key space within which lesbians and gay men work, however complex the negotiations involved in such a location. The homoerotics of a recent chart-topping film such as *Universal Soldier*, which works through a long love affair between Dolph Lundgren and Jean-Claude Van Damme, is extremely self-consciously presented.
5 Though other traditions of course exist, oppositional film criticism and practice has a strong history of commitment to a realist aesthetic, which has been perceived as a way of communicating the 'truth' of those existences which have been excluded from representation.
6 Interview with Kathryn Bigelow (ibid.: 313).
7 Freud cites Rank who argues that the 'immortal soul' represents one of the first of such doubles (Freud 1919/1988: 356).
8 In Freud's work of course narcissism is complexly developed as a term associated with homosexuality, representing a love of self expressed in object choice, or a stage to be surmounted. As a refusal to grow up, to accept one's place of authority or of submission to authority, I have identified the hero's infantile insistence on his own existence as being of structuring importance to the action picture.
9 Accompanying the release of *Point Break*, the *Guardian* ran an interview with Bigelow, by Mark Salisbury, under the title 'Hollywood's Macho Woman' (21 November 1991: 27). The introduction to the piece ran as follows:

> Kathryn Bigelow has been asked this particular question a lot. No matter how delicately you phrase it, how much you skirt around the issue, it comes down to the same thing; Why does she make the kind of movies

> she makes? As the sole woman director regularly working in the traditionally male-dominated action movie arena, Bigelow has had to contend with critics ill-at-ease with her proficiency with the medium. Moreover, she does it better than most of her male counterparts.

This particular version manages to evade the fact that Hollywood film production in general, rather than a genre in particular, is male dominated, certainly in terms of the prestigious position of director.

10 Interview with Kathryn Bigelow, *Empire* (December 1991: 76).

11 Interview with Patrick Swayze, *Empire* (December 1991: 70).

12 Interview with Patrick Swayze, *For Him* (November 1991: 39). This interview ran under the title 'Lone Star Straight', both a pun on the star's Texas origins and a bizarre assertion of heterosexuality! The interview cited in note 11, above, ran under the title 'Cry Baby'.

13 Gail Ching-Liang Low (1989) makes this point very well in relation to nineteenth-century imperialist discourses.

FILMOGRAPHY

LIST OF ABBREVIATIONS

d Director
l.p. Leading players
p Producer
p.c. Production company
sc Screenplay

Above the Law Hong Kong, 1986
p.c.: American Imperial; *p*: Leonard K. C. Ho; *d*: Cory Yuen; *sc*: Barry Wong, Szeto Cheuk Hon; *l.p.*: Yuen Biao (*Jason Chen*), Cynthia Rothrock (*Sandy Jones*), Melvin Wong (*Superintendent Wong*). 87 mins.

Action Jackson USA, 1988
p.c.: Lorimar. A Silver Pictures production; *p*: Joel Silver; *d*: Craig R. Baxley; *sc*: Robert Reneau; *l.p.*: Carl Weathers (*Jericho 'Action' Jackson*), Craig T. Nelson (*Peter Dellaplane*), Vanity (*Sydney Ash*), Sharon Stone (*Patrice Dellaplane*), Thomas F. Wilson (*Officer Kornblau*), Bill Duke (*Captain Armbruster*), Robert Davi (*Tony Moretti*), Jack Thibeau (*Detective Ketterwell*), Roger Aaron Brown (*Officer Lack*), Stan Foster (*Albert*). 96 mins.

Alien GB, 1979
p.c.: 20th Century Fox (London). A Brandywine–Roland Shusett Production; *p*: Gordon Carroll, David Giler, Walter Hill; *d*: Ridley Scott; *sc*: Dan O'Bannon; *l.p.*: Tom Skerritt (*Captain Dallas*), Sigourney Weaver (*Ripley*), Veronica Cartwright (*Lambert*), Harry Dean Stanton (*Brett*), John Hurt (*Kane*), Ian Holm (*Ash*), Yaphet Kotto (*Parker*). 117 mins.

Aliens USA, 1986
p.c.: 20th Century Fox. A Brandywine Production; *p*: Gale Anne Hurd; *d*: James Cameron; *sc*: James Cameron; *l.p.*: Sigourney Weaver (*Ripley*), Carrie Henn (*'Newt'*), Michael Biehn (*Corporal Hicks*), Paul Reiser (*Carter J. Burke*), Lance Henriksen (*Bishop*), Bill Paxton (*Private Hudson*), William Hope (*Lieutenant Gorman*), Jenette Goldstein (*Private Vasquez*), Al Matthews (*Sergeant Apone*), Mark Rolston (*Private Drake*), Ricco Ross (*Private Frost*), Colette Hiller (*Corporal Ferro*), Daniel Kash (*Private Spunkmeyer*), Cynthia Scott (*Corporal Dietrich*), Tip Tipping (*Private Crowe*), Trevor Steedman (*Private Wiezbowski*). 137 mins.

A.W.O.L. USA, 1990
p.c.: Wrong Bet Productions. For Imperial Entertainment; *p*: Ash R. Shah, Eric Karson; *d*: Sheldon Lettich; *sc*: Sheldon Lettich, Jean-Claude Van Damme; *l.p.*: Jean-Claude Van Damme (*Lyon Gaultier*), Harrison Page (*Joshua*), Deborah Rennard (*Cynthia*), Lisa Pelikan (*Helene*), Ashley Johnson (*Nicole*), Brian Thompson (*Russell*), Voyo (*Sergeant Harthog*), Michael Qissi (*Moustafa*), George McDaniel (*Adjutant*). 108 mins.

Basic Instinct USA, 1992
p.c.: Carolco/Le Studio Canal¢; *p*: Alan Marshall; *d*: Paul Verhoeven; *sc*: Joe Eszterhas; *l.p.*: Michael Douglas (*Nick Curran*), Sharon Stone (*Catherine Tramell*), George Dzundza (*Gus*), Jeanne Tripplehorn (*Dr Beth Garner*), Denis Arndt (*Lieutenant Walker*), Leilani Sarelle (*Roxy*). 128 mins.

Black Belt Jones USA, 1973
p.c.: Sequoia Films. For Warner Bros; *p*: Fred Weintraub, Paul Heller; *d*: Robert Clouse; *sc*: Oscar Williams; *l.p.*: Jim Kelly (*Black Belt Jones*), Gloria Hendry (*Sidney*), Malik Carter (*Pinky*), Scatman Crothers (*Pop*), Alan Weeks (*Toppy*), Eric Laneuville (*Quincy*). 85 mins.

Blue Steel USA, 1990
p.c.: Lightning Pictures. In association with Precision Films, Mack-Taylor Productions; *p*: Edward R. Pressman, Oliver Stone; *d*: Kathryn Bigelow; *sc*: Kathryn Bigelow, Eric Red; *l.p.*: Jamie Lee Curtis (*Megan Turner*), Ron Silver (*Eugene Hunt*), Clancy Brown (*Nick Mann*), Elizabeth Pena (*Tracy Perez*), Louise Fletcher (*Shirley Turner*), Philip Bosco (*Frank Turner*). 102 mins.

Braddock: Missing in Action 3 USA, 1988
p.c.: Cannon Films/Cannon International; *p*: Menahem Golan, Yoram Globus; *d*: Aaron Norris; *sc*: James Bruner, Chuck Norris. Based on characters created by Arthur Silver, Larry Levinson, Steve Bing; *l.p.*: Chuck Norris (*Colonel James Braddock*), Aki Aleong (*General Quoc*), Roland Harrah III (*Van Tan Cang*), Miki Kim (*Lin Tang Cang*). 103 mins.

China O'Brien USA, 1988
p.c.: Golden Harvest; *p*: Fred Weintraub, Sandra Weintraub; *d*: Robert Clouse; *sc*: Robert Clouse; *l.p.*: Cynthia Rothrock (*Lori 'China' O'Brien*), Richard Norton (*Matt Conroy*), Keith Cooke (*Dakota*). 86 mins.

Cleopatra Jones and the Casino of Gold USA/Hong Kong, 1975
p.c.: Warner Bros (Los Angeles)/Shaw Brothers (Hong Kong); *p*: William Tennant, Run Run Shaw; *d*: Chuck Bail; *sc*: William Tennant. Based on characters created by Max Julien; *l.p.*: Tamara Dobson (*Cleopatra Jones*), Stella Stevens (*Dragon Lady*), Tanny (*Mi Ling*), Norman Fell (*Stanley Nagel*), Albert Popwell (*Matthew Johnson*). 96 mins.

Cobra USA, 1986
p.c.: Cannon; *p*: Menahem Golan, Yoram Globus; *d*: George Pan Cosmatos; *sc*: Sylvester Stallone, based on the novel *Fair Game* by Paula Gosling; *l.p.*: Sylvester Stallone (*Marion 'Cobra' Cobretti*), Brigitte Nielson (*Ingrid*), Reni Santoni (*Gonzales*), Andrew Robinson (*Detective Monte*), Brian Thompson (*Night Slasher*). 87 mins.

Commando USA, 1985
p.c.: 20th Century Fox. A Silver Pictures production; *p*: Joel Silver; *d*: Mark L. Lester; *sc*: Steven E. de Souza; *l.p.*: Arnold Schwarzenegger (*John Matrix*), Rae Dawn Chong (*Cindy*), Dan Hedaya (*General Arius*), Vernon Wells (*Bennett*). 90 mins.

Conan the Barbarian USA, 1981
p.c.: Dino De Laurentiis Corporation. An Edward R. Pressman production; *p*: Buzz Feitshans, Raffaella De Laurentiis; *d*: John Milius; *sc*: John Milius, Oliver Stone. Based on the character created by Robert E. Howard; *l.p.*: Arnold Schwarzenegger (*Conan*), James Earl Jones (*Thulsa Doom*), Max Von Sydow (*Kind Osric*), Sandahl Bergman (*Valaria*). 129 mins.

Conan the Destroyer USA, 1984
p.c.: Dino De Laurentiis Corporation. An Edward R. Pressman production. For Universal; *p*: Raffaella De Laurentiis; *d*: Richard Fleischer; *sc*: Stanley Mann; *l.p.*: Arnold Schwarzenegger (*Conan*), Grace Jones (*Zula*), Wilt Chamberlain (*Bombaata*), Mako (*Akira*), Tracey Walter (*Malak*), Sarah Douglas (*Queen Tamaris*) Olivia D'Abo (*Princess Jehnna*). 101 mins.

Dark Angel USA, 1989
p.c.: Vision p.d.g.; *p*: Jeff Young; *d*: Craig R. Baxley; *sc*: Jonathon Tydor, Leonard Maas Jnr; *l.p.*: Dolph Lundgren (*Jack Caine*), Brian Benben (*Laurence Smith*), Betsy Brantley (*Diane Pollon*), Matthias Hues (*Talec*), David Ackroyd (*Switzer*), Jim Haynie (*Captain Malone*). 91 mins.

Die Hard USA, 1988
p.c.: 20th Century Fox; *p*: Lawrence Gordon, Joel Silver; *d*: John McTiernan; *sc*: Jeb Stuart and Steven E. de Souza; *l.p.*: Bruce Willis (*John McClane*), Bonnie Bedelia (*Holly Gennaro McClane*), Reginald Veljohnson (*Sergeant Al Powell*), Paul Gleason (*Dwayne T. Robinson*), De'Voreaux White (*Argyle*), Hart Bochner (*Ellis*), James Shigeth (*Tagaki*), Alan Rickman (*Hans Gruber*), Alexander Godunov (*Karl*). 132 mins.

Die Hard 2 USA, 1990
p.c.: 20th Century Fox. A Gordon Company/Silver Pictures production; *p*: Lawrence Gordon, Joel Silver, Charles Gordon; *d*: Renny Harlin; *sc*: Steven E. de Souza, Doug Richardson. Based on the novel *58 Minutes* by Walter Wager; Oliver Wood; *l.p.*: Bruce Willis (*John McClane*), Bonnie Bedelia (*Holly McClane*), Reginald Veljohnson (*Al Powell*), John Amos (*Captain Grant*), Dennis Franz (*Carmine Lorenzo*). 123 mins.

Fatal Beauty USA, 1987
p.c.: MGM. In association with CST Communications; *p*: Leonard Kroll; *d*: Tom Holland; *sc*: Hilary Henkin, Dean Riesner; *l.p.*: Whoopi Goldberg (*Rita Rizzoli*), Sam Elliott (*Mike Marshak*), Ruben Blades (*Carl Jimenez*), Harris Yulin (*Conrad Kroll*), John P. Ryan (*Lieutenant Kellerman*). 104 mins.

First Blood USA, 1982
p.c.: Carolco. For Anabasis; *p*: Buzz Feitshans; *d*: Ted Kotcheff; *sc*: Michael Kozoll, William Sackheim and Sylvester Stallone. Based on the novel by David Morrell; *l.p.*: Sylvester Stallone (*John Rambo*), Richard Crenna (*Colonel Trautman*), Brian Dennehy (*Sheriff Will Teasle*), David Caruso (*Mitch*), Jack Starrett (*Galt*). 93 mins.

Getting Physical USA, 1984 (TV movie)
p.c.: CBS Entertainment; *p*: Marcy Gross and Ann Weston; *d*: Steven H. Stern; *Teleplay*: Laurian Leggett. Story by Laurian Leggett, Marcy Gross and Ann Weston; *l.p.*: Alexandra Paul (*Kendal Gibley*), Sandahl Bergman (*Nadine*), David Naughton (*Mickey*). 110 mins.

Hard to Kill USA, 1990
p.c.: Warner Bros. In association with Adelson–Todman–Simon Productions; *p*: Gary Adelson, Joel Simon, Bill Todman Jnr; *d*: Bruce Malmuth; *sc*: Steven McKay; *l.p.*: Steven Seagal (*Mason Storm*), Kelly Le Brock (*Andy Stewart*), Bill Sadler (*Vernon Trent*), Frederick Coffin (*Kevin O'Malley*), Bonnie Burroughs (*Felicia Storm*), Andrew Bloch (*Captain Dan Hulland*). 95 mins.

Heartbreak Ridge USA, 1986
p.c.: Malpaso. For Warner Bros; *p*: Clint Eastwood; *d*: Clint Eastwood; *sc*: James Carabatsos; *l.p.*: Clint Eastwood (*Sergeant Thomas Highway*), Marsha Mason (*Aggie*), Everett McGill (*Major Powers*), Moses Gunn (*Sergeant Webster*), Mario Van Peebles (*'Stitch' Jones*). 130 mins.

Invasion USA USA, 1985
p.c.: Cannon Films; *p*: Menahem Golan, Yoram Globus; *d*: Joseph Zito; *sc*: James Bruner, Chuck Norris; *l.p.*: Chuck Norris (*Matt Hunter*), Richard Lynch (*Rostov*), Melissa Prophet (*McGuire*). 107 mins.

Karate Kid, The USA, 1984
p.c.: Columbia-Delphi Productions II; *p*: Jerry Weintraub; *d*: John G. Avildsen; *sc*: Robert Mark Kamen; *l.p.*: Ralph Macchio (*Daniel La Russo*), Noriyuki 'Pat' Morita (*Miyagi*), Elisabeth Shue (*Ali*), Martin Kove (*Kresse*), Randee Heller (*Lucille La Russo*). 127 mins.

Kickboxer USA, 1989
p.c.: Kings Road Entertainment; *p*: Mark DiSalle; *d*: Mark DiSalle, David Worth; *sc*: Glenn Bruce; *l.p.*: Jean Claude Van Damme (*Kurt Sloane*), Dennis Alexio (*Eric Sloane*), Dennis Chan (*Xian*), Tong Po (*Tong Po*), Haskell Anderson (*Winston Taylor*), Rochelle Ashana (*Mylee*). 103 mins.

Last Boy Scout, The USA, 1991
p.c.: Warner Bros. A Silver Pictures production; *p*: Joel Silver, Michael Levy; *d*: Tony Scott; *sc*: Shane Black; *l.p.*: Bruce Willis (*Joe Hallenbeck*), Damon Wayans (*Jimmy Dix*), Chelsea Field (*Sarah Hallenbeck*), Noble Willingham (*Sheldon Marcone*), Taylor Negron (*Milo*), Danielle Harris (*Darian Hallenbeck*). 105 mins.

Lethal Weapon USA, 1987
p.c.: Warner Bros. A Silver Pictures production; *p*: Richard Donner, Joel Silver; *d*: Richard Donner; *sc*: Shane Black; *l.p.*: Mel Gibson (*Martin Riggs*), Danny Glover (*Roger Murtaugh*), Gary Busey (*Joshua*), Mitchell Ryan (*General McAllister*), Tom Atkins (*Michael Hunsaker*), Darlene Love (*Trish Murtaugh*), Traci Wolfe (*Rianne Murtaugh*). 109 mins.

Lethal Weapon 2 USA, 1989
p.c.: Warner Bros. A Silver Pictures production; *p*: Richard Donner, Joel Silver; *d*: Richard Donner; *sc*: Jeffrey Boam; *l.p.*: Mel Gibson (*Martin Riggs*), Danny Glover (*Roger Murtaugh*), Joe Pesci (*Leo Getz*), Joss Ackland (*Arjen Rudd*), Derrick

O'Connor (*Pieter Vorstedt*), Patsy Kensit (*Rika Van Den Haas*), Darlene Love (*Trish Murtaugh*), Traci Wolfe (*Rianne Murtaugh*). 114 mins.

Lock Up USA, 1989
p.c.: White Eagle Productions/Carolco Pictures. A Gordon Company production; *p*: Tony Munafo; *d*: John Flynn; *sc*: Richard Smith, Jeb Stuart, Henry Rosenbaum; *l.p.*: Sylvester Stallone (*Frank Leone*), Donald Sutherland (*Warden Drumgoole*), John Amos (*Meissner*), Sonny Landham (*Chink*), Tom Sizemore (*Dallas*), Frank McRae (*Eclipse*), Darlanne Fluegel (*Melissa*), William Allen Young (*Braden*), Larry Romano (*First Base*). 109 mins.

Missing In Action USA, 1984
p.c.: Canon Productions; *p*: Menahem Golan, Yoram Globus; *d*: Joseph Zito; *sc*: James Bruner; *l.p.*: Chuck Norris (*Colonel James Braddock*), M. Emmett Walsh (*Tuck*), David Tress (*Senator Porter*), Leonore Kasdorf (*Ann*), James Hong (*General Iran*), Ernie Ortega (*Colonel Vinh*), Pierrino Mascarino (*Jacques*), E. Erich Anderson (*Massucci*). 101 mins.

Missing In Action 2: The Beginning USA, 1984
p.c.: Canon Productions; *p*: Menahem Golan, Yoram Globus; *d*: Lance Hool; *sc*: Arthur Silver, Larry Levinson, Steve Bing; *l.p.*: Chuck Norris (*Colonel James Braddock*), Soon-Tech Oh (*Colonel Yin*), Steven Williams (*Captain David Nester*), Bennett Ohta (*Colonel Ho*), Cosie Costa (*Lieutenant Anthony Mazilli*). 95 mins.

Nico USA, 1988
p.c.: Warner Bros; *p*: Steven Seagal, Andrew Davis; *d*: Andrew Davis; *sc*: Steven Pressfield, Ronald Shusett, Andrew Davies; *l.p.*: Steven Seagal (*Nico Toscani*), Pam Grier (*Delores Jackson*), Henry Silva (*Zagon*), Ron Dean (*Lukich*). 99 mins. US Title: 'Above the Law'.

Perfect USA, 1985
p.c.: Columbia; *p*: James Bridges; *d*: James Bridges; *sc*: Aaron Latham and James Bridges; *l.p.*: Jamie Lee Curtis (*Jessie Wilson*), John Travolta (*Adam Lawrence*), Anne De Salvo (*Frankie*), Jann Wenner (*Mark Roth*), Marilu Henner (*Sally*), Laraine Newman (*Linda*), Matthew Reed (*Roger*). 120 mins.

Platoon USA, 1986
p.c.: Hemdale Film Corporation; *p*: Arnold Kopelson; *d*: Oliver Stone; *sc*: Oliver Stone; *l.p.*: Tom Berenger (*Sergeant Barnes*), Willem Dafoe (*Sergeant Elias*), Charlie Sheen (*Chris Taylor*). 120 mins.

Point Break USA, 1991
p.c.: Largo Entertainment; *p*: Peter Abrams, Robert L. Levy; *d*: Kathryn Bigelow; *sc*: W. Peter Iliff; *l.p.*: Patrick Swayze (*Bodhi*), Keanu Reeves (*Johnny Utah*), Gary Busey (*Angelo Pappas*), Lori Petty (*Tyler*), John McGinley (*Ben Harp*), James Le Gros (*Roach*), John Philbin (*Nathanial*), Bojesse Christopher (*Grommet*), Julian Reyes (*Alvarez*), Daniel Beer (*Babbit*), Chris Pederson (*Bunker Weiss*). 122 mins.

Predator USA, 1987
p.c.: 20th Century Fox. In association with Amercent Films/American Entertainment Partners; *p*: Lawrence Gordon, Joel Silver, John Davies; *d*: John McTiernan; *sc*: Jim Thomas, John Thomas; *l.p.*: Arnold Schwarzenegger (*Major Alan 'Dutch' Schaeffer*), Carl Weathers (*Dillon*), Elpidia Carrillo (*Anna*), Bill Duke (*Mac*), Jesse

Ventura (*Blain*), Sonny Landham (*Billy*), Richard Chaves (*Poncho*), R. G. Armstrong (*General Phillips*), Shane Black (*Hawkins*), Kevin Peter Hall (*Predator*). 106 mins.

Predator 2 USA, 1990
p.c.: 20th Century Fox; *p*: Lawrence Gordon, Joel Silver, John Davies; *d*: Stephen Hopkins; *sc*: Jim Thomas, John Thomas; *l.p.*: Kevin Peter Hall (*The Predator*), Danny Glover (*Harrigan*), Gary Busey (*Keyes*), Ruben Blades (*Danny*), Maria Conchita Alonso (*Leona*), Bill Paxton (*Jerry*), Robert Davi (*Heinemann*), Adam Baldwin (*Garber*), Kent McCord (*Captain Pilgram*), Morton Downey Jnr (*Pope*). 108 mins.

Pumping Iron USA, 1977
p.c.: White Mountain; *p*: George Butler, Jerome Gary; *d*: George Butler, Robert Fiore; *sc*: George Butler. Based on the book by Charles Gaines, George Butler; *narrator*: Charles Gaines; *with*: Arnold Schwarzenegger, Lou Ferrigno, Matty Ferrigno, Mike Katz. 86 mins.

Pumping Iron II: The Women USA, 1984
p.c.: Bar Belle Productions. A White Mountain film. In association with Gym Tech USA; *p*: George Butler; *d*: George Butler; *sc*: Charles Gaines, George Butler; *with*: Bev Francis, Rachel McLish, Lori Bowen Rice, Carla Dunlap, Steve Michalik, Krish Alexander, Sherry Atton. 107 mins.

Rambo: First Blood Part II USA, 1985
p.c.: Carolco. For Anabasis; *p*: Buzz Feitshans; *d*: George Pan Cosmatos; *sc*: Sylvester Stallone, James Cameron. Based on characters created by David Morrell; *l.p.*: Sylvester Stallone (*John Rambo*), Richard Crenna (*Colonel Trautman*), Julie Nickson (*Co Bao*), Charles Napier (*Marshall Murdock*), Steven Berkoff (*Lieutenant Podovsky*), Martin Kove (*Ericson*), Andy Wood (*Banks*), George Kee Cheung (*Sergeant Tay*), William Ghent (*Captain Vinh*). 96 mins.

Rambo III USA, 1988
p.c.: Carolco Pictures; *p*: Buzz Feitshans; *d*: Peter MacDonald; *sc*: Sylvester Stallone, Sheldon Lettich; *l.p.*: Sylvester Stallone (*John Rambo*), Richard Crenna (*Colonel Trautman*), Marc de Jonge (*Colonel Zaysen*), Spiros Focas (*Masoud*), Sasson Gabai (*Mousa*), Doudi Shoua (*Hamid*). 102 mins.

Red Sonja USA, 1985
p.c.: Dino De Laurentiis. For MGM/UA; *p*: Christian Ferry; *d*: Richard Fleischer; *sc*: Clive Exton, George MacDonald Fraser. Based on the character created by Robert E. Howard; *l.p.*: Arnold Schwarzenegger (*Kalidor*), Brigitte Nielson (*Red Sonja*), Sandahl Bergman (*Queen Gedren*), Paul Smith (*Falkon*), Ernie Reyes Jnr (*Prince Tarn*). 89 mins.

RoboCop USA, 1987
p.c.: Orion Pictures; *p*: Arne Schmidt; *d*: Paul Verhoeven; *sc*: Edward Neumeier, Michael Miner; *l.p.*: Peter Weller (*Murphy/RoboCop*), Nancy Allen (*Lewis*), Daniel O'Herlihy (*Old Man*), Ronny Cox (*Dick Jones*), Kurtwood Smith (*Clarence Boddicker*), Miguel Ferrer (*Robert Morton*). 102 mins.

RoboCop 2 USA, 1990
p.c.: Orion Pictures; *p*: Jon Davison; *d*: Irvin Kershner; *sc*: Frank Miller, Walon Green; *l.p.*: Peter Weller (*RoboCop*), Nancy Allen (*Anne Lewis*), Belinda Bauer (*Dr Juliette Faxx*), Daniel O'Herlihy (*Old Man*), Tom Noonan (*Cain*), Gabriel Damon (*Hob*), Willard Pugh (*Mayor Kuzak*). 116 mins.

Rocky USA, 1976
p.c.: United Artists; *p*: Irwin Winkler, Robert Chartoff; *d*: John G. Avildsen; *sc*: Sylvester Stallone; *l.p.*: Sylvester Stallone (*Rocky Balboa*), Talia Shire (*Adrian Balboa*), Burt Young (*Paulie*), Carl Weathers (*Apollo Creed*), Burgess Meredith (*Mickey*). 119 mins.

Rocky II USA, 1979
p.c.: United Artists; *p*: Irwin Winkler, Robert Chartoff; *d*: Sylvester Stallone; *sc*: Sylvester Stallone; *l.p.*: Sylvestor Stallone (*Rocky Balboa*), Talia Shire (*Adrian Balboa*), Burt Young (*Paulie*), Carl Weathers (*Apollo Creed*), Burgess Meredith (*Mickey*). 119 mins.

Rocky III USA, 1982
p.c.: United Artists. A Robert Chartoff–Irwin Winkler production; *p*: Irwin Winkler, Robert Chartoff; *d*: Sylvester Stallone; *sc*: Sylvester Stallone; *l.p.*: Sylvester Stallone (*Rocky Balboa*), Talia Shire (*Adrian Balboa*), Burt Young (*Paulie*), Carl Weathers (*Apollo Creed*), Burgess Meredith (*Mickey*), Tony Burton (*Duke*), Mr T (*Clubber Lang*), Hulk Hogan (*Thunderlips*). 99 mins.

Rocky IV USA, 1985
p.c.: United Artists; *p*: Irwin Winkler, Robert Chartoff; *d*: Sylvester Stallone; *sc*: Sylvester Stallone; *l.p.*: Sylvester Stallone (*Rocky Balboa*), Talia Shire (*Adrian Balboa*), Burt Young (*Paulie*), Carl Weathers (*Apollo Creed*), Brigitte Nielson (*Ludmilla*), Tony Burton (*Duke*), Dolph Lundgren (*Ivan Drago*). 91 mins.

Rocky V USA, 1990
p.c.: United Artists. In association with Star Partners III; *p*: Irwin Winkler, Robert Chartoff; *d*: John G. Avildsen; *sc*: Sylvester Stallone; *l.p.*: Sylvester Stallone (*Rocky Balboa*), Talia Shire (*Adrian Balboa*), Burt Young (*Paulie*), Sage Stallone (*Rocky Jnr*), Burgess Meredith (*Mickey*), Tommy Morrison (*Tommy Gunn*), Richard Gant (*George Washington Duke*), Tony Burton (*Tony*). 104 mins.

Running Man, The USA, 1987
p.c.: Taft Entertainment/Keith Barish Productions; *p*: Tim Zinnemann, George Linder; *d*: Paul Michael Glaser; *sc*: Steven E. de Souza. Based on the novel by Richard Bachman [Stephen King]; *l.p.*: Arnold Schwarzenegger (*Ben Richards*), Maria Conchita Alonso (*Amber Mendez*), Yaphet Kotto (*Laughlin*), Jim Brown (*Fireball*), Jesse Ventura (*Captain Freedom*), Erland Van Lidth (*Dynamo*), Marvin J. McIntyre (*Weiss*), Gus Rethwisch (*Buzzsaw*), Professor Toru Tanaka (*Professor Subzero*), Mick Fleetwood (*Mic*), Dweezil Zappa (*Stevie*), Richard Dawson (*Damon Killian*) 101 mins.

Silence of the Lambs, The USA, 1990
p.c.: Orion Pictures. A Strong Heart/Demme production; *p*: Edward Saxon, Kenneth Utt, Ron Bozman; *d*: Jonathon Demme; *sc*: Ted Tally. Based on the novel by Thomas Harris; *l.p.*: Jodie Foster (*Clarice Starling*), Anthony Hopkins (*Dr*

Hannibal Lecter), Scott Glenn (*Jack Crawford*), Ted Levine (*Jame Gumb*), Anthony Heald (*Dr Frederick Chilton*). 118 mins.

Tango and Cash USA, 1989
p.c.: Warner Bros. A Guber–Peters Company production; *p*: Peter MacDonald; *d*: Andrei Konchalovsky; *sc*: Randy Feldman; *l.p.*: Sylvester Stallone (*Ray Tango*), Kurt Russell (*Gabriel Cash*), Jack Palance (*Yves Perret*), Teri Hatcher (*Kiki*), Michael J. Pollard (*Owen*), Brion James (*Requin*), Geoffrey Lewis (*Police Captain*), James Hong (*Quan*), Robert Z'Dar (*Face*), Marc Alaimo (*Lopez*). 102 mins.

Terminator, The USA, 1984
p.c.: Cinema '84. A Pacific Western production. For Orion; *p*: Gale Anne Hurd; *d*: James Cameron; *sc*: James Cameron, Gale Anne Hurd; *l.p.*: Arnold Schwarzenegger (*Terminator*), Linda Hamilton (*Sarah Connor*), Michael Biehn (*Kyle Reese*), Paul Winfield (*Traxler*), Lance Henrikson (*Vukovich*). 107 mins.

Terminator 2: Judgement Day USA, 1991
p.c.: Carolco Pictures. A Pacific Western production. In association with Lightstorm Entertainment; *p*: James Cameron; *d*: James Cameron; *sc*: James Cameron, William Wisher; *l.p.*: Arnold Schwarzenegger (*The Terminator*), Linda Hamilton (*Sarah Connor*), Edward Furlong (*John Connor*), Robert Patrick (*T1000*), Earl Boen (*Doctor Silverman*), Joe Morton (*Miles Dyson*). 135 mins.

Thelma and Louise USA, 1991
p.c.: Pathe Entertainment Inc.; *p*: Ridley Scott, Mimi Polk; *d*: Ridley Scott; *sc*: Callie Khouri; *l.p.*: Susan Sarandon (*Louise Sawyer*), Geena Davies (*Thelma Dickinson*), Harvey Kietel (*Hal Slocombe*), Michael Madsen (*Jimmy*), Christopher McDonald (*Darryl*), Brad Pitt (*JD*). 129 mins.

Total Recall USA, 1990
p.c.: Carolco; *p*: Buzz Feitshans, Ronald Shusett; *d*: Paul Verhoeven; *sc*: Ronald Shusett, Dan O'Bannon, Gary Goldman. Inspired by the short story 'We Can Remember It For You Wholesale' by Philip K. Dick; *l.p.*: Arnold Schwarzenegger (*Douglas Quaid*), Rachel Ticotin (*Melina*), Sharon Stone (*Lori Quaid*), Ronny Cox (*Cohaagen*), Michael Ironside (*Richter*), Marshall Bell (*George/Kuato*), Mel Johnson Jnr (*Benny*). 113 mins.

Uncommon Valour USA, 1983
p.c.: Paramount; *p*: John Milius, Buzz Feitshans; *d*: Ted Kotcheff; *sc*: Joe Gayton; *l.p.*: Gene Hackman (*Colonel Jason Rhodes*), Robert Stack (*Hugh MacGregor*), Fred Ward (*Wilkes*), Reb Brown (*Blaster*), Randell 'Tex' Cobb (*Sailor*), Patrick Swayze (*Scott*), Harold Sylvestor (*Johnson*), Tim Thomerson (*Charts*), Lau Nga Lai (*Lai Fun*), Kwan Hi Lim (*Jiang*). 105 mins.

BIBLIOGRAPHY

Adair, G. (1989) *Hollywood's Vietnam*, London: Heinemann.

Bad Object Choices (eds) (1991) *How Do I Look? Queer Film and Video*, Seattle: Bay Press.

Baehr, H. and Dyer, G. (eds) (1987) *Boxed In: Women and Television*, London: Pandora.

Baldwin, J. (1991) *Nobody Knows My Name*, Harmondsworth: Penguin.

Balio, T. (ed.) (1990) *Hollywood in the Age of Television*, London: Unwin Hyman.

Barker, M. (ed.) (1984) *Video Nasties*, London: Pluto.

Basinger, J. (1986) *The World War II Combat Film*, New York: Columbia University Press.

Bhabha, H. K. (1984) 'Of Mimicry and Man: The Ambivalence of Colonial Discourse', *October* 28: 125–33.

—— (1985) 'Sly Civility', *October* 34: 71–80.

—— (ed.) (1990) *Nation and Narration*, London: Routledge.

Bogle, D. (1991) *Toms, Coons, Mulattoes, Mammies, & Bucks*, New York: Continuum (2nd edition).

Boone, J. A. and Cadden, M. (eds) (1990) *Engendering Men: The Question of Male Feminist Criticism*, London: Routledge.

Boss, P. (1986) 'Vile Bodies and Bad Medicine', *Screen* 27, 1: 14–24.

Botcherby, S. (1991) 'Thelma and Louise Go Shooting', *Trouble and Strife* 22: 15–18.

—— and Garland, R. (1991) 'Hardware Heroines', *Trouble and Strife* 21: 40–6.

Bristow, J. (1988) 'How Men Are', *New Formations* 6: 119–31.

Britton, A. (1986) 'Blissing Out: The Politics of Reaganite Entertainment', *Movie* 31–2: 1–42.

Brophy, P. (1986) 'Horrality – the Textuality of Contemporary Horror Films', *Screen* 27, 1: 2–13.

Brunsdon, C. (1982) 'A Subject for the Seventies', *Screen* 23, 3–4: 20–9.

Burgin, V., Donald, J. and Kaplan, C. (eds) (1986) *Formations of Fantasy*, London: Methuen.

Burnett, R. (1985) 'The Tightrope of Male Fantasy', *Framework* 26–7: 76–84.

Butler, J. (1990) *Gender Trouble: Feminism and the Subversion of Identity*, London: Routledge.

Buxton, D. (1989) *From the Avengers to Miami Vice*, Manchester: Manchester University Press.

Carroll, N. (1982) 'The Future of Allusion: Hollywood in the Seventies (and Beyond)', *October* 20: 51–81.

Chapman, R. and Rutherford, J. (eds) (1988) *Male Order: Unwrapping Masculinity*, London: Lawrence & Wishart.

Chase, A. (1977) 'The Strange Romance of 'Dirty Harry' Callahan and Ann Mary Deacon', *The Velvet Light Trap* 17: 13–18.
Ching-Liang Low, G. (1989) 'White Skins/Black Masks: The Pleasures and Politics of Imperialism', *New Formations* 9: 83–103.
Clark, M. (1985) 'Vietnam: Representations of the Self and War', *Wide Angle* 17, 4: 4–11.
Cohen, S. and Hark, I. R. (eds) (1993) *Screening the Male*, London: Routledge.
Cook, P. (1982) 'Masculinity in Crisis?', *Screen* 23, 3–4: 39–46.
Coward, R. (1984) *Female Desire*, London: Paladin.
Creed, B. (1986) 'Horror and the Monstrous-Feminine – An Imaginary Abjection', *Screen* 27, 1: 44–70.
—— (1987) 'From Here to Modernity: Feminism and Postmodernism', *Screen* 28, 2: 47–67.
Cubitt, S. (1988) 'Time Shift', *Screen* 29, 2: 74–81.
Dargis, M. (1991) 'Roads to Freedom', *Sight and Sound* July: 15–18.
Ditmar, L. and Michaud, G. (1990) *From Hanoi to Hollywood*, New York: Rutgers University Press.
Doane, M. A. (1991) *Femmes Fatales*, London: Routledge.
Doherty, T. (1986) 'Review of *Rambo*', *Film Quarterly* Spring: 50–4.
Donald, J. (ed.) (1989) *Fantasy and the Cinema*, London: BFI.
—— and Rattansi, A. (eds) (1992) *'Race', Culture and Difference*, London: Sage/Open University Press.
Dyer, R. (1977) 'Entertainment and Utopia', *Movie* 24.
—— (1979) *Stars*, London: BFI.
—— (1982) 'Don't Look Now', *Screen* 23, 3–4: 61–73.
—— (1987) *Heavenly Bodies*, London: BFI/Macmillan.
—— (1988) 'White', *Screen* 29, 4: 44–64.
Epstein, J. and Straub, K. (eds) (1991) *Body Guards: The Cultural Politics of Gender Ambiguity*, London: Routledge.
Errigo, A. (1991) 'Action': Interview with Kathryn Bigelow, *Empire* 30: 76.
Fanon, F. (1985) *The Wretched of the Earth*, Harmondsworth: Penguin.
—— (1986) *Black Skins, White Masks*, London: Pluto.
Fiedler, L. A. (1990) 'Mythicizing the Unspeakable', *Journal of American Folklore* 103: 390–9.
Flaherty, J. (1982) 'Rocky's Road', *Film Comment* 18, 4: 58–63.
Foster, A. (1988) 'Heroes, Fools and Martyrs', *Ten.8* 28: 54–63.
Freud, S. (1914/1987) 'On Narcissism: An Introduction', Penguin Freud Library, vol. 11, pp. 59–97.
—— (1919/1988) 'The 'Uncanny', Penguin Freud Library, vol. 14, pp. 335–76.
Fuss, D. (1989) *Essentially Speaking: Feminism, Nature and Difference*, London: Routledge.
—— (ed.) (1991) *Inside/Out: Lesbian Theories, Gay Theories*, London: Routledge.
Gaines, J. and Herzog, C. (eds) (1990) *Fabrications: Costume and the Female Body*, London: Routledge/AFI.
Glaessner, V. (1974) *Kung Fu: Cinema of Vengeance*, London: Lorrimar.
Glass, F. (1989) 'The "New Bad Future": *RoboCop* and 1980s' Sci-Fi Films', *Science as Culture* 5: 7–49.
—— (1990) 'Totally Recalling Arnold: Sex and Violence in the New Bad Future', *Film Quarterly* 44, 1: 2–13.
Gledhill, C. (ed.) (1987) *Home Is Where the Heart Is*, London: BFI.
—— (ed.) (1991) *Stardom: Industry of Desire*, London: Routledge.
Gomery, D. (1983) 'The American Film Industry of the 1970s', *Wide Angle* 5, 4: 52–9.

Hebdige, D. (1979) *Subculture: The Meaning of Style*, London: Methuen.
—— (1988) *Hiding in the Light*, London: Routledge.
Hill, V. and Tasker, Y. (1992) 'Tonight I Made No Difference', *Over Here* 10, 2.
Hirsch, M. and Keller, E. F. (eds) (1990) *Conflicts in Feminism*, London: Routledge.
Holmlund, C. A. (1989) 'Visible Difference and Flex Appeal: The Body, Sex, Sexuality, and Race in the *Pumping Iron* Films', *Cinema Journal* 28, 4: 38–51.
Hong Kingston, M. (1977) *The Woman Warrior*, London: Picador.
—— (1981) *China Men*, London: Picador.
Jackson, B. (1990) 'The Perfect Informant', *American Journal of Folklore* 103: 400–16.
James, R. (1992) 'Women of Substance', *Film Review* January: 20–5.
Jameson, F. (1984) 'Postmodernism or the Cultural Logic of Late Capitalism', *New Left Review* 146: 53–92.
Jardine, A. and Smith, P. (eds) (1987) *Men in Feminism*, London: Methuen.
Jeffords, S. (1989) *The Remasculinization of America*, Bloomington: Indiana University Press.
Jones, A. (1991) 'James Cameron's Judgement Day', *Starburst* 158: 12–17.
Kaplan, E. A. (ed.) (1980) *Women in Film Noir*, London: BFI.
—— (1983) *Women and Film: Both Sides of the Camera*, London: Methuen.
—— (1987) *Rocking Around The Clock: Music Television, Postmodernism, and Consumer Culture*, London: Routledge.
Keen, B. (1987) 'Play It Again, Sony: The Double Life of Home Video Technology', *Science as Culture* 1: 7–42.
Kerr, P. (1980) 'The Vietnam Subtext', *Screen* 21, 2: 67–72.
King, S. B. (1990) 'Sonny's Virtues: The Gender Negotiations of *Miami Vice*', *Screen* 31, 3: 281–95.
Kruger, B. and Mariani, P. (eds) (1989) *Remaking History*, Seattle: Bay Press.
Krutnik, F. (1991) *In a Lonely Street: Film Noir, Genre, Masculinity*, London: Routledge.
Kuhn, A. (ed.) (1990) *Alien Zone*, London: Verso.
Lapsley, R. and Westlake, M. (1988) *Film Theory: An Introduction*, Manchester: Manchester University Press.
Larkins, R. (1970) 'Hollywood and the Indian', *Focus on Film* 2: 44–63.
Leab, D. J. (1975) *From Sambo to Superspade*, London: Secker & Warburg.
Lifton, R. J. (1974) *Home from the War*, London: Wildwood House.
Louvre, A. and Walsh, J. (eds) (1988) *Tell Me Lies About Vietnam*, Milton Keynes: Open University Press.
Lury, C., Franklin, S. and Stacey, J. (eds) (1991) *Off-centre: Feminism and Cultural Studies*, London: HarperCollins.
McClellan, J. (1990) 'Female Fury: Cynthia Rothrock', *i-D* 79: 74–7.
—— (1992) Interview with Jean-Claude Van Damme, *The Face* 42: 38–44.
Mann, K. B. (1989–90) 'Narrative Entanglements: *The Terminator*', *Film Quarterly* 43, 2: 17–27.
Mapplethorpe, R. (1983) *Lady: Lisa Lyons*, New York: Viking Press.
Medhurst, A. (1990) 'Pitching Camp', *City Limits* 10–17 May: 19.
Mercer, K. (1988) 'The Boy Who Fell To Earth', *Marxism Today* July: 34–5.
—— (1992) 'Back to my Routes: A Postcript to the 80s', *Ten.8* 2, 3: 32–9.
Morley, D. (1987) *Family Television*, London: Comedia.
Morley, D. and Robins, K. (1992) 'Techno-Orientalism: Futures, Foreigners and Phobias', *New Formations* 16: 136–56.
Mulvey, L. (1989) *Visual and Other Pleasures*, London: Macmillan.
Murphy, K. (1991) 'Only Angels Have Wings', *Film Comment* 24, 4: 26–9.
Neale, S. (1976) 'New Hollywood Cinema', *Screen* 17, 2: 117–22.

—— (1980) *Genre*, London: BFI.
—— (1983) 'Masculinity as Spectacle', *Screen* 24, 6: 2–16.
Nesteby, J. R. (1982) *Black Images in American Films, 1896-1954*, Lanham: University Press of America.
Norris, C., with Hyams, J. (1990) *The Secret of Inner Strength*, London: Arrow.
Parker, A., Russo, M., Sommer, D. and Yaeger, P. (eds) (1992) *Nationalisms and Sexualities*, London: Routledge.
Patton, P. and Poole, P. (eds) (1985) *War/Masculinity*, Sydney: Intervention Publications.
Petley, J. (1984) 'A Nasty Story', *Screen* 25, 2: 68–74.
Pribram, E. D. (ed.) (1988) *Female Spectators*, London: Verso.
Radway, J. (1986) 'Identifying Ideological Seams: Mass Culture, Analytic Method, and Political Practice', *Communication* 9: 93–123.
—— (1987) *Reading the Romance*, London: Verso.
Robins, D. and Cohen, P. (1978) *Knuckle Sandwich: Growing Up in the Working-class City*, Harmondsworth: Penguin.
Ross, A. (1986) 'Masculinity and *Miami Vice*: Selling In', *Oxford Literary Review* 8, 1/2: 143–54.
Rovin, J. (1985) *Stallone! A Hero's Story*, London: Hodder & Stoughton.
Ryall, T. (1975/6) 'Teaching through Genre', *Screen Education* 17: 27–33.
Said, E. (1980) *Orientalism*, London: Routledge & Kegan Paul.
Schulze, L. J. (1986) '*Getting Physical*: Text/Context/Reading and the Made-for-Television Movie', *Cinema Journal* 25, 2: 35–50.
Smith, J. (1973a) 'Between Vermont and Violence: Film Portraits of Vietnam Veterans', *Film Quarterly* 26, 4: 10–17.
—— (1973b) 'Look Away, Look Away, Look Away, Movie Land', *Journal of Popular Film* 1: 29–46.
Stecopoulos, H. and Uebel, M. (eds) (forthcoming) *Back to the Raft: Race and the Subject of Masculinities*, Duke University Press.
Taubin, A. (1991) 'Killing Men', *Sight and Sound* May: 16–18.
Theweleit, K. (1987) *Male Fantasies*, Cambridge: Polity Press.
Todorov, T. (1977) *The Poetics of Prose*, Oxford: Blackwell.
Vendler, H. (ed.) (1990) *Contemporary American Poetry*, London: Faber & Faber.
Wallace, M. (1990) *Invisibility Blues*, London: Verso.
Walsh, J. and Aulich, J. (eds) (1989) *Vietnam Images: War and Representation*, London: Macmillan.
Watney, S. (1986) 'The Banality of Gender', *Oxford Literary Review* 8: 13–22.
—— (1987) *Policing Desire*, London: Comedia/Methuen.
Webster, D. (1988) *Looka Yonder!: The Imaginary America of Populist Culture*, London: Routledge.
—— (1989) '"Whodunnit? America Did": *Rambo* and Post-Hungerford Rhetoric', *Cultural Studies* 3, 2: 173–93.
White, E. (1980) *States of Desire: Travels in Gay America*, London: Picador.
Willemen, P. (1981) 'Anthony Mann: Looking at the Male', *Framework* 15–17: 16.
Williamson, J. (1983) 'Images of "Woman" – The Photographs of Cindy Sherman', *Screen* 24, 6: 102–6.
—— (1986) 'The Problems of Being Popular', *New Socialist*, September: 14–15.
—— (1988) 'Short Circuit of the New Man', *New Statesman*, 20 May: 28–9.
Winship, J. (1987) *Inside Women's Magazines*, London: Pandora.
Wood, R. (1986) *Hollywood from Vietnam to Reagan*, New York: Columbia University Press.
Yacowar, M. (1989) 'The White Man's Mythic Invincibility', *Jump Cut* 34: 2–4.
Yearwood, G. L. (1982) 'The Hero in Black Film', *Wide Angle* 5, 2: 42–50.

Zavitzianos, G. (1977) 'The Object in Festishism, Homeovestism and Transvestism', *International Journal of Psycho-Analysis* 58: 487–95.
Zizek, S. (1989) *The Sublime Object of Ideology*, London: Verso.

INDEX

Above the Law 22, 25
action cinema 6–9, 30–1, 59–60, 75–6, 79–80, 91, 98, 125, 153; critical status of 5–6, 7–9, 65, 70–1, 92–3, 107–8, 154–5
action hero 77; black men as 37–9, 40–2, 47–53; body of 3–5, 65, 78–80, 106–7, 125–8; and femininity 69; as outsider 62–3, 98–100, 104–5
action heroine 2–3, 14–34, 132–52; black women as 21–3, 31–4; in Hong Kong cinema 24; and masculinity 132–4, 146–50; and motherhood 15, 27, 32, 152
Action Jackson 41–2
Alexandra, Karen 33
Alien 15, 18, 31, 51, 134, 148
Alien[3] 153
Aliens 15, 49, 135, 138–9, 146–7, 148–9, 150–2
Allen, Nancy 27
All the President's Men 107
Alonso, Maria Conchita 47, 149
anti-semitism 162
audiences 6, 59, 63, 64–5, 71, 93, 107–8, 145–6
Avengers, The 19
A.W.O.L. 40, 128

Backdraft 89, 129
Back to the Future 3 67
Barbarella 19
Barton Fink 153
Basic Instinct 134, 139–40, 146
Basinger, Jeanine 68,70
Biao, Yuen 25
Big Trouble in Little China 89
Bigelow, Kathryn 13, 147, 153, 155, 156–7, 160, 163, 164
Billy Jack 99
Black Belt Jones 21, 22–3
Blade Runner 56, 75
blaxspoitation 21–3, 37–9
Blue Steel 3, 13, 31, 147–8, 155, 158–62
bodybuilding 9–10, 77–83, 118–23; in action cinema 1–2, 14, 73–6, 132, 149–50; and fascist imagery 1, 81–2; and women 79, 141–6
Bogle, Donald 4, 21, 23, 33, 38, 43, 45
Born on the Fourth of July 93
boxing 106, 126–7
Braddock: Missing in Action 3 101–2
Britton, Andrew 58–9, 61
buddie movies 89, 163–4; and male bonding 36; and racial difference 43–7; and women 20, 134, 155
Butch Cassidy and the Sundance Kid 45
Butler, Judith 115, 127, 146, 165

Cagney and Lacey 20
Cameron, James 15, 83
Chapman, Rowena 60, 120
Charlie's Angels 18, 21
Chase, Anthony 70–1
China O'Brien 22, 25–6, 30, 136, 147
China O'Brien 2 25–6, 29
Chong, Rae Dawn 28, 40
Christian imagery 39–40, 74, 127
class 5–6, 79, 106–7, 109, 118, 126, 136
Cleopatra Jones and the Casino of Gold 23
Cobra 62, 124, 125

Commando 28, 81, 88, 91, 94, 104–5, 127–8, 130
Conan the Destroyer 19, 21, 29, 40
Cook, Pam 114, 125, 161
Creed, Barbara 9, 73, 78, 111–12, 128
Curtis, Jamie Lee 3, 143, 161–2
Cyborg 40

Death Warrant 16, 29, 36, 40, 42–3, 128
Death Wish 69
Deer Hunter, The 94, 99
Die Hard 4, 7, 44–5, 60, 61–5, 68, 71, 87, 88, 91, 114, 129
Die Hard 2 105, 129
Dirty Harry 17, 41, 70, 124
Dobson, Tamara 21, 23
double 71, 156–8, 163
drugs 112–13; and blackness 32, 42, 47–8
Duel in the Sun 117–18
Dyer, Richard 72, 76, 77, 111, 118–19

Eastwood, Clint 43, 68–9, 86–7
Ellison, Mary 100
Enter the Dragon 21, 24
ethnicity 106, 120, 127
Evil Dead, The 55

Fanon, Frantz 126–7, 132–3
Fargas, Antonio 36
Fatal Beauty 4, 30, 31–4, 35, 37, 48, 88, 147, 148, 153 fatherhood 31, 83, 88, 128–30; and action heroine 20, 25, 26, 147, 161; in cinema 3, 73
femininity 14, 17–18, 19, 77–8, 115–17, 141–6
feminism 20, 120–1, 133; and film 116, 135–6, 150, 153–4
fetishism 32; and death 154; and weaponry 147, 161
Fiedler, Leslie 8, 98, 102, 110
film noir 140
First Blood 16, 39, 84, 92, 94, 98, 103, 105, 106, 127
Flaming Star 66
Ford, Harrison 74, 111
Full Metal Jacket 96, 104, 121
Fung, Richard 69

genre 7, 54–5; evolution of 67–70; hybrids of 57–8; self-reflexivity of 59
Getting Physical 143–4, 145
Ghost 31, 32, 164
Gibson, Mel 4, 43, 45, 75, 130
Glaessner, Verina 24
Glover, Danny 4, 35, 43, 45, 76, 130, 155
Goldberg, Whoopi 4, 30, 31–3, 88, 148, 152, 155
Goude, Jean-Paul 21
Green Berets, The 100
Grier, Pam 21, 23, 36

Hamburger Hill 100, 101
Hamilton, Linda 83, 138, 142–3, 149
Haskell, Molly 20
Heartbreak Ridge 43, 68, 75, 121
Hendry, Gloria 21
Hoberman, J. 106
Holmlund, Christine 145–6
homeovestism 128–9
homoeroticism 29, 89, 121, 127–8, 154–5, 162–4; and racial difference 36, 45–7; and violence 42; and women 15–16
Hong Kingston, Maxine 133
Hong Kong cinema 5, 15, 21, 22, 23–6, 69, 73, 102
Hudson Hawk 62, 74, 88
Hughs, Langston 100

identification 33, 117; and identity 5; and nation 99–100
independent woman stereotype 18–19, 20, 22–3
Indiana Jones and the Temple of Doom 2, 91, 137
Invasion USA 104, 113
I Spit On Your Grave 21, 152

Jackson, Bruce 103
'Japanisation' 63
Jeffords, Susan 95, 99, 101
Johnson, Don 36
Johnstone, Sheila 127
Jones, Grace 21, 27, 29
Julia 18
Julien, Isaac 120, 165

Kickboxer 17
Kelly, Jim 21, 24
Kindergarten Cop 82, 129
King, Scott Benjamin 114
Klute 18
Kruger, Barbara 11
Kung Fu 69

Lapsley, Robert 97
Last Boy Scout, The 44, 62, 74, 87–8, 90, 124, 130
Lee, Bruce 21, 24, 69, 123
lesbian audiences 3, 29, 146; images 29–30, 140, 145–6
Lethal Weapon 17, 43, 45–6, 58, 130
Lethal Weapon 2 15, 17, 45–7, 87
Lethal Weapon 3 75
Levey, Michael 61
Lock Up 17, 29, 85, 90, 127, 154–5
Look Who's Talking 88, 129
Louvre, Alf 78, 92, 94, 102
Lundgren, Dolph 9, 28, 74, 86
Lyons, Lisa 142

Mad Max 55
Made in LA 113
Making Mr Right 10–13
Malcolm, Derek 65, 108
Manhunter 113
Mann, Michael 112, 113
Mao Ying, Angela 23–4
Mapplethorpe, Robert 35, 116, 142
martial arts movie 23–6, 74
masculinity 1, 11–12, 44–5, 62, 63, 94–108, 109–131, 162–5; and star images 73–90; study of 71, 73, 114; and weaponry 46–7, 53; and women 139, 149–50
Masters of the Universe 28
Medhurst, Andy 111, 130
Mercer, Kobena 35, 116, 120, 133, 165
Miami Vice 36, 43, 112–14, 122
Missing in Action 58, 62, 98, 101
Missing in Action 2: The Beginning 101
Moonlighting 60, 64–5, 87
Mortal Thoughts 152
Mr T 4, 17
Ms 45/Angel of Vengeance 21, 152
Mulvey, Laura 16, 17, 79, 104, 114–15, 117, 118, 135, 136
Murphy, Kathleen 137
music video 66, 112

narcissism 158; and bodybuilding 78, 81, 119, 122
nationhood 62, 97–101
Neale, Steve 58, 115, 118
Near Dark 155–8
Nesteby, James R. 4
new man 1, 11, 85, 94–5, 117, 120–1, 165
Nickson, Julia 26, 40
Nico/Above the Law 23, 36
Nielson, Brigitte 14, 29
Norris, Chuck 9, 62, 74, 98, 101, 123–4

Officer and a Gentleman, An 43
Once Upon A Time in the West 69

Parenthood 3, 73, 129
Parents 73
Perfect 143, 144
Pesci, Joe 47, 87
phallic woman 31, 39, 139
Place, Janey 140
Platoon 8, 66, 96, 97, 100, 101, 103, 104, 107, 137
Point Break 13, 155, 162–5
Policewoman 18
populism 62, 98, 101, 102, 104, 105, 108, 112; and action hero 65, 114, 125, 147, 148
postmodernism 54–7, 91; and masculinity 73–4, 110–14, 128, 130
Predator 49, 61, 65, 91, 94, 105
Predator 2 4, 35, 47–53, 76, 133, 149, 155
Presley, Elvis 66
Pretty Woman 128
Pumping Iron 78
Pumping Iron II: The Women 143, 144–6

racial discourse 2, 4–5, 35–53, 96–7; and black women 21–3, 31–4; and male bonding 36, 40, 43–7; and nation 99–101; and sexuality 24, 37–43, 79, 118, 127, 133; in the western 69, 118
Raging Bull 114, 125–6
Raiders of the Lost Ark 27, 75

Rambo: First Blood Part II 7–9, 26, 27, 28, 40, 58, 62, 69, 71, 86, 91–2, 93–100, 102–4, 105–8, 116, 119, 120, 122, 125
Rambo III 39, 55, 78, 84, 94, 99, 101, 127
rape 24, 29, 134, 151–2, 161; as narrative device 16–17, 20–1
Reanimator 57
Red Sonja 19, 29–30, 32
Reeves, Steve 2, 122
Return of the Living Dead 57
rites of passage narrative 70, 96, 104, 137
River's Edge 153
road movies 29, 134, 152, 155
RoboCop 27, 28, 32, 48, 65, 150–1
RoboCop 2 2, 27
Rocky 39, 43, 55, 83–4, 99, 120, 126, 127
Rocky II 106, 123
Rocky III 4, 17
Rocky IV 4, 43, 71, 125
Rocky V 75
Root, Jane 145
Ross, Andrew 112, 113
Rothrock, Cynthia 5, 15, 24–6
Roundtree, Richard 37
Running Man, The 83
Russell, Kurt 89
Rutherford, Jonathan 94–6, 107

St Jacques, Raymond 100
Schulze, Laurie 141, 144, 146
Schwarzenegger, Arnold 1, 2, 9, 28, 29, 30, 47, 49, 61, 65, 74, 78, 80–3, 86, 90, 91, 104, 112, 119, 124
Scott, Ridley 56, 134
Seagal, Steven 23
Segal, Lynne 117–18
Shaft 37, 38–9, 127, 135
Sherman, Cindy 11
Shootist, The 68
Silence of the Lambs 18, 31, 135, 146–7, 162
Simpson, O.J. 2
Spielberg, Stephen 59
Stallone, Sylvester 1, 9, 43, 62, 65, 74, 78–9, 80, 83–7, 89, 90, 91, 92, 101, 112, 121, 122–3, 154
star images 74–90, 122–3, 164–5
Starsky and Hutch 36
Star Wars 55, 58, 59, 70, 75
Stay Hungry 82
Stepfather, The 73
Stone, Sharon 41, 140
Sudden Impact 21
Swayze, Patrick 164–5

Takei, George 100
Tango and Cash 29, 43, 84–5, 88–9, 121
Taxi Driver 124
teen movie 66–8, 70
Terminator, The 65, 82, 124, 138, 153
Terminator 2 3, 18, 27, 56, 83, 128, 138, 143, 149–50, 152
Thelma and Louise 3, 18, 26, 29, 31, 43, 62, 134–9, 140, 150, 151–2, 153–4, 155, 156, 161
Thief/Violent Streets 113
Thomas, Philip Michael 36
Three Men and a Baby 3, 129
Tightrope 68, 71, 121
Todorov, Tzvetan 55
Top Gun 104
Total Recall 26–7, 28, 83, 150–1
Twin Peaks 153
Twins 83, 124

uncanny 155–8

Van Damme, Jean-Claude 36, 40, 73, 74, 128
vanity 41
Van Peebles, Mario 43
Van Peebles, Melvin 37
Verhoeven, Paul 65
video 7, 56, 92
Vietnam War 68, 92; in American film 8–9, 49, 61–2, 93–4, 96–7, 98–104, 105, 107, 108
View to a Kill, A 27
violence 92, 107; and masculinity 95; and narrative 65

Walkerdine, Valerie 71, 106, 123, 155
Wallace, Michele 31
Wall Street 128
Walsh, Jeffrey 80, 101
war movie 47, 97, 121
Watney, Simon 116–17
Wayans, Damon 87, 88
Wayne, John 53, 68, 76, 100

Way of the Dragon 123
Weathers, Carl 4, 41, 43, 83
westerns 66–70, 163; racial difference
in 69, 118
Westlake, Michael 97
Williamson, Fred 2
Williamson, Judith 11, 12
Willis, Bruce 4, 45, 62, 64–5, 74, 87–8
Wings of the Apache 104
Wonderwoman 18
Wood, Robin 58–9, 63

Yacowar, Maurice 63–5
Yearwood, Gladstone L. 39, 40
Young Guns 57, 66–8, 69, 70

Zavitzianos, George 128–9
Zizek, Slavoj 117